The Spice Islands Cook Book

RECIPE DEVELOPMENT BY LOUISE DRIGGS

ILLUSTRATIONS BY ALICE HARTH

BOOK DESIGN BY ADRIAN WILSON

THE SPICE ISLANDS Cook Book

BY THE SPICE ISLANDS HOME ECONOMICS STAFF

LANE BOOKS   MENLO PARK, CALIFORNIA

THE SPICE ISLANDS® COOK BOOK is dedicated to the thousands of men and women who cook for fun and pleasure as well as for everyday family needs.

It is our hope that this book will answer the frequently-asked question: How do I use spices and herbs? The recipes contained herein have been selected with one thought in mind—to enhance foods by the knowledgeable use of seasonings.

The recipes range from the simple to the gourmet level. None is difficult, and all are delectable. Each of them was prepared under the direction of skilled home economists in the modern test kitchens of Spice Islands. Every recipe was taste-tested by a trained taste panel, and only the very finest of them were selected for inclusion in this book.

In developing and testing these recipes, Spice Islands seasonings were used exclusively—we hope that you will use the same full-flavored seasonings when you make these recipes in your own kitchen.

We receive countless letters each month requesting information on Spice Islands—its farm, its processing, its products, and its recipes and booklets. If you would like additional information, please write to us at 100 East Grand Avenue, South San Francisco, California.

F. Calgiuri

SPICE ISLANDS COMPANY

Library of Congress Catalog Card 61-15588
Title Number 264

Fifth Printing July 1965
Copyright © 1961
Lane Magazine & Book Company, Menlo Park, California

Printed in the United States of America by Stecher-Traung Lithograph Corporation

CONTENTS

SPICE ISLANDS

THE ROMANCE
OF SPICES

TAKE A JAR OF CINNAMON from your spice shelf, unscrew the cap, and sniff
its pungent fragrance. It is a familiar scent, one that you can rely on to grace
a pudding, an eggnog, or a sweet roll. You know it as a common seasoning,
respected, but obtainable in any store. Yet, it has not always been so easily
taken for granted!

Cinnamon is one of dozens of aromatic seasonings known as *Spices* — a
magic word that has stirred men's dreams and aroused their cupidity since
the beginning of recorded history. Over the centuries, the quest for spices
has sent thousands of men to their deaths on dangerous caravan trails and
uncharted oceans, has caused raids and wars, and has inspired men to venture into the unknown and to discover continents of whose existence no man
had even dreamed.

The origin of spices is lost in antiquity. Historians tell us that they were in
use long before the dawn of the written record. Early Chinese writings mention the trading and use of spices in that country in the year 200 B.C. The
Chinese are known to have had a flourishing spice business beginning early
in the first century of the Christian era. Rome entered the spice trade during
the latter half of the first century. It enjoyed an extensive and lucrative trade
with both China and what is now India, dealing principally in spices, silks,
satins, aromatic woods, and fragrant oils.

Desirable as they were, these exotic goods were in extremely short supply.
They had to be carried by camel caravan over long, tortuous overland routes
that started in southern India, ran northwest through Afghanistan, Persia,
Syria, and into Arabia, and crossed the Red Sea into Egypt where they were
transshipped to Mediterranean ports. The caravans were beset by bandits
and constantly at the mercy of the elements. Consequently, spices were not
only in short supply but were quite expensive as well. In the ninth century,
cloves and mace sold for the equivalent of $18 per pound. Pepper was so
expensive that it was sold by the individual peppercorn!

These high prices attracted unscrupulous traders who made great fortunes
by adulterating the few pounds of spices they were able to obtain and selling
them at astronomical prices. In time, the practice of adulteration became so

widespread that the authorities in Rome, Bagdad, and Alexandria decreed that spice adulteration would be punishable by death. Apparently a large number of these entrepreneurs literally lost their heads over their spices!

You may rightly wonder why the people of an earlier day would pay fantastic prices for a few grains of spices, but the answer is a simple one. Their diet was coarse, monotonous, and unpalatable by modern standards. Food spoiled quickly. Spices served a dual purpose: not only did they add flavor to otherwise flavorless food, but the anti-oxidant qualities of certain spices also inhibited spoilage — particularly of meats. Is it any wonder that spices were one of the most valued commodities in the trade centers of ancient society!

Even though the demand for spices spread like wild-fire throughout early civilization, the supply remained short. This shortage was aided and abetted by those who owned the dusty, plodding caravans. Mostly Arabians, the caravan masters were wise in the ways of the desert and wilderness, and they soon controlled the bulk of the spice traffic. To solidify their lucrative monopoly, these wily traders took pains to keep secret the sources of their valuable cargoes. They discouraged possible competition by exaggerating the dangers of the trails and by spreading fantastic stories of monsters, dragons, and fierce wildmen. These tales served their purpose well, and for several hundred years the secrets of the Indies were known to few.

It was a Venetian by the name of Marco Polo who at last unlocked the secret and helped to break the spice monopoly. During the years 1271 to 1295 A. D., he traveled extensively through the Near East, central and southern Asia, and many of the then-unknown islands and island chains in the Pacific.

After his return to Venice, Marco Polo published an account of his three trips to the Orient. He gave a glowing description of the people and the golden-towered cities that he had visited; but perhaps most important of all, he divulged the great secret on which he had stumbled — the sources of the spice trade. He told of seeing Ginger growing in China, Cinnamon in Ceylon, Pepper in Borneo, and of the Nutmeg and Clove trees growing on volcanic islands jutting out of the Indian and Pacific oceans. Furthermore, he had returned from his last trip part way by sea, and he thus proved that there might be a sea passage to the Indies that was less perilous than the land routes.

Marco Polo's book astonished the world. It stirred men to want to visit the fabled lands he had described; but the overland routes were too long and hazardous, and few men were bold enough to try them. For the next two hundred years, expeditions sailed out of European ports in search of a sea lane that might give an easier passage to the fabled land of Cathay, the island of Zipangu (Japan), and the mysterious islands where flourished the spices that the medieval world had come to value so highly.

Sea voyages, too, were unbelievably dangerous. The ships were clumsy, leaky, and cramped. What maps existed were treacherously unreliable. Shipboard diet and primitive medical care were almost certain to take the lives of a part of each crew on a long voyage. So risky was the venture that crews were usually impressed from the prisons. Many of the expeditions that embarked from Spanish and Portuguese ports were never heard from again, and those that did return often came back with only half of their original crews, the rest having died from scurvy.

Nevertheless, many brave navigators sailed out into the unknown in search of a practical route to the East and its wealth of spices. In their quest, they pushed the boundaries of the known world back thousands of miles and opened whole new continents to exploration and settlement.

The names of the few who returned safely from these voyages are well known in history. Columbus, seeking a westward passage to the Indies, thought he had touched the outposts of Cathay when he reached the islands of the Caribbean. Another Portuguese sailor, Vasco de Gama rounded the continent of Africa in 1498 and reached the spice-rich port of Calicut, India. His success emboldened other seafarers to carry on the search for the mythical islands that were known to exist somewhere off the coast of China.

It was the Magellan round-the-world expedition of 1519-23 that finally charted a course to the Spice Islands. With a fleet of five small ships, he left Spain in the summer of 1519 and after two years of adventure and hardship dropped anchor in Philippine waters. Here Magellan was killed in an uprising of the natives, but the remnants of his expedition continued south and discovered the cluster of volcanic islands west of New Guinea where Cloves; Nutmeg, Cinnamon, Pepper, and other spices grew in profusion. The Magellan expedition continued on its way and finally returned to Spain in 1523 with the news of this discovery so important to the spice trade. (Of the five ships and 265 sailors who started on this long voyage, only one vessel and 18 sailors returned to Spain!)

The islands that the expedition discovered were given by Spain to Portugal to administer under a papal treaty. The Portuguese carried on a profitable trade for two hundred years before the islands were seized by the Dutch, who administered them until the formation of the Indonesian Republic. Today the Spice Islands, known also as the Moluccas, continue to produce an abundance of aromatic, flavorful spices that work their wonders for us as they did for people hundreds of years ago.

HOW TO USE
SEASONINGS

For your guidance in the use of spices, herbs, and the other seasonings, we make the following suggestions:

How Much To Use: Generally figure ¼ teaspoon of dried herbs for each 4 servings. This usually measures to the "pinch" so often recommended. In many respects, herbs and spices are to cooking what accessories are to fashion: too much can be ruinous, so use them with restraint.

How To Use: Before adding the measured amount of an herb to a recipe, crush it in palm of one hand with the fingertips of the other hand. This will give quicker flavor release.

When To Use: Cooked foods such as stews, soups, and sauces will taste best if herbs are added during the last hour of cooking. Uncooked foods such as salad dressings, fruits, and juices need time for the flavors to "marry"; add herbs as long before serving as possible.

When Not To Use: While there are many herbs or spices that may well complement a dish, be selective. Unless you are following a tested recipe, do not combine too many at one time. Also, one herb course to a meal is plenty. A meal in which every dish is herbed is a culinary catastrophe.

Which To Use: The correct herb or spice or combination for any food is the one that tastes right to you. Remember that seasoning is not a science but an expressive art — and you are the artist. When experimenting with a new herb, crush some of it and let it warm in your hand; then sniff it and taste it. If it is delicate, you can be bold and adventurous. If it is very strong and pungent, be cautious.

APPETIZERS &
HORS D'OEUVRES

APPETIZERS AND HORS D'OEUVRES should be prepared with thought and care so that they are appealing to the eye, tempting to the taste, and festive enough to suit the occasion.

If you are serving a small group of guests, here is a perfect opportunity to serve those savory hot tidbits that are too time-consuming to prepare for a large party. You may limit the selection to one or two exceptional appetizers to accompany cocktails served on the patio or in the living room. Or you may decide to serve an *hors d'oeuvre* course at the table as a prelude to the meal.

The large cocktail party, on the other hand, calls for a wide assortment of finger food that can be prepared well ahead of the guests' arrival and that will hold up during the party with a minimum of attention from the hostess. Dips, spreads, and trays of appetite-provoking canapés are popular for this type of entertaining.

One or two hot dips or appetizers, kept warm in chafing dishes, may be included in the selection—but unless you provide plates and a place for guests to sit, don't serve food that is awkward to eat, or messy and likely to drip or crumble. Serve flavors, textures, shapes, and colors in wide variety—a smooth, creamy pâté; zesty chili-flavored cashews; a dip with the crunch of Toasted Onions.

Pickled Mushrooms à la Grecque

 Serve 4 or 5 mushrooms on crisp lettuce as an opening course.

1 pound fresh medium-size button mushrooms	1 teaspoon Onion Powder
⅛ teaspoon Thyme	3 tablespoons Red Wine Vinegar
2 or 3 Whole Black Peppercorns	2 tablespoons olive oil
⅛ teaspoon Fennel Seed	¼ teaspoon Lemon Peel
1 piece (1 inch) Bay Leaf	3 teaspoons Beau Monde Seasoning
½ teaspoon Garlic Powder	½ teaspoon Parsley

Wash mushrooms in cold water; trim off the tip of the stalk. Crush Thyme, Peppercorns, and Fennel Seed and combine with mushrooms in saucepan. Add Bay Leaf, Garlic Powder, Onion Powder, Vinegar, olive oil, Lemon Peel, Beau Monde, and Parsley. Cook over low heat, turning mushrooms frequently, until the mushrooms are tender, about 15 minutes. Pour mushrooms and marinade into glass jar or refrigerator dish. Chill for several hours or, preferably, overnight. Serve cold. Makes 6 servings.

Chili Cashews

1 tablespoon olive oil	1 can (12 oz.) salted cashews,
10 Chili Pequins	peanuts, or mixed nuts
¼ teaspoon Garlic Powder	¼ teaspoon Chili Powder

Pour olive oil into heavy frying pan. Crush Chili Pequins and add to oil along with Garlic Powder; mix well with oil. Add nuts and toast over medium heat for 7 or 8 minutes, stirring constantly. Mix seasonings and nuts together thoroughly. When nuts are toasted, sprinkle with Chili Powder; stir so Chili Powder is well mixed with nuts. Pour into serving bowl. Makes about 2 cups.

Tea Eggs

Adapted from a Chinese recipe, these eggs make interesting hors d'oeuvres. They look like enormous olives.

1 dozen hard-cooked eggs	1 teaspoon Anise Seed
1 quart boiling water	4 tablespoons Soy Sauce
3 tablespoons Orange Pekoe and Pekoe Tea	1½ tablespoons salt

Shell eggs carefully so white is unbroken. Pour boiling water over tea; let steep for 5 minutes. Strain and combine with Anise Seed, Soy Sauce, and salt. Add hard-cooked eggs and simmer for 1 hour. Chill eggs in liquid. Eggs will keep indefinitely if covered with liquid and kept in refrigerator. Makes 1 dozen.

Gurkas Dilisas

These cucumber tidbits with their Dill Stuffing are a specialty of a famous Norwegian restaurant. They can be made hours ahead and still stay crisp and crunchy.

3 or 4 small young cucumbers
1 flat tin (2 oz.) anchovy filets
2 packages (3 oz. each) cream cheese
1 teaspoon Dill Weed

1 teaspoon Shredded Green Onions
1 tablespoon mayonnaise
1/16 teaspoon Cayenne Pepper
Dairy sour cream
Chervil

Scrub cucumbers but do not peel; cut off ends. Cut into 1-inch lengths. Scoop out center seedy portion with sharp paring knife or grapefruit knife. Drain anchovy filets and chop. Mix together with cream cheese, Dill Weed, Shredded Green Onions, and mayonnaise. Season with Cayenne; blend well. Stuff mixture into cucumber sections. Chill for several hours. Just before serving, top each piece with a small spoonful of sour cream. Sprinkle with Chervil. Serve very cold. Makes about 2 dozen hors d'oeuvres.

Ten Minute Pizza

3 English muffins
⅓ cup chili sauce
1 teaspoon Spaghetti Sauce Seasoning

1 cup shredded sharp Cheddar cheese

Tear muffins in two. Toast lightly. Combine chili sauce and Spaghetti Sauce Seasoning. Spread on muffin halves. Sprinkle with shredded cheese. Toast in broiler until cheese is melted. Cut each muffin half into quarters. Serve hot. Makes 24 appetizers.

Chicken Liver-Bacon Rolls

½ pound chicken livers
3 tablespoons Soy Sauce
1 tablespoon sherry
¼ teaspoon Garlic Powder

1 teaspoon Horseradish
20 canned or fresh whole button mushrooms
½ pound bacon

Wash chicken livers and cut into two or three pieces, depending on size of livers. Combine Soy Sauce, sherry, Garlic Powder, and Horseradish. Pour over chicken livers and let marinate for several hours in the refrigerator. Drain canned mushrooms, or wash and cut stems from fresh mushrooms. Cut each bacon slice into thirds. Wrap piece of chicken liver and a mushroom in a bacon strip. Fasten with small skewers or toothpicks. Broil rolls until bacon is crisp and chicken livers cooked, turning once or twice. Serve hot. Makes about 20 hors d'oeuvres.

Broiled Shrimp Indienne

An authentic Far Eastern recipe — the touch of cooling mint with the other seasonings provides the interest.

1 pound large raw shrimp, fresh or frozen
¼ cup olive oil
1 teaspoon Ground Turmeric
½ teaspoon Garlic Powder
¼ teaspoon Cracked Black Pepper

1 teaspoon Beau Monde Seasoning
1 teaspoon Chili Powder
1 tablespoon Red Wine Vinegar
1 teaspoon Sweet Basil
2 teaspoons Spearmint

Wash, shell, and de-vein shrimp. Combine olive oil, Turmeric, Garlic Powder, Pepper, Beau Monde, Chili Powder, and Vinegar. Crush Sweet Basil and Spearmint and stir into sauce. Pour over shrimp and marinate for at least 2 or 3 hours at room temperature. Broil or grill for 10 to 15 minutes, or until shrimp are done, basting 2 or 3 times with sauce. Makes 2 or 3 servings.

Cumin Seed Wafers

Serve these hot from the oven with your favorite cocktail or soft drink. Or cool and serve as an accompaniment to a salad.

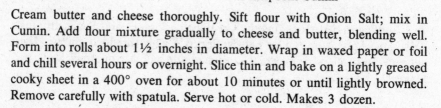

¾ cup soft butter
1 cup shredded sharp Cheddar cheese

2 cups sifted all-purpose flour
½ teaspoon Onion Salt
1½ teaspoons Cumin

Cream butter and cheese thoroughly. Sift flour with Onion Salt; mix in Cumin. Add flour mixture gradually to cheese and butter, blending well. Form into rolls about 1½ inches in diameter. Wrap in waxed paper or foil and chill several hours or overnight. Slice thin and bake on a lightly greased cooky sheet in a 400° oven for about 10 minutes or until lightly browned. Remove carefully with spatula. Serve hot or cold. Makes 3 dozen.

Piquant Cheese Canapé

Try this sometime, spread on English muffin halves and toasted in the broiler.

1 package (8 oz.) sharp Cheddar cheese spread
2 tablespoons soft butter
¼ teaspoon Cracked Black Pepper

½ teaspoon Onion Salt
¼ teaspoon Garlic Powder
1 teaspoon Worcestershire sauce
Paprika

Let cheese warm slightly to soften. Cream thoroughly with butter. Mix in Pepper, Onion Salt, Garlic Powder, and Worcestershire sauce. Heap in small bowl. Sprinkle with Paprika. Serve with crisp crackers; or spread on crackers and sprinkle with Paprika. Makes about 1 cup.

Olive Canapé Spread

4 teaspoons Chicken Seasoned Stock Base

2 tablespoons boiling water

1 teaspoon Instant Minced Onions

1 teaspoon bottled meat sauce or Worcestershire sauce

1 package (8 oz.) cream cheese

½ cup chopped ripe olives

Mix Chicken Seasoned Stock Base with boiling water in bowl. Add Onions and meat sauce; let stand for 5 to 10 minutes. Blend in cream cheese until smooth; stir in chopped olives. Spread on crisp crackers, rounds of Melba toast, or rye wafers. Makes 2½ cups.

Smoked Oyster Spread

Serve as a spread, or add a little more milk or cream for a dip.

2 packages (3 oz. each) cream cheese

2 tablespoons light cream or milk

1 teaspoon Beau Monde Seasoning

2 teaspoons bottled meat sauce

1 can (3⅔ oz.) smoked oysters

1 tablespoon Instant Toasted Onions

1 teaspoon Chervil

Soften cream cheese with fork; blend in cream or milk until smooth. Mix in Beau Monde and bottled meat sauce. Cut oysters into small pieces and mix into cheese with Toasted Onions. (Thin with additional cream or milk if desired.) Sprinkle with Chervil. Serve with crisp crackers, potato chips, or corn chips. Makes 1½ cups.

Chicken Liver Paté Tarragon

Made in the blender, this paté has a smooth, creamy texture and a delicate liver flavor.

6 chicken livers

2 tablespoons butter

¼ teaspoon Garlic Powder

1 teaspoon Chicken Seasoned Stock Base

1 tablespoon sherry

2 packages (3 oz. each) cream cheese

¼ teaspoon Tarragon

½ teaspoon Beau Monde Seasoning

2 tablespoons dairy sour cream

Wash chicken livers and cut into small pieces. Melt butter in small frying pan. Stir in Garlic Powder, chicken livers, and Chicken Seasoned Stock Base. Sauté until livers are no longer red. Put livers in electric blender. Add sherry to frying pan and scrape up drippings. Add to livers in blender along with cream cheese, Tarragon, Beau Monde, and sour cream. Blend thoroughly. Chill and spread on crisp crackers or rounds of Melba toast or rye wafers. Makes about 1½ cups.

Paté Beau Monde

Make this canapé spread ahead and store in the freezer to have on hand for holiday entertaining.

2 packages (3 oz. each) cream cheese	¼ teaspoon Thyme
1 tablespoon water	¼ teaspoon Marjoram
2½ teaspoons Beau Monde Seasoning	¼ teaspoon Summer Savory
	2 teaspoons Parsley

Soften cream cheese with a fork; blend in water and Beau Monde. Crush Thyme, Marjoram, and Summer Savory and mix into cheese along with Parsley. Chill for several hours for flavors to blend. Spread on crisp crackers or use to fill small stalks of celery. Makes about ½ cup.

BEAU MONDE DIP

Omit water and add 3 or 4 tablespoons of light cream to make of dipping consistency. Serve with potato or corn chips or crisp raw vegetables.

Mushroom Liver Paté

This smokey-flavored paté makes a savory spread for your appetizer tray.

¼ pound liverwurst	3 tablespoons milk
1 teaspoon Powdered Mushrooms	½ teaspoon Caraway Seed
1 package (3 oz.) cream cheese	½ teaspoon Old Hickory Smoked Salt

Mash liverwurst and blend in Powdered Mushrooms, cream cheese, and milk. When smooth and thoroughly blended, crush Caraway Seed and mix in along with Old Hickory. Chill in refrigeator for about an hour or so for flavors to develop. Serve with rye or wheat wafers or rye melba toast. Makes 1½ cups.

Paté Neapolitan

To serve this as a dip, thin with 3 or 4 tablespoons of light milk or cream and surround with potato or corn chips.

| 2 packages (3 oz. each) cream cheese | ½ teaspoon Beau Monde Seasoning |
| 1 tablespoon water | 1 teaspoon Spaghetti Sauce Seasoning |

Soften cream cheese with a fork; blend in water and Beau Monde. Add Spaghetti Sauce Seasoning and mix thoroughly. Chill for an hour or so for flavors to blend. Spread on crisp crackers or use to fill small stalks of celery. Makes about ½ cup.

Smoky Seafood Dip

🌱 Surround a bowl of Smoky Seafood Dip with large, cooked chilled shrimp, small lobster tails or cubes of lobster, or crab legs; pass toothpicks for spearing. You'll find this your most popular appetizer.

½ cup mayonnaise
½ cup dairy sour cream
¼ teaspoon Hot Mustard
¼ teaspoon Garlic Powder
2 teaspoons Instant Minced Onions

1 tablespoon Tarragon White Wine Vinegar
Dash Cayenne Pepper
1 teaspoon Old Hickory Smoked Salt

Blend together mayonnaise, sour cream, Mustard, Garlic Powder, Onions, and Vinegar. Add Cayenne and Old Hickory; mix well. Chill sauce for an hour or so for flavors to blend. Makes about 1 cup.

Shrimp and Toasted Onion Dip

🌱 Spice Parisienne gives zesty seasoning, and Instant Toasted Onions contribute a crunchy texture.

2 packages (3 oz. each) cream cheese
4 tablespoons light cream or milk
½ cup cooked or canned chopped shrimp

1 tablespoon Soy Sauce
1 tablespoon Garlic Wine Vinegar
⅛ teaspoon Spice Parisienne
2 tablespoons Instant Toasted Onions

Soften cream cheese with fork; blend in cream or milk until smooth. Add chopped shrimp, Soy Sauce, Vinegar, and Spice Parisienne. Mix well and stir in Toasted Onions. Let stand for about 1 hour for flavors to blend. Serve with potato chips, corn chips, crisp crackers, or Melba toast. Makes 1½ cups.

Guacamole

🌱 If Guacamole cannot be served shortly after it is made, top with a thin coating of mayonnaise to prevent the avocado from darkening. Stir mayonnaise in when ready to serve.

2 Chili Pequins
1 tablespoon Garlic Wine Vinegar
2 very ripe avocados
1 tablespoon Instant Toasted Onions

1 teaspoon Chili Con Carne Seasoning Powder
2 teaspoons Beau Monde Seasoning

Crush Chili Pequins in bowl and add Vinegar. Let stand for about 15 minutes. Peel avocados; remove seeds, add to Chili Pequins. Mash and mix well. Stir in Toasted Onions, Chili Con Carne Seasoning Powder, and Beau Monde. Makes 1½ cups.

Dill 'n' Onion Dip

⅔ cup mayonnaise
⅔ cup dairy sour cream
1 tablespoon Shredded Green
    Onions

1 tablespoon Parsley
1 teaspoon Dill Weed
1 teaspoon Beau Monde Seasoning

Blend mayonnaise and sour cream. Mix in Shredded Green Onions, Parsley, Dill Weed, and Beau Monde. Chill for an hour or so for flavors to blend. Serve with potato or corn chips, crisp crackers, or crisp raw vegetables. Makes 1½ cups.

Nippy Cottage Cheese Dip

1 pint country-style or small curd
    cottage cheese
½ cup yoghurt
2 teaspoons Beau Monde Seasoning

2 teaspoons Parsley
½ teaspoon Lemon Peel
1 teaspoon Worcestershire sauce

Press cottage cheese through fine wire sieve. Combine with yoghurt, Beau Monde, Parsley, Lemon Peel, and Worcestershire sauce. Let stand for an hour or so for flavors to blend. Serve in a chilled bowl surrounded by crisp raw vegetables, cooked whole shrimp, or Melba toast. Makes 2½ cups.

Smoky Cheese and Onion Dip

2 teaspoons Instant Minced Onions
2 teaspoons water
2 packages (3 oz. each) cream
    cheese

3 or 4 tablespoons light cream or
    milk
½ teaspoon Old Hickory Smoked Salt

Rehydrate Onions in water. Soften cream cheese with fork; blend in Onions and cream or milk. Season with Old Hickory Smoked Salt. Serve with potato or corn chips or crisp crackers. Makes about ½ cup.

Toasted Onion-Sour Cream Dip

1 cup dairy sour cream
1½ tablespoons Instant Toasted
    Onions

3 teaspoons Beef Stock Base
½ teaspoon Worcestershire sauce
Dash Cayenne Pepper

Mix together sour cream, Toasted Onions, Beef Stock Base, Worcestershire sauce, and Cayenne; blend thoroughly. Let stand for an hour or so for flavors to blend. Serve with potato or corn chips, crisp crackers, or chilled raw vegetables. Makes 1½ cups.

SALADS

A SALAD IS as individual as the person who combines it. It may be bold, gay, whimsical, fancy, or casual. It is an ever-changing personal design, which can be varied to fit the mood of the cook, the weather, the rest of the menu, the occasion, the season, or the ingredients on hand.

There is a lot of showmanship in every good cook, and the salad she creates—whether it be a preamble to dinner, a hearty main dish, or a congenial accent to accompany the entrée—provides a very effective means by which she can display her inventive genius.

The artful addition of unexpected flavor accents contributes greatly to the personality of a salad. It is here that herbs, seasonings, and flavorful vinegars play one of their most important roles. The tasty crunchiness of Toasted Onions makes a salad of citrus fruits outstanding. Tuna salad takes on an exotic character with the addition of chopped Crystallized Ginger and toasted almonds. The pungent goodness of Oregano flatters chilled tomato slices. Crisp zucchini slices become a special treat when marinated in a well-seasoned dressing and served with avocado and olives.

And the gourmet's favorite—fresh, crisp greens, tossed lightly with the simplest of dressings—becomes a masterpiece to excite the most discriminating palate when enlivened by just the right seasonings.

Fruit Salad with Chervil Dressing

🌱 There's enough dressing for 6 salads. Take your pick of any kind of fruit—the flavors in this dressing will go with almost any combination.

Fresh or canned fruit, such as
  pears, peaches, pineapple,
  bananas, melons, grapes
Salad greens
⅔ cup White Wine Vinegar
¼ teaspoon Marjoram

4 teaspoons sugar
½ teaspoon Ground Nutmeg
½ teaspoon Orange Peel
¼ teaspoon Lemon Peel
⅔ cup olive oil
2 teaspoons Chervil

Arrange chilled fruits on crisp lettuce or other salad greens. Pour Vinegar into jar. Crush Marjoram and add to Vinegar with sugar, Nutmeg, Orange and Lemon Peel. Shake well to dissolve sugar. Add olive oil and Chervil. Shake again; pour over fruit. Serve at once. Makes 1½ cups dressing.

Orange and Grapefruit Salad with Toasted Onion Dressing

🌱 The flavor and crispness of the Toasted Onions is unusually good with citrus fruit.

3 oranges, pared and sectioned
2 grapefruit, pared and sectioned
1 large avocado, peeled and
  cut into wedges
Salad greens
½ teaspoon Salad Herbs
1½ teaspoons Garlic Salt
½ teaspoon Paprika

⅛ teaspoon Medium Grind Black
  Pepper
½ teaspoon sugar
¼ cup Eschalot Wine Vinegar
½ cup olive oil
1 tablespoon Instant Toasted Onions
1 teaspoon Orange Peel

Arrange orange, grapefruit, and avocado sections on salad greens. Crush Salad Herbs and sprinkle over fruit. Chill thoroughly. Combine Garlic Salt, Paprika, Pepper, sugar, and Vinegar in a jar. Screw on top and shake until seasonings are well blended. Add olive oil, Toasted Onions, and Orange Peel. Just before serving, shake dressing well and pour over fruit. Makes 6 servings.

Orange-Rice Salad

❧ Serve with spicy barbecued foods or as an accompaniment to baked ham.

1 tablespoon Chicken Seasoned
    Stock Base
1¼ cups boiling water
½ cup rice
¼ teaspoon Salad Herbs
1 teaspoon Orange Peel
2 tablespoons Instant Toasted Onions

1 cup thinly sliced celery
1 can (11 oz.) mandarin oranges,
    drained
2 tablespoons Soy Sauce
3 tablespoons White Wine Vinegar
¼ cup olive or salad oil
Endive or romaine

Add Chicken Seasoned Stock Base to boiling water; add rice; cover and steam until done. Chill well. Fluff rice with fork. Crush Salad Herbs and sprinkle over rice with Orange Peel. Add Toasted Onions, sliced celery, and mandarin oranges. Toss gently to mix. Combine Soy Sauce, Vinegar and oil; shake well and pour over salad. Mix well but carefully. Garnish with endive or romaine. Serve very cold. Makes 6 servings.

Dilled Green Beans

❧ Prepare these beans a day or so ahead.

1 can (1 lb.) green beans or
    ¾ pound cooked fresh green
    beans
⅓ cup Red Wine Vinegar

½ teaspoon Beau Monde Seasoning
½ teaspoon Dill Weed
3 tablespoons olive oil
1 tablespoon Instant Toasted Onions

Drain beans. Heat Vinegar and pour over beans. When beans cool, add Beau Monde, Dill Weed, and olive oil. Toss lightly to combine thoroughly. Chill well, preferably overnight. Just before serving, sprinkle with Toasted Onions. Makes 4 servings.

Caraway Cole Slaw

❧ A good salad to serve with pork chops or roast pork.

3 cups finely chopped or
    shredded cabbage
2 teaspoons Beau Monde Seasoning
1 tablespoon sugar
½ teaspoon salt
¼ teaspoon Hot Mustard

1 tablespoon Shredded Green Onions
2 tablespoons Basil White Wine
    Vinegar
½ cup dairy sour cream
½ teaspoon Caraway Seed

Chill cabbage thoroughly. Combine Beau Monde, sugar, salt, Mustard, and Shredded Green Onions. Blend in Vinegar and sour cream. Crush Caraway Seed and add to dressing. Just before serving pour over cabbage and mix well. Makes 6 servings.

Ensalada Zucchini

🌱 Careful! Don't overcook the zucchini. This unusual salad will rate raves at your next buffet supper or barbecue.

1 pound zucchini or Italian squash
½ cup water
1 teaspoon Mei Yen Seasoning
2 teaspoons Garlic Salt
¼ teaspoon Paprika
¼ teaspoon Medium Grind Black Pepper
¼ teaspoon sugar
¼ cup Basil White Wine Vinegar
⅓ cup olive or salad oil
1 large ripe avocado
6 to 8 large pimiento-stuffed olives
Salad greens
1 tablespoon Instant Toasted Onions

Scrub zucchini; cut off stem ends and slice into 1-inch thick slices. Cook in water and Mei Yen Seasoning for 5 to 7 minutes; drain. Combine Garlic Salt, Paprika, Pepper, sugar, Vinegar, and oil. Shake to combine well. Pour over zucchini. Marinate the zucchini in dressing several hours or overnight. Just before serving, drain off dressing. Peel and slice avocado; cut olives in half lengthwise. Arrange zucchini, avocado, and olives on platter. Garnish with crisp salad greens. Add Toasted Onions to dressing; shake dressing well again and spoon over salad. Makes 4 servings.

Gourmet Buffet Salad

🌱 There'll be enough dressing to make this salad twice or for double the amount of salad greens. Use a sharp knife to cut the greens in fine shreds.

1 cup shredded cabbage
1 cup shredded spinach
1 cup shredded chicory or curly endive
1 cup shredded lettuce
4 or 5 anchovy fillets
2 tablespoons crumbled Blue or Roquefort cheese
1 tablespoon Instant Toasted Onions
¼ teaspoon Garlic Powder
1 teaspoon Beau Monde Seasoning
½ teaspoon Paprika
¼ teaspoon Mild Mustard
¼ teaspoon Cracked Black Pepper
2 tablespoons Eschalot Wine Vinegar
6 tablespoons salad oil (include oil drained from anchovy fillets as part of 6 tablespoons)
½ cup dairy sour cream

Toss salad greens together in salad bowl. Cut anchovy fillets in small pieces and sprinkle over greens along with cheese and Toasted Onions. In a small bowl mix together Garlic Powder, Beau Monde, Paprika, Mustard, Pepper, and Vinegar. Beat in oil and sour cream. Pour half of dressing over salad greens. Toss until greens are coated with dressing. Makes 6 servings.

Tomatoes Rossi

4 ripe tomatoes
1 teaspoon Oregano
1 flat tin (2 oz.) anchovy fillets
5 tablespoons olive oil

3 tablespoons Basil White Wine Vinegar
Watercress

Scald and peel tomatoes; chill. Cut each tomato into four slices. Arrange on platter or on 4 individual salad plates. Crush Oregano and sprinkle over the tomatoes. Top each tomato slice with an anchovy fillet. Spoon oil and Vinegar over tomatoes. Garnish with watercress, if desired. Makes 4 servings.

Tossed Salad Orientale

2 cups cooked rice, well chilled
2 tablespoons Instant Toasted Onions
1 cup well-drained cooked or canned bean sprouts
¼ cup sliced radishes
¼ cup slivered green pepper
½ cup thinly sliced celery

1 cup broken curly endive, lettuce, or other greens
1 teaspoon Mei Yen Seasoning
4 teaspoons Soy Sauce
⅛ teaspoon Garlic Powder
2 tablespoons White Wine Vinegar
4 tablespoons olive oil
Salad greens

Combine rice, Toasted Onions, bean sprouts, radishes, green pepper, celery, and endive. Mix together Mei Yen, Soy Sauce, Garlic Powder, Vinegar, and oil. Beat well and pour over rice. Toss lightly but thoroughly. Heap in a salad bowl lined with lettuce, endive, or other greens. Makes 6 servings.

Tuna Salad Waikiki

Make this salad, too, with 2 cups diced, cooked leftover chicken or turkey or with canned chicken.

2 cans (7 oz. each) solid pack tuna
1 cup thinly sliced celery
2 tablespoons diced pimiento
2 tablespoons chopped Crystallized Ginger
¾ cup slivered, toasted almonds
¼ cup dairy sour cream

¼ cup mayonnaise
1 tablespoon White Wine Vinegar
1 teaspoon Beau Monde Seasoning
6 to 8 slices pineapple, chilled
Salad greens
Ripe olives

Drain tuna and separate into large size pieces. Combine with celery, pimiento, Ginger, and almonds. Blend together sour cream, mayonnaise, Vinegar, and Beau Monde. Pour over tuna and mix carefully but thoroughly. Drain chilled pineapple and arrange on salad greens. Heap tuna salad on pineapple slice. Garnish with ripe olives, if desired. Serve at once. Makes 6 to 8 servings.

Chef's Salad with Salad Herbs

❦ Perfect main course for a summer meal. Try it, too, using crab, shrimp, ham, or cold roast veal.

5 or 6 cups broken salad greens such as romaine, watercress, red or bibb lettuce, head lettuce
1 cup slivered, cold cooked chicken, turkey, or tongue
½ cup slivered Swiss cheese
4 hard-cooked eggs, cut in quarters
2 slices bread
1 tablespoon butter

½ teaspoon Onion Powder
1 teaspoon Beau Monde Seasoning
¼ teaspoon Hot Mustard
¼ teaspoon Cracked Black Pepper
2½ tablespoons White Wine Vinegar
6 tablespoons olive oil
4 tablespoons dairy sour cream
½ teaspoon Salad Herbs

Fill large salad bowl with greens. Arrange slivered chicken, turkey, or tongue, cheese, and eggs on top of the greens. Cut bread into croutons. Melt butter in frying pan; stir in Onion Powder. Add croutons and toast over low heat, tossing croutons as they brown. When lightly browned and crisp, sprinkle over salad. Blend together Beau Monde, Mustard, Pepper, and Vinegar. Add oil and sour cream and beat well with a fork. Crush Salad Herbs and add to the dressing. Pour over salad and toss lightly until salad is coated with dressing. Serve at once. Makes 6 servings.

Shrimp and Lima Bean Salad

❦ Smooth and crunchy textures combine in this flavorful entrée salad.

1 package frozen small green lima beans, cooked, or 2 cups cooked fresh or canned green limas
¾ pound fresh cooked shrimp or 2 cans (6 oz.) shrimp
1 cup thinly sliced celery
1 tablespoon Instant Toasted Onions
1 tablespoon chopped pimiento

¼ teaspoon Salad Herbs
1 teaspoon Beau Monde Seasoning
½ teaspoon Paprika
¼ teaspoon Medium Grind Black Pepper
¼ cup Basil White Wine Vinegar
½ cup salad oil
Ripe olives and radishes

Drain beans thoroughly; combine with shrimp, sliced celery, Toasted Onions, and pimiento. Crush Salad Herbs and sprinkle over salad. Combine Beau Monde, Paprika, Pepper, and Vinegar in jar. Shake until well blended. Add oil and shake again. Pour just enough dressing over salad to moisten well. Toss gently with fork to mix thoroughly. Chill well and garnish with ripe olives and radishes. Makes 6 servings.

Cucumber Aspic

🌿 Good with broiled trout or lobster — or with cold sliced chicken or turkey.

1 envelope unflavored gelatin
1¼ cups cold water
1½ tablespoons sugar
1 teaspoon Beau Monde Seasoning
⅓ cup White Wine Vinegar

¾ cup well-drained grated cucumber
1 tablespoon Shredded Green Onion
1 teaspoon Dill Weed
Mayonnaise or dairy sour cream

Add gelatin to cold water. When softened, heat slowly until gelatin is dissolved. Stir in sugar, Beau Monde, and Vinegar. Chill until syrupy. Mix in cucumber, Onion, and Dill Weed. Pour into 3-cup mold and chill until firm. Serve with mayonnaise or dairy sour cream. Makes 4 servings.

Crab Mousse Ring

1½ cups fresh cooked crab or
    2 cans (6 oz. each) crabmeat
3 tablespoons lemon juice
2 tablespoons Basil White Wine
    Vinegar
1 teaspoon Mei Yen Seasoning
2 teaspoons Horseradish
½ teaspoon Medium Grind Black
    Pepper

½ teaspoon salt
1 envelope unflavored gelatin
¼ cup cold water
½ cup heavy cream
1 cup mayonnaise
2 hard-cooked eggs
Tomato wedges and
    cucumber slices

Mix crab with lemon juice, Vinegar, Mei Yen, Horseradish, Pepper, and salt. Let stand about 30 minutes for flavors to develop. Soften gelatin in cold water and dissolve over hot water. Whip cream in large bowl; mix in mayonnaise and gelatin. Add crab. Oil an 8-inch ring mold. Slice hard-cooked eggs and arrange egg slices in mold. Pour in crab mixture. Chill until firm, at least 1 hour. Unmold and garnish with tomato wedges and cucumber slices. Makes 8 servings.

Molded Borscht Ring

1 envelope unflavored gelatin
¼ cup cold water
1 can (1 lb.) shoestring beets
3 tablespoons sugar

⅓ cup Red Wine Vinegar
1 tablespoon Instant Minced Onion
Dairy sour cream
Dill Weed or Chervil

Soften gelatin in cold water. Drain liquid from beets. Combine with sugar and Vinegar; heat to simmering. Dissolve gelatin in hot liquid. Chill until syrupy. Stir in beets and Onions. Pour into 3-cup ring mold. Chill until firm. Serve with dairy sour cream sprinkled with Dill Weed or Chervil. Makes 6 servings.

SALAD DRESSINGS

The old saying that "a salad is only as good as its dressing" is true whether it be a simple tossed green salad or an elaborate "centerpiece" salad.

Classic French Dressing

Always a favorite with those who like good food. Use Basil Vinegar instead of Tarragon for a change in flavor.

1 teaspoon salt
¼ teaspoon Cracked Black Pepper
4 tablespoons Tarragon Red Wine Vinegar

4 tablespoons Garlic Wine Vinegar
1 cup olive or salad oil

Mix salt and Pepper with Vinegar. Add oil and shake or beat. Pour over salad greens and toss until leaves are coated. Serve at once. Makes 1½ cups.

SALAD HERB FRENCH DRESSING

Use 1 teaspoon of Garlic Salt instead of salt and add 1 teaspoon Paprika. Substitute Red Wine Vinegar for the flavored Vinegar. Just before tossing salad, sprinkle with 1 to 1½ teaspoons Salad Herbs.

FRENCH DRESSING AUX FINES HERBES

To Classic French Dressing, add 1 teaspoon Paprika, ¼ teaspoon crushed Oregano, ¼ teaspoon crushed Sweet Basil, and ¼ Bay Leaf.

Poppy Seed Dressing

Poppy Seed Dressing will keep for two or three weeks in the refrigerator without separating. Serve it on fresh fruit salad sprinkled with Salad Herbs.

1 cup sugar
2 tablespoons Hot Mustard
¾ teaspoon Onion Powder
1/16 teaspoon Garlic Powder
1½ teaspoons salt

2½ tablespoons Poppy Seed
3 tablespoons lemon juice
½ cup White Wine Vinegar
2 cups olive oil

Blend together the sugar, Mustard, Onion Powder, Garlic Powder, salt, and Poppy Seed. Stir in lemon juice and Vinegar; mix with an electric beater at medium speed. Add olive oil, one tablespoon at a time, continuing to beat with electric beater. After all oil is added, beat at high speed for 15 minutes. Dressing will be rather thick, but will thin out when added to fruit. Or dressing can be thinned with fruit juice. Makes 3 cups.

Roquefort Dressing

❧ Use on any salad calling for a Roquefort Dressing.

3 to 4 ounces Roquefort cheese (6 tablespoons)
⅛ teaspoon Cracked Black Pepper
1 teaspoon Onion Salt

¼ teaspoon Paprika
¼ teaspoon sugar
⅓ cup Garlic Wine Vinegar
4 tablespoons olive oil

Mash cheese with fork. Blend in Pepper, Onion Salt, Paprika, and sugar. Add Vinegar and olive oil; mix thoroughly. Pour over salad greens and toss until all leaves are coated with dressing. If dressing is made ahead of time, shake or mix thoroughly just before serving. Makes ¾ cup.

Sour Cream Dressing

❧ A simple dressing—delicious for coleslaw, sliced cucumbers, fruit, or salad greens.

1 cup dairy sour cream
3 tablespoons water
2 tablespoons Basil White Wine Vinegar

1 teaspoon salt
1½ tablespoons sugar
⅛ teaspoon Cayenne Pepper

Combine sour cream, water, Vinegar, salt, sugar, and Cayenne. Mix well and serve at once. Makes 1¼ cups.

Parmesan Herb Dressing

❧ Serve on cooked, chilled artichokes, cauliflower, string beans, or asparagus, or on wedges of lettuce. A good sauce for hot vegetables, too.

1 egg
1 teaspoon Beau Monde Seasoning
¼ teaspoon Garlic Powder
¼ teaspoon Onion Powder
¼ teaspoon Paprika

¼ teaspoon Cracked Black Pepper
¼ cup Tarragon White Wine Vinegar
¼ cup grated Parmesan cheese
1 cup olive oil
½ teaspoon Salad Herbs

Beat egg; blend in Beau Monde, Garlic Powder, Onion Powder, Paprika, Pepper, Vinegar, and cheese. Add the oil, a tablespoon or two at a time, beating until thoroughly blended after each addition. Continue beating until thick and very smooth. Crush Salad Herbs and stir in dressing. Chill for flavors to develop. Makes 2 cups.

RELISHES AND PICKLES

Spicy, pickled fruits or vegetables are the perfect accompaniment to all kinds of meats, fish, or poultry. They add zest to menus and turn ordinary food into party fare.

Spiced Apricots

Serve hot or cold with chicken, ham, or roast meats.

1 can (1 lb. 13 oz.) whole apricots
2 tablespoons brown sugar
½ teaspoon Pumpkin Pie Spice
1 tablespoon White Wine Vinegar

Drain syrup from apricots. Measure 1 cup of syrup and add brown sugar, Pumpkin Pie Spice, and Vinegar. Add apricots and simmer for 15 to 20 minutes. Serve hot or cold. Makes 6 to 8 servings.

Turkish Oranges

An intriguing addition to a buffet, try Turkish Oranges as an opening course or tossed with romaine lettuce for a delicious salad.

6 large oranges
½ cup pitted ripe olives
1 tablespoon Instant Minced Onions
⅛ teaspoon Cayenne Pepper
2 teaspoons Beau Monde Seasoning
4 tablespoons White Wine Vinegar
4 tablespoons olive oil

Pare oranges with sharp knife; cut in slices and remove seeds and the white membrane from center. Cut ripe olives into wedges. Alternate layers of oranges, olives, and Onions in a bowl. Combine Cayenne, Beau Monde, Vinegar, and olive oil. Stir well and pour over oranges. Chill for an hour or so for flavors to develop. Serve cold. Makes 6 servings.

Dilly Carrots

Serve these piquant tidbits as an hors d'oeuvres, or as a garnish for a molded salad or cold meat plate.

8 to 10 small young carrots
½ cup Basil White Wine Vinegar
½ cup water
1 teaspoon Dill Weed
1 teaspoon Beau Monde Seasoning

Scrape and trim carrots; cut in quarters lengthwise. Add Vinegar, water, Dill Weed, and Beau Monde. Cover and simmer for about 20 minutes or until carrots are crisp-tender. Chill for several hours or overnight in liquid. Makes about 1 pint.

Gingered Pineapple Slices

1 can (1 lb. 13 oz.) pineapple slices
½ cup sugar
2 tablespoons White Wine Vinegar

¼ cup dry white wine
1 piece Whole Ginger

Drain pineapple syrup into saucepan. Add sugar, Vinegar, and wine to syrup. Cut Whole Ginger into two or three pieces lengthwise and add to syrup. Simmer for 5 minutes. Add pineapple slices, bring back to simmering and cook for 5 minutes, basting frequently. Cool; refrigerate overnight or longer. Makes 7 or 8 servings.

Spiced Cantaloupe

1 medium or large-size cantaloupe
⅔ cup fruit juice (syrup from canned or cooked fruit, or canned fruit juice, such as pineapple or grapefruit juice)
½ teaspoon Whole Cloves

¼ cup brown sugar
¼ cup White Wine Vinegar
1 piece (½ inch) Stick Cinnamon
1 tablespoon chopped Crystallized Ginger

Pare cantaloupe; cut into wedges or cubes. Arrange in flat glass dish. Combine fruit juice, Cloves, brown sugar, Vinegar, Cinnamon, and Ginger in saucepan. Bring to a boil and simmer for about 10 minutes. Pour over cantaloupe. Chill in refrigerator overnight. Serve cold. Makes about 1 pint.

Fresh Tomato Relish

Good with hamburgers and broiled or barbecued meats.

5 or 6 medium-size tomatoes, peeled and diced
2 tablespoons Instant Toasted Onions
1 tablespoon Green Bell Peppers
3 tablespoons olive or salad oil
2 tablespoons Basil White Wine Vinegar

1 teaspoon sugar
1 teaspoon salt
¼ teaspoon Medium Grind Black Pepper
¼ teaspoon Salad Herbs

Peel tomatoes and dice into small cubes, discarding seeds. Add Toasted Onions, Green Peppers, oil, Vinegar, sugar, salt, and Pepper. Crush Salad Herbs and stir into relish. Chill for several hours for flavors to blend. Makes 2 cups.

SOUPS

THESE SOUPS are a far cry from the old-fashioned kind that simmered for days on the back of the stove—but they have lost nothing in the way of flavor and character. Thanks to the contributions of the seasoning shelf, many of today's soups can be made in a few minutes. Some of the heartier ones require two or three hours of cooking, but preparation time is cut to a minimum.

Beef Stock Base and Chicken Seasoned Stock Base provide a rich flavor background in just a few seconds. Fragrant herbs add their mysterious flavors to the soup pot, but without the tedious chopping that was once necessary. Sometimes vegetable spices—Onions, or Garlic, or Mushrooms—join with them to give full-bodied flavor to a hearty soup.

Skillful seasoning works quick wonders, too, with canned soups. Try cream of chicken soup with a dash of Cumin Seed, or tomato soup with Oregano, or onion soup with a little Marjoram, or clam chowder with Thyme.

In choosing a soup, consider the entire menu. If you are serving tomatoes with the main course, don't serve a tomato soup. Consider, too, the type of meal you are serving. A rich entrée calls for a light soup; a highly seasoned one needs a bland beginning. A thick, hearty soup is a meal in itself and for accompaniments needs only a crisp salad, French bread or crusty rolls, and a simple, light dessert.

Consommé Barraca

🌱 Be sure the Chicken Stock has cooled before combining with the eggs so the consommé will be smooth.

3 tablespoons Chicken Seasoned
    Stock Base
4 cups boiling water
4 egg yolks

¼ cup light cream
¼ cup sherry
1 teaspoon Arrowroot
1 teaspoon Shredded Green Onions

Dissolve Chicken Seasoned Stock Base in boiling water. Let cool until just warm. Beat egg yolks, cream, sherry, and Arrowroot until smooth. Beat into Chicken Stock. Heat over low heat, stirring constantly, until soup is hot and has thickened slightly. Do not allow to boil. Pour into soup cups. Sprinkle each serving with ¼ teaspoon Shredded Green Onions. Serve at once. Makes 4 servings.

Beef Broth with Caraway

🌱 A real quickie with a distinctive flavor.

6 teaspoons Beef Stock Base
3 cups boiling water
¼ teaspoon Caraway Seeds

1 teaspoon Arrowroot
1 tablespoon cold water

Dissolve Beef Stock Base in boiling water. Crush Caraway Seeds and add to broth. Simmer for about 15 minutes. Strain out seeds. Mix Arrowroot with cold water; stir into broth. Simmer until broth thickens slightly, stirring constantly. Serve at once. Makes 4 servings.

Green Pea Soup

🌱 Made in just a few minutes from a can of peas, this beautiful looking soup has real gourmet flavor.

1 can (1 lb.) green peas or
    2 cups cooked fresh or
    frozen peas
2 tablespoons Chicken Seasoned
    Stock Base
1 cup hot water

1 teaspoon Onion Powder
2 teaspoons Mei Yen Seasoning
1 cup light cream
    Dash Ground White Pepper
1 teaspoon Chervil

Purée undrained peas in an electric blender or food mill. Dissolve Chicken Seasoned Stock Base in hot water. Combine puréed peas and Chicken Stock in top of double boiler. Add Onion Powder, Mei Yen, cream, and Pepper. Heat over hot water. Just before serving sprinkle with Chervil. Makes 6 servings.

Tomato Bouillon Curry

4 teaspoons Beef Stock Base
2 cups boiling water
1 can (10½ oz.) condensed
    tomato soup

½ teaspoon Curry Powder
¼ cup cold water
½ teaspoon Mei Yen Seasoning

Dissolve Beef Stock Base in boiling water. Add condensed tomato soup and blend until smooth. Mix Curry Powder with cold water and stir into soup along with Mei Yen. Heat just to simmering. Serve hot. Makes 4 servings.

Purée Mongole

It takes only a minute or two to make this gourmet soup.

1 can (1 lb.) peas
2 tablespoons tomato paste
1 teaspoon Chicken Seasoned
    Stock Base

1 cup light cream
2 teaspoons Mei Yen Seasoning
2 tablespoons sherry
1 teaspoon Chervil

Blend peas and their liquid and tomato paste in blender; strain through wire sieve. Add Chicken Seasoned Stock Base. Heat, stirring constantly. When hot, add cream and Mei Yen. Heat just to simmering, but do not boil. Add sherry and sprinkle with Chervil. Makes 4 servings.

Cream of Corn Soup

When fresh corn is in season, substitute fresh for canned corn. Cut the kernels from 4 medium-size ears and add an extra ½ cup hot water. Add extra Mei Yen to taste.

2 tablespoons Instant Minced Onions
2 tablespoons Green Bell Peppers
¼ cup water
2 tablespoons butter
1 can (1 lb.) whole kernel corn

1 tablespoon Chicken Seasoned
    Stock Base
1 teaspoon Mei Yen Seasoning
1½ cups hot water
1 cup light cream
½ teaspoon Sweet Basil

Rehydrate Onions and Green Peppers in ¼ cup water for about 5 minutes. Melt butter; add Onions and Green Peppers; simmer gently 4 to 5 minutes. Add undrained corn, Chicken Stock Base, Mei Yen, and hot water. Cover and simmer for about 30 minutes. Let cool slightly; pour into electric blender and blend until smooth. Press through wire sieve. Add light cream. Crush Basil and stir into soup. Heat just to boiling. Serve hot. Makes 6 servings.

Sour Cream Potato Soup

❧ This filling potato soup, with its unusual Cumin flavor, is good to serve for luncheon or supper.

5 cups water
2½ cups diced potatoes
2 tablespoons Beef Stock Base
½ teaspoon Medium Grind Black Pepper
2 teaspoons Beau Monde Seasoning

1 teaspoon Ground Cumin
1 teaspoon Arrowroot
1 cup light cream
1 cup dairy sour cream
1 teaspoon Chervil

Combine water, diced potatoes, and Beef Stock Base in a 3-quart kettle. Simmer until potatoes are very tender; mash potatoes but do not drain. Add Pepper, Beau Monde, and Cumin; simmer for 10 minutes. Blend Arrowroot into cream and stir slowly into soup. Blend sour cream into soup; heat just to boiling. Sprinkle with Chervil and serve at once. Makes 8 servings.

Cream of Artichoke Soup

❧ If you're looking for something just a little out of the ordinary, you'll like this artichoke soup. Serve it hot or icy cold.

6 small artichoke hearts, fresh or frozen
1 quart boiling water
1 tablespoon Beau Monde Seasoning
2 tablespoons Chicken Seasoned Stock Base
1 quart hot water

1 teaspoon salt
⅛ teaspoon Cracked Black Pepper
1 cup light cream
2 teaspoons Arrowroot
1 tablespoon cold water
1 teaspoon Chervil

If using fresh artichokes, trim and pull off outer leaves. Place in kettle and add boiling water and Beau Monde. Cover and cook until tender. Drain and chop coarsely. Remove tough portion. Dissolve Chicken Seasoned Stock Base in hot water; add chopped artichoke hearts. Season with salt and Pepper. Stir in cream. Mix Arrowroot with cold water; stir into soup. Heat soup, stirring constantly, just until boiling and slightly thickened. Sprinkle with Chervil. Serve at once or chill and serve cold. Makes 6 servings.

Chilled Clam Madrilène

3 cups tomato juice
1 teaspoon Mei Yen Seasoning
1 teaspoon Onion Salt
⅛ teaspoon Lemon Peel

½ teaspoon Dill Weed
1 bottle (8 oz.) clam juice
½ cup dairy sour cream
Shredded Green Onions or Chervil

Combine tomato juice, Mei Yen, Onion Salt, Lemon Peel, and Dill Weed. Simmer for 10 minutes; stir in clam juice. Cool and beat in sour cream with rotary beater or electric mixer. Chill until very cold. Serve in soup cups; garnish with Shredded Green Onions or Chervil. Makes 6 servings.

Chicken Avocado Soup

Such a lovely color and so easy to do, for it requires no cooking.

2 tablespoons Chicken Seasoned
   Stock Base
2 cups boiling water
1 medium-size ripe avocado

1 tablespoon lime juice
½ teaspoon Beau Monde Seasoning
⅛ teaspoon Cracked Black Pepper

Dissolve Chicken Seasoned Stock Base in boiling water. Let cool slightly. Peel and dice avocado. Combine with Chicken Stock in electric blender; blend until smooth. Add lime juice, Beau Monde, and Pepper. Blend again for two or three seconds. Chill thoroughly. Serve very cold. Makes 4 servings.

Chilled Cream of Cucumber Soup

Especially refreshing on a hot day.

2 large cucumbers
1 tablespoon Instant Minced Onions
4 cups water
4 tablespoons Chicken Seasoned
   Stock Base

½ teaspoon Bouquet Garni for Soup
1 cup light cream
1 teaspoon Shredded Green Onions

Peel cucumbers and cut into 1-inch pieces. Combine in saucepan with Onions, water, and Chicken Seasoned Stock Base. Bring to a boil; crush Bouquet Garni and add. Simmer until cucumbers are tender, about 30 to 40 minutes. Cool slightly and purée in electric blender or food mill. Chill several hours or overnight. Stir in cream. Just before serving sprinkle with Shredded Green Onions. Makes 6 servings.

Vichysoisse

 Though traditionally served icy cold, Vichysoisse is delicious, too, served as a hot soup.

8 large leeks
2 tablespoons butter
2 tablespoons Chicken Seasoned
   Stock Base
3½ cups boiling water
1½ cups thinly sliced, raw potatoes

1½ teaspoons Mei Yen Seasoning
   Powder
⅛ teaspoon Ground White Pepper
1½ cups light cream
Shredded Green Onions

Wash leeks; cut off green tops. Slice leeks very thin. Melt butter in saucepan; add leeks. Cover and cook over low heat for 10 minutes, but do not brown. Combine Chicken Seasoned Stock Base and boiling water. Add to leeks along with potatoes, Mei Yen, and Pepper. Simmer until potatoes and leeks are done. Press through wire sieve. Cool; add cream. Chill until icy cold. Or heat just to boiling and serve very hot. Sprinkle each serving with Shredded Green Onions. Makes 6 servings.

VICHYSOISSE WITH ONIONS

Make as for Vichysoisse substituting for the leeks 2 tablespoons Instant Minced Onions rehydrated in 2 tablespoons water. Sprinkle with Dill Weed instead of Shredded Green Onions.

MUSHROOM VICHYSOISSE

Make as for Vichysoisse with Onions adding 1 teaspoon Powdered Mushrooms to the boiling water along with the Chicken Seasoned Stock Base. Garnish with Chervil or Parsley.

Clam Bisque

Double this recipe for more servings; it's quick and easy to make.

1 can (7 oz.) minced clams
2 cups milk
½ teaspoon Dill Seed
½ teaspoon Beau Monde Seasoning

1 tablespoon butter
1 teaspoon Arrowroot
1 tablespoon water

Drain clams; combine clam juice with milk and Dill Seed in top of double boiler. Place over hot water. When thoroughly heated, add minced clams, Beau Monde, and butter. Mix Arrowroot with water; stir into hot bisque. Keep over simmering water for 10 to 15 minutes, stirring occasionally. Serve hot. Makes 2 or 3 servings.

Mushroom-Oyster Stew

🌿 Oyster stew that's elegantly different!

1 pint (or 12-oz. jar) fresh oysters
3 tablespoons butter
1 teaspoon Beau Monde Seasoning
⅛ teaspoon Spice Parisienne
1 teaspoon Powdered Mushrooms

1 teaspoon Chicken Seasoned
   Stock Base
1 cup hot water
1 cup light cream or rich milk
1 tablespoon brandy or cognac

Drain oysters, reserving liquor. Cut in half if very large. Melt butter; add oysters, Beau Monde, and Spice Parisienne. Cook until oysters are plump and edges curl. Add Powdered Mushrooms, Chicken Seasoned Stock Base, and hot water. Heat to simmering, stirring occasionally. Add milk and oyster liquor. When soup again is simmering, stir in brandy or cognac. Serve at once. Makes 4 servings.

Lobster Potage

🌿 The unusual combination of herbs and seasonings is the flavor secret in this elegant soup. Serve small cups for an opening course, a plate or large bowl as a main course for a soup supper party.

1 pound fresh or frozen lobster meat
   or lobster tails, or 2 cans (6½
   oz. each) lobster meat
2 tablespoons Instant Minced Onions
2 tablespoons water
2 tablespoons olive oil
½ cup thinly sliced carrots
¼ cup thinly sliced celery
2 cups hot water

2 tablespoons Chicken Seasoned
   Stock Base
1½ cups dry white wine
1/32 teaspoon Powdered Saffron
½ teaspoon Paprika
¼ teaspoon Curry Powder
1 cup light cream
¼ teaspoon Dill Weed
¼ teaspoon Parsley

Separate lobster meat into bite-size pieces. Rehydrate Instant Onions in water. Sauté Onions in olive oil until golden. Add carrots, celery, hot water, Chicken Seasoned Stock Base, wine, Saffron, Paprika, and Curry Powder. Simmer until vegetables are tender, about 30 minutes. Add lobster and cream; heat just to boiling. Sprinkle with Dill Weed and Parsley. Serve hot. Makes 6 to 8 servings.

Old Hickory Fish Chowder

Chowder in the New England tradition — with a robust smoky flavor.

1 pound halibut, haddock, cod, or other firm, white fish, fresh or frozen

2 cups cubed potatoes

3 cups water

2 tablespoons Instant Minced Onions

¼ teaspoon Celery Seed

½ teaspoon salt

⅛ teaspoon Medium Grind Black Pepper

2 cups rich milk

2 teaspoons Old Hickory Smoked Salt

1 tablespoon butter

¼ teaspoon Rosemary

Cut fish into cubes; remove any skin and bones. Place in 3-quart kettle or saucepan. Add potatoes, water, Onions, Celery Seed, salt, and Pepper. Simmer for 30 to 35 minutes or until fish and potatoes are done. Add milk, Old Hickory, and butter; heat just to boiling. Crush Rosemary and sprinkle on chowder. Serve in large soup plates or bowls as a main course accompanied by crisp crackers. Makes 4 servings.

Fish Chowder Ménagère

This robust soup, a complete meal in itself, is borrowed from a collection of prized Scandinavian recipes.

2 pounds white fish such as sole, bass, or flounder

2 tablespoons Instant Minced Onions

2 tablespoons water

1 tablespoon butter

1 tablespoon olive oil

1½ cups thinly sliced carrots

¼ cup thinly sliced celery

2 cups hot water

1 tablespoon Chicken Seasoned Stock Base

½ teaspoon salt

¼ teaspoon Medium Grind Black Pepper

1 teaspoon Bouquet Garni for Soup

1 cup light cream

1 egg yolk

¼ teaspoon Dill Weed

Toasted French Bread or Melba Toast

Cut fish into chunks. Rehydrate Onions in water. Heat butter and olive oil in 3-quart kettle or saucepan. Add Onions and cook until golden. Add carrots, celery, hot water, Chicken Seasoned Stock Base, salt, and Pepper. Simmer until the vegetables are done, about 30 minutes. Crush Bouquet Garni and add to soup along with fish. Simmer until fish is done, about 15 minutes. Beat cream and egg yolk together; stir into soup. Heat, but do not boil. Sprinkle with Dill Weed. Ladle chowder over toast and serve at once. Makes 6 to 8 servings.

Old-Fashioned Bean Soup

An excellent soup for a Lenten lunch — it's as hearty, filling, and flavorful as if there had been a ham-bone in the pot, but the flavor comes from Old Hickory Smoked Salt.

1 cup navy or pea beans	¼ cup diced carrots
1 quart warm water	½ cup chopped celery
1 teaspoon Beau Monde Seasoning	¼ teaspoon Bouquet Garni for Soup
¼ teaspoon Garlic Powder	2 tablespoons tomato paste
1 tablespoon Instant Minced Onions	1 quart milk
1 piece (1 inch) Bay Leaf	1 tablespoon Old Hickory Smoked Salt
3 or 4 Whole Black Peppercorns	

Wash and pick over beans. Combine beans and water in a large kettle and simmer gently for 1 hour. Add Beau Monde, Garlic Powder, Instant Onions, Bay Leaf, Whole Black Peppercorns, carrots, celery, Bouquet Garni, and tomato paste. Continue cooking until beans are tender. Mash with a potato masher or put beans through food mill. Add milk and heat just to simmering. Stir in Old Hickory and serve at once. Makes 8 servings.

Corn Chowder

A hearty chowder, satisfying enough for a main course. For a meatless chowder, omit the bacon, use butter instead of bacon drippings, and season with Old Hickory Smoked Salt.

6 slices bacon	1 teaspoon Beau Monde Seasoning
2 tablespoons Instant Minced Onions	1½ teaspoons salt
1 tablespoon Green Bell Peppers	¼ teaspoon Paprika
3 tablespoons cold water	1 piece (1 inch) Bay Leaf
½ cup chopped celery	¼ teaspoon Bouquet Garni for Soup
1 cup diced potatoes	1 teaspoon Arrowroot
2 cups hot water	2 cups light cream or rich milk
1 can (12 oz.) whole kernel corn	1 teaspoon Parsley

Cut bacon into small pieces. Fry until crisp; drain and set aside. Pour off all but 1 tablespoon bacon drippings. Rehydrate Onions and Green Peppers in cold water. Sauté Onions, Peppers, and celery in drippings until lightly browned. Add potatoes, water, undrained corn, Beau Monde, salt, Paprika, and Bay Leaf. Crush Bouquet Garni and stir into soup. Simmer until vegetables are tender, about 45 minutes. Just before ready to serve, moisten Arrowroot in a tablespoon of the milk; stir into soup along with rest of milk. Heat to boiling, stirring occasionally. Sprinkle with Parsley and crisp bacon bits. Serve hot. Makes 6 servings.

Old Hickory Split Pea Soup

 Garnish with thin rings of frankfurter, crumbled crisp bacon, or cubes of leftover baked ham. Or top with a few crisp croutons for a smokey-flavored meatless soup.

1 package (12 oz.) split peas	1 tablespoon Instant Minced Onions
6 cups water	¼ teaspoon Thyme
1 teaspoon salt	1 piece (½ inch) Bay Leaf
1 cup coarsely chopped celery and celery leaves	1 teaspoon Old Hickory Smoked Salt
1 cup sliced carrots	

Combine peas, water, salt, celery, carrots, and Onions in a large kettle. Bring to a boil; crush Thyme and add to soup along with Bay Leaf. Simmer until peas are very soft, about 2 hours. Press through wire sieve or food mill; or purée in electric blender. Heat to simmering; stir in Old Hickory. Serve hot. Makes 6 servings.

Minestrone Soup

 This thick soup is a whole meal when served with hot French bread or rolls. If you prefer a thinner soup, dissolve a teaspoon of Beef Stock Base in a cup of hot water and add to soup.

2 quarts water	1 cup cut green beans, fresh, frozen, or canned
3 tablespoons Beef Stock Base	1 cup peas, fresh, frozen, or canned
2 teaspoons salt	1 cup lima beans, fresh, frozen, or cooked dried
3 tablespoons olive oil	
3 tablespoons Instant Minced Onions	½ cup diced zucchini or other Italian squash
¼ teaspoon Garlic Powder	½ cup shredded Swiss chard or spinach
3 tablespoons tomato paste	
½ cup diced carrots	½ cup elbow macaroni
½ cup diced celery	Grated Romano or Parmesan cheese
1 teaspoon Parsley	
½ teaspoon Bouquet Garni for Soup	

Combine water, Beef Stock Base, salt, olive oil, Onions, Garlic Powder, and tomato paste in a large kettle. Bring to a boil and simmer for 10 to 15 minutes. Add carrots, celery, Parsley, and Bouquet Garni. Continue simmering for 20 to 30 minutes. Then add green beans, peas, lima beans, zucchini, and chard or spinach. When vegetables are almost tender, add macaroni and continue simmering until vegetables and macaroni are done. Serve in soup plates, sprinkled generously with grated Romano or Parmesan cheese. Makes 6 servings.

MEATS

NEW AND UNUSUAL recipes combine here with old favorites prepared in excitingly different ways. Spices and other seasonings bring intriguing flavors to familiar dishes — try Beef Stroganoff with Dill Weed, German Meat Balls in Caraway Sauce, Lamb Chops in Sherried Orange Sauce, Ham Slice with Curried Cherry Sauce, or Meat Loaf with Sweet-Sour Glaze.

Seasonings also lend a touch of international to meat recipes. Rogan Jaush, a pungently seasoned curry, is from the classic cuisine of India. The West Indies are represented in the unusual seasonings of Caribbean Pork and Bean Stew. From northern China comes a recipe for Beef Short Ribs Mandarin-Style, distinctly flavored with Anise Seed, Ginger, and Soy Sauce. Veal Scaloppine, made with Spaghetti Sauce Seasoning, takes just minutes to prepare, yet is reminiscent of Scaloppine sauces served in the finest Italian restaurants.

Here, too, you'll find budget meats lifted to new positions of elegance by the discriminating use of interesting and unusual seasonings. Chuck steak will tempt the gourmet when sauced with wine and Rosemary. Leftover lamb goes into a flavor-rich and hearty casserole that needs only a salad and a tasty bread to round out the meal. Ground beef becomes a special treat in an herb-flavored meat loaf. A savory stuffing turns economical breast of veal into a distinctive delicacy.

BEEF

Delightful seasoning touches add zest to these beef dishes which run the gamut from economy fare to elegant steaks and roasts.

Roast Prime Ribs of Beef

🌾 Don't overdo the herbs on this choice cut of meat — about ⅛ teaspoon for each rib of beef is enough.

2-rib prime rib of beef roast (about 4 to 5 pounds)
¼ teaspoon Bouquet Garni for Beef
½ teaspoon salt

⅛ teaspoon Medium Grind Black Pepper
1 teaspoon Beef Stock Base
2 cups hot water

Wipe meat with damp cloth. Combine ⅛ teaspoon of Bouquet Garni with salt and Pepper and rub into sides and fat of meat. Place meat in open roasting pan, fat side up, and roast in a 325° oven 20 to 30 minutes per pound, depending on rareness desired. Dissolve Beef Stock Base in 1 cup hot water; crush remaining ⅛ teaspoon Bouquet Garni and add to stock. Baste meat frequently. When meat is done, place on heated platter. Skim off excess fat and pour remaining 1 cup hot water into pan. Simmer, stirring constantly, until drippings are dissolved. Carve meat and serve with the pan gravy. Makes 6 servings.

Rotisserie Beef Roast

🌾 Roast meat in oven or portable rotisserie, or cook on a barbecue rotisserie over charcoal. Use a meat thermometer for accurate timing of roast.

4-pound boned and rolled beef roast (cross-rib, rib, or sirloin tip)
½ teaspoon Garlic Chips
2 teaspoons Beef Stock Base
1 cup hot water

1 teaspoon Mei Yen Seasoning
1 teaspoon Bouquet Garni for Beef
¼ cup Red Wine Vinegar
¼ cup salad oil

Insert Garlic Chips under fat and into roast, distributing as evenly as possible. Dissolve Beef Stock Base in hot water; add Mei Yen. Crush Bouquet Garni and add to beef stock with Vinegar and oil. Pour over roast and let marinate for several hours at room temperature. Fasten roast securely on spit. Roast at 325° for about 1½ hours or until done as desired. Baste frequently with marinade. When meat is done, remove from spit and carve. Heat any remaining marinade and combine with meat juices. Spoon over slices of meat. Makes 8 servings.

Chuck Steak Rosemary

🌿 Budget steaks make a gourmet meal when treated with a little Meat Tenderizer and served with a wine sauce seasoned with Rosemary.

1½ to 2-pound chuck steak, cut 1½ inches thick
1 teaspoon Unseasoned Meat Tenderizer
3 tablespoons butter
⅛ teaspoon Garlic Powder
¼ teaspoon Hot Mustard

1 tablespoon Shredded Green Onions
1 teaspoon Parsley
½ cup dry red wine
1 teaspoon Beef Stock Base
⅛ teaspoon Rosemary

Sprinkle meat evenly on both sides with Meat Tenderizer. Pierce generously with fork. Let stand at room temperature about 1½ hours. Broil or grill to desired doneness. Melt butter in saucepan. Stir in Garlic Powder, Mustard, Shredded Green Onions, Parsley, and wine; add Beef Stock Base. Bring to a boil. Crush Rosemary and stir into sauce. Simmer for 4 or 5 minutes. Pour over broiled steak. Serve at once. Makes 4 servings.

Roulades of Beef

2 pounds thinly sliced round steak
1 envelope (4 servings) instant mashed potatoes
2 teaspoons Instant Minced Onions
1 cup chopped fresh mushrooms or 1 can (4 oz.) mushroom stems and pieces, drained
1 tablespoon butter or shortening
1 teaspoon Bouquet Garni for Beef

3 tablespoons flour
½ teaspoon salt
⅛ teaspoon Fine Grind Black Pepper
1 tablespoon Beef Stock Base
1 cup hot water
½ cup dairy sour cream
2 tablespoons sherry
1 teaspoon Chervil

Cut steak into 6 or 8 pieces. Make mashed potatoes according to package directions, adding Instant Onions to liquid. Sauté mushrooms in butter or shortening in heavy frying pan; add to mashed potatoes. Crush ½ teaspoon Bouquet Garni and mix into potatoes. Spread pieces of meat with mashed potato. Roll up steak to form rolls and tie with string. Combine flour, salt, and Pepper. Dip beef rolls in seasoned flour. Brown in same frying pan in which mushrooms were cooked. Dissolve Beef Stock base in hot water; crush remaining ½ teaspoon Bouquet Garni and add to beef stock. Pour over browned meat rolls. Cover and cook over low heat until meat is tender, about 45 minutes. When meat is done, remove string. Arrange rolls on heated platter; skim off fat from gravy in pan. Blend in sour cream. Heat just to boiling; stir in sherry. Pour over meat rolls. Sprinkle with Chervil and serve at once. Makes 6 servings.

London Broil

Use this marinade on chuck or other budget steaks, as well as on flank steak. It's flavorful and helps to tenderize the less choice cuts. Broil or barbecue as preferred.

1 to 1½-pound flank steak
1 tablespoon tomato paste
1 cup hot water
1½ teaspoons Garlic Salt
¼ cup Red Wine Vinegar

¼ teaspoon Cracked Black Pepper
⅛ teaspoon Cracked Bay Leaf
¼ teaspoon Bouquet Garni for Beef
2 tablespoons salad oil

Score flank steak well. Combine tomato paste with hot water; add Garlic Salt and stir until dissolved. Add Vinegar, Pepper, and Bay Leaf. Crush Bouquet Garni and stir into marinade along with salad oil. Pour over steak in glass pan or bowl. Let marinate several hours at room temperature, or overnight in refrigerator, turning the steak several times. Drain steak; broil quickly, about 5 to 7 minutes on each side, basting with marinade. Cut into thin slices diagonally across grain. Heat remaining marinade and spoon over steak. Serve hot. Makes 4 servings.

Gingered Steak Strips

Gingered Steak, typical of the Malay states, makes an unusual supper dish. Serve it just like you would a curry.

1 piece (1 inch) Whole Ginger
1½ to 2 pounds sirloin or round steak, cut ½ inch thick
2 tablespoons butter
1 tablespoon coarsely chopped blanched almonds
2 teaspoons Mei Yen Seasoning
1 teaspoon Chili Powder
¼ teaspoon Garlic Powder
3 tablespoons Instant Minced Onions

3 tablespoons water
2 teaspoons Beef Stock Base
2 cups hot water
2 tablespoons plum jam
1 tablespoon Red Wine Vinegar
1 tablespoon Arrowroot
1 tablespoon cold water
2 tablespoons sherry

Soak piece of Ginger in cold water several hours or overnight. Chop finely to make about 1 teaspoon. Cut steak into 2-inch strips. Brown lightly in butter in heavy frying pan. Add almonds, Ginger, Mei Yen, Chili Powder, and Garlic Powder. Rehydrate Onions in water and stir into browned meat. Dissolve Beef Stock Base in hot water and pour over meat. Add plum jam and Vinegar. Cover and simmer slowly until meat is tender, about 40 minutes. Mix Arrowroot with cold water and stir into steak. When sauce is thickened, add sherry. Serve hot. Makes 6 servings.

Steak au Poivre

🌱 Pepper Steak is considered a man's dish, but women seem to like it, too. If you want your steak with less "bite," scrape off the Pepper kernels before serving. Try preparing venison steaks this way, too—using Meat Tenderizer if the venison seems tough.

1 to 1½-pound steak (New York, top sirloin, or any preferred cut)

1 tablespoon Whole Black Peppercorns

1 tablespoon olive oil

Salt to taste

¼ cup brandy or cognac

About an hour before cooking steak, remove from refrigerator. Crush Peppercorns by wrapping in cloth and crushing with a wooden mallet or rolling pin. Press Pepper firmly into both sides of steak. Let stand at room temperature. Heat olive oil in heavy frying pan. Pan broil steak to desired doneness. Season to taste with salt and place on hot platter. Pour brandy into frying pan. Set aflame, if desired. (Do this very carefully; brandy may flare up.) Stir to extinguish flame. When sauce is bubbling, pour over steak. Cut in strips to serve. Makes 2 servings.

Pot Roast of Beef, Bouquet Garni

3½ to 4-pound beef pot roast (chuck, rump, or round)

2 tablespoons flour

1 teaspoon Beau Monde Seasoning

1 teaspoon salt

¼ teaspoon Fine Grind Black Pepper

2 tablespoons Instant Minced Onions

2 tablespoons water

1 tablespoon Powdered Mushrooms

1 teaspoon Beef Stock Base

1 cup hot water

1 teaspoon Bouquet Garni for Beef

Potatoes, carrots, or other vegetables

½ cup cold water

Combine flour, Beau Monde, salt, and Pepper. Coat meat with seasoned flour. Cut off some of the fat and fry out in a large heavy frying pan or Dutch oven. Brown roast on all sides in hot fat. Meanwhile, rehydrate the Onions in water. When meat is well browned, remove from pan. Pour off excess fat. Add Onions and cook until lightly browned. Return meat to pan. Dissolve Powdered Mushrooms and Beef Stock Base in hot water. Pour over meat. Crush Bouquet Garni for Beef and add to pot roast. Cover pan tightly and cook over low heat for 2 to 3 hours or until meat is tender. Or cook pot roast in a 350° oven for 2 to 3 hours. About 40 minutes before serving time, add potatoes, carrots, or other vegetables. When meat and vegetables are done, arrange on heated platter. Blend remaining seasoned flour with cold water and stir into gravy. Cook until gravy is thickened and smooth, stirring constantly. Makes 6 servings.

Beef Stroganoff with Dill Weed

🌿 A different version of a favorite recipe. Serve Paprika Noodles (page 106) as an accompaniment.

1½-pound sirloin steak, cut ½ inch thick
4 tablespoons butter
1 teaspoon Mei Yen Seasoning
¼ teaspoon Fine Grind Black Pepper
¼ pound fresh mushrooms or 1 can (4 oz.) sliced mushrooms

2 teaspoons Beef Stock Base
2 teaspoons Onion Powder
2 cups hot water
2 teaspoons Arrowroot
1 tablespoon cold water
½ cup dairy sour cream
½ teaspoon Dill Weed

Trim meat and cut into thin strips. Brown in butter; season with Mei Yen and Pepper. Slice fresh mushrooms or drain canned mushrooms. When meat is browned, add mushrooms. Cook for 4 or 5 minutes, stirring frequently. Dissolve Beef Stock Base and Onion Powder in hot water and pour over meat. Cover and simmer for 1 hour or until meat is very tender, stirring occasionally. Mix Arrowroot with cold water and stir into meat. When sauce is thickened, blend in sour cream and Dill Weed. Serve hot. Makes 6 servings.

Beef Short Ribs Mandarin-Style

🌿 This recipe comes from a friend who formerly lived in Northern China. Anise Seeds give the different flavor. Serve with rice or noodles.

2½ to 3 pounds beef short ribs, cut into serving-size pieces
12 Anise Seeds
2 tablespoons Soy Sauce
½ cup dry red wine
⅛ teaspoon Garlic Powder

⅛ teaspoon Ground Ginger
2 teaspoons Beef Stock Base
2 teaspoons Powdered Mushrooms
1 cup hot water
¼ teaspoon Bouquet Garni for Beef

Place short ribs in deep bowl. Crush Anise Seeds thoroughly. Combine with Soy Sauce, wine, Garlic Powder, and Ginger. Pour over ribs. Marinate for several hours at room temperature or overnight in the refrigerator. Drain short ribs and brown in heavy frying pan. Pour off excess fat. Add Beef Stock Base and Powdered Mushrooms to hot water; combine with marinade. Pour over browned ribs. Crush Bouquet Garni and sprinkle over meat. Cover tightly and simmer slowly for 2 to 2½ hours or until ribs are very tender. Thicken sauce, if desired, with 2 teaspoons Arrowroot mixed with 1 tablespoon cold water. Makes 4 or 5 servings.

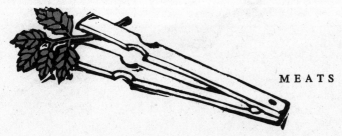

Chili Con Carne

🌿 Serve this alone or with beans, enchiladas, or tamales, or as a sauce for barbecued hamburgers or hot dogs.

1 pound round steak, ground or
    diced small
2 cups water
2 teaspoons Instant Minced Onions
3 tablespoons Chili Con Carne
    Seasoning

1 cup canned tomatoes
¾ teaspoon salt
1½ teaspoons Paprika

Brown meat lightly in heavy frying pan. Add water, Onions, Chili Con Carne Seasoning, tomatoes, salt, and Paprika. Simmer for 3 to 3½ hours. Makes 4 servings.

Beef Stew with Vegetables

🌿 Vegetables in this savory stew can be varied—use string beans, lima beans, celery, or turnips instead of the vegetables called for. Serve with mashed potatoes, noodles, or steamed rice.

2 pounds lean beef stew meat, cut
    into 1½-inch cubes
3 tablespoons flour
1 teaspoon Beau Monde Seasoning
1 teaspoon salt
¼ teaspoon Fine Grind Black Pepper
⅛ teaspoon Garlic Powder
2 tablespoons shortening or oil
1 teaspoon Beef Stock Base

2 tablespoons tomato paste
1 cup hot water
¼ cup dry red wine
1 teaspoon Bouquet Garni for Beef
1 can (4 oz.) sliced or whole mush-
    rooms, undrained
6 small whole onions
3 or 4 carrots
1 cup frozen or fresh peas

Trim any excess fat from meat. Combine flour, Beau Monde, salt, Pepper, and Garlic Powder. Coat meat with seasoned flour. Brown in hot shortening or oil in a heavy kettle or Dutch oven. Sprinkle any remaining seasoned flour over meat. Combine Beef Stock Base, tomato paste, and hot water; add wine to stock and pour over browned meat. Crush Bouquet Garni and add to stew along with mushrooms and mushroom liquid. Cover and cook slowly for 2 to 3 hours, or until meat is tender. Stir occasionally. About 30 minutes before meat is to be served, add onions and carrots; cook for about 20 minutes, then add peas and continue cooking until meat and vegetables are done. Serve hot. Makes 4 or 5 servings.

Baked Beef Hash

🌿 Just the right seasonings dress up leftovers.

2 to 3 cups diced leftover roast beef
2 to 3 cups diced cooked potatoes
2 tablespoons Instant Toasted
    Onions
¼ cup dry red wine

2 tablespoons tomato catsup
¾ cup light cream
2 tablespoons Soy Sauce
½ teaspoon Paprika
1 teaspoon Chervil

Combine meat, potatoes, and Toasted Onions. Pour wine over meat mixture. Combine catsup, cream, Soy Sauce, and Paprika. Mix carefully into hash. Spoon into casserole or baking dish. Bake in a 400° oven until thoroughly heated. Sprinkle with Chervil just before serving. Makes 6 servings.

German Meat Balls in Caraway Sauce

🌿 Quite different in texture and flavor from the ordinary meat balls. Especially good served with mashed or baked potatoes.

1 cup coarsely grated raw potato
1 pound lean ground beef
1 teaspoon Beau Monde Seasoning
¼ teaspoon Fine Grind Black Pepper
1 tablespoon Parsley
½ teaspoon Onion Powder

1 teaspoon Lemon Peel
1 egg
2 teaspoons Arrowroot
2½ cups hot water
4 teaspoons Beef Stock Base

Drain any excess liquid from potatoes. Combine potatoes with ground beef, Beau Monde, Pepper, Parsley, Onion Powder, Lemon Peel, and egg. Mix very thoroughly. Form into 1½-inch balls. Dip each meat ball in Arrowroot. Combine hot water and Beef Stock Base in large kettle with tight-fitting cover. Bring to boiling; drop each meat ball carefully into boiling stock. Cover and simmer for 30 minutes. Lift meat balls out into a hot serving dish; keep hot while making sauce. Makes 4 or 5 servings.

CARAWAY SAUCE

Stock from meat balls
¼ teaspoon Fine Grind Black Pepper
½ teaspoon Caraway Seeds

1 teaspoon Arrowroot
1 tablespoon cold water

Add Pepper and Caraway Seeds to stock in which meat balls were cooked. Simmer for about 10 minutes. Mix Arrowroot with cold water and stir into stock. Cook, stirring constantly, until sauce has thickened. Pour sauce over meat balls and serve hot.

Meat Loaf with Herbs

🌿 Vary the liquid in this meat loaf recipe for interesting flavor — try part red or white wine, beef stock (made by adding a teaspoon of Beef Stock Base to ¾ cup hot water), or the liquid drained from cooked or canned vegetables.

1 cup soft bread crumbs
¾ cup milk or tomato sauce, tomato juice, or diluted condensed tomato soup
1 teaspoon Bouquet Garni for Beef
2 tablespoons Instant Minced Onions
1 tablespoon Green Bell Peppers

½ teaspoon Horseradish
1 teaspoon Beau Monde Seasoning
1 teaspoon salt
¼ teaspoon Hot Mustard
1 egg
1½ pounds lean ground beef

Place bread crumbs in large bowl. Heat milk or other liquid to simmering; pour over crumbs. Crush Bouquet Garni and mix into bread crumb mixture along with Onions, Green Peppers, Horseradish, Beau Monde, salt, and Mustard. Beat in egg. Add ground beef and mix thoroughly. Shape into loaf and place in flat roasting pan. Bake uncovered in a 350° oven for 1½ hours. Make gravy from pan drippings if desired. Slice loaf and serve hot. Makes 6 servings.

Meat Loaf with Sweet-Sour Glaze

🌿 Spaghetti Sauce Seasoning gives lots of flavor to this glistening meat loaf.

1 pound lean ground beef
¼ pound ground pork
¼ pound ground veal
1 can (8 oz.) tomato sauce
1½ cups soft bread crumbs
1 teaspoon Green Bell Peppers

1 tablespoon Instant Minced Onions
1 teaspoon Beau Monde Seasoning
1 teaspoon Spaghetti Sauce Seasoning
¼ teaspoon Fine Grind Black Pepper
1 egg

Mix ground meats together; or have ground meats mixed at the market. Heat tomato sauce and pour over bread crumbs. Mix in Green Peppers, Onions, Beau Monde, Spaghetti Sauce Seasoning, and Black Pepper. Beat in egg. Combine with ground meat and mix thoroughly. Shape into loaf and place in flat roasting pan. Bake, uncovered, in a 350° oven for 1½ hours. For the last half hour baste frequently with Glaze. Serve hot. Makes 6 to 8 servings.

GLAZE

3 tablespoons brown sugar
3 tablespoons Red Wine Vinegar

½ teaspoon Hot Mustard
2 teaspoons Worcestershire sauce

Mix brown sugar, Vinegar, Mustard, and Worcestershire sauce until well blended.

VEAL

Savory sauces flatter this delicate meat. Veal is a favorite of European chefs, and you'll find a number of classic continental recipes here.

Bohemian Veal Roast

❧ Mashed potatoes or noodles are good with this rich-flavored gravy.

4½ to 5 pounds boneless veal rump roast
3 tablespoons butter
1 pint dairy sour cream
2 tablespoons Beef Stock Base
2 tablespoons Instant Minced Onions
2 teaspoons Dill Seed
2 teaspoons Mei Yen Seasoning
¼ teaspoon Medium Grind Black Pepper

Wipe meat with damp cloth. Melt butter in Dutch oven or heavy, deep frying pan or kettle. Brown roast on all sides. Place rack under meat. Mix thoroughly sour cream, Beef Stock Base, Onions, Dill Seed, Mei Yen, and Pepper. Spread over top and sides of roast. Cover and cook over low heat until meat is tender, about 3 hours. Or bake in a 325° oven until tender. Arrange veal on hot platter. Pour gravy from roasting pan into bowl or gravy boat. Carve meat and spoon gravy over slices. Makes 8 servings.

Veal Paprika

❧ Wonderful for a party — serve it at the table for a sit-down supper or from a chafing dish at a buffet. If you prefer, use veal steak cut into strips instead of veal stew meat.

2 to 2½ pounds boneless veal stew meat, cut into 1½-inch cubes
¼ cup butter
½ cup Instant Minced Onions
½ cup water
4 teaspoons Beef Stock Base
2 cups hot water
½ cup dry white wine
1 teaspoon salt
½ teaspoon Mei Yen Seasoning
¼ teaspoon Thyme
1 tablespoon Paprika
1 teaspoon Lemon Peel
½ cup dairy sour cream
2 tablespoons sherry

Wipe meat with damp cloth. Brown slowly in butter. Meanwhile, rehydrate Onions in water. When meat is browned, add Onions and cook for 5 minutes or until Onions are lightly browned. Dissolve Beef Stock Base in hot water and pour over veal. Add wine, salt, and Mei Yen. Crush Thyme and stir into veal along with Paprika and Lemon Peel. Cover and cook over low heat for 1½ to 2 hours or until meat is tender. Just before serving, stir in sour cream. Heat thoroughly but do not boil. Add sherry; serve at once. Makes 6 servings.

Veal Italienne

For a delectable dinner, serve this with plain buttered rice and green peas.

1-pound veal steak, cut ½ inch thick
2 tablespoons Instant Minced Onions
2 tablespoons water
2 tablespoons olive oil
¼ teaspoon Garlic Powder
1 teaspoon Powdered Mushrooms
1½ teaspoons Beau Monde Seasoning
⅛ teaspoon Spice Parisienne
½ cup dry white wine

Wipe meat with damp cloth; cut into 2-inch squares. Rehydrate Onions in water. Heat olive oil in heavy frying pan. Stir in Onions and Garlic Powder; cook gently for 5 minutes. Add veal and continue to cook over low heat, turning veal frequently, for 20 minutes. Stir in Powdered Mushrooms, Beau Monde, Spice Parisienne, and wine. Cover and cook for another 20 minutes or until veal is tender. Serve hot. Makes 4 servings.

Stuffed Veal Roll

A hearty entrée for a winter day — it's economical, too.

3 to 3½-pound breast of veal, boned
1 can (4½ oz.) deviled ham
⅛ teaspoon Thyme
1½ cups soft bread crumbs
2 tablespoons Instant Toasted Onions
4 tablespoons butter
½ teaspoon salt
¼ teaspoon Fine Grind Black Pepper
1½ cups hot water
2 teaspoons Beef Stock Base
1 teaspoon Chervil
½ cup light cream
2 teaspoons Arrowroot
1 tablespoon cold water

Wipe meat with damp cloth; spread out flat with boned surface up. Spread with deviled ham. Crush Thyme and combine with bread crumbs and Toasted Onions. Melt 2 tablespoons of butter and pour over crumbs; toss thoroughly and spread on top of deviled ham. Roll veal up, skewer, and tie securely with string. Melt remaining butter in Dutch oven or heavy frying pan; brown meat. Season with salt and Pepper. Combine hot water, Beef Stock Base, and ½ teaspoon Chervil. Pour over veal roll. Cover and simmer slowly until tender, about 1½ hours; or bake in a 325° oven until tender. When done, remove veal to hot platter; cut string and remove skewers. Add light cream to liquid in Dutch oven. Mix Arrowroot with cold water; stir into gravy. Cook, stirring constantly, until gravy is thickened and smooth. Sprinkle with remaining ½ teaspoon Chervil. Cut veal roll into 1-inch-thick slices and spoon gravy over meat. Makes 6 servings.

Saffron Veal Strips

The subtle flavor of Saffron makes veal a distinctive delicacy. If you should care for a stronger Saffron flavor, add the merest speck at a time.

2 pounds veal steak
¼ cup butter
⅛ teaspoon Garlic Powder
1/32 teaspoon Powdered Saffron
1 teaspoon Beau Monde Seasoning
½ teaspoon salt
¼ teaspoon Cracked Black Pepper

½ teaspoon Thyme
1 tablespoon Instant Minced Onions
2 cups rich milk
1 tablespoon Arrowroot
1 tablespoon cold water

Cut meat into strips about ½ inch wide. Remove bones and connective tissue. Melt butter in heavy frying pan. Add veal strips and brown lightly. Mix thoroughly Garlic Powder, Saffron, Beau Monde, salt, and Pepper. Sprinkle over veal; turn meat and stir until coated with seasonings. Crush Thyme; sprinkle Thyme and Onions over veal. Cover and cook over very low heat until meat is tender, about 45 minutes. If meat becomes too dry, add a small amount of hot water. Add milk. Mix Arrowroot with cold water. Stir into meat. Cook, stirring constantly, until sauce is thickened and smooth. Serve hot. Makes 6 servings.

Sherried Veal with Herbs

Rich and flavorful — serve it with wild rice, brown rice, or cracked wheat. Use frozen veal cutlets instead of veal steak if preferred.

1½ pounds veal steak, cut ¼ inch thick
3 tablespoons flour
1½ teaspoons Mei Yen Seasoning
⅛ teaspoon Garlic Powder
½ teaspoon Onion Powder
¼ teaspoon Fine Grind Black Pepper
3 tablespoons salad oil

½ cup dry sherry
½ cup water
1 can (4 oz.) sliced mushrooms
⅛ teaspoon Rosemary
½ cup dairy sour cream
½ teaspoon Parsley

Cut veal steak into serving-size pieces. Combine flour, Mei Yen, Garlic Powder, Onion Powder, and Pepper. Dip meat in seasoned flour. Brown in hot oil in heavy frying pan. When meat is well browned, remove from pan. Add remaining seasoned flour to drippings in pan. Stir until lightly browned. Add sherry, water, and undrained mushrooms; stir until sauce has thickened slightly. Crush Rosemary and stir into sauce. Return meat to pan. Cover and cook very slowly until veal is tender, about 45 minutes. Arrange veal on hot platter. Stir sour cream into sauce in pan. Pour over meat. Sprinkle with Parsley and serve hot. Makes 6 servings.

Veal and Ham Rolls

 No fussing at the last minute when serving Veal and Ham Rolls. Everything can be done ahead and the cheese added at the last.

1½ pounds veal steak, cut ¼ inch thick

6 thin slices boiled ham

1 cup cooked rice

1 tablespoon Instant Minced Onions

3 tablespoons chopped celery

1 teaspoon Spaghetti Sauce Seasoning

2 tablespoons butter

2 teaspoons Chicken Seasoned Stock Base

1½ cups hot water

1 tablespoon tomato paste

1 teaspoon Spaghetti Sauce Seasoning

¼ teaspoon Lemon Peel

½ teaspoon Chervil

½ cup shredded Monterey Jack cheese

Cut bone from veal steaks; cut into six serving-size pieces. Cover each slice of veal with a slice of ham. Combine cooked rice, Onions, celery, and Spaghetti Sauce Seasoning. Divide into equal parts and spoon onto veal and ham. Roll up, then tie securely with string. Brown rolls in butter in heavy frying pan. Arrange browned rolls in baking dish. Dissolve Chicken Seasoned Stock Base in hot water. Add tomato paste, Spaghetti Sauce Seasoning, and Lemon Peel. Pour over rolls. Cover tightly and bake in a 350° oven for 45 minutes to 1 hour or until meat is tender. Just before serving, remove strings, sprinkle with Chervil and shredded cheese. Continue baking for 10 to 15 minutes or until cheese is melted. Serve at once. Makes 6 servings.

Quick Veal Scaloppine

1 pound thinly sliced veal

1 egg

3 teaspoons Spaghetti Sauce Seasoning

½ teaspoon salt

¼ cup grated Parmesan cheese

¼ cup fine dry French bread crumbs

¼ cup olive or salad oil

½ cup dry white wine

1 can (8 oz.) tomato sauce

1 can (2 oz.) sliced mushrooms

Pound veal thoroughly and cut into serving-size pieces. Beat egg well with 1 teaspoon Spaghetti Sauce Seasoning and salt. Combine Parmesan cheese and bread crumbs. Dip veal in beaten egg and then in bread crumb mixture. Place on waxed paper or aluminum foil and let stand for 30 minutes for coating to dry. Brown quickly in heavy frying pan in hot oil. Arrange on hot platter and keep warm while making sauce. Combine wine, tomato sauce, undrained mushrooms, and remaining 2 teaspoons Spaghetti Sauce Seasoning. Pour into frying pan and simmer for 5 to 10 minutes. Pour over veal and serve at once. Makes 4 servings.

Savory Veal Loaf

🌿 A delicious meat loaf to serve cold on a hot summer day.

3 slices white bread
1 tablespoon Beef Stock Base
1 cup hot water
½ cup tomato sauce
1 egg

1 teaspoon Onion Powder
2 teaspoons Poultry Seasoning
¼ teaspoon Sweet Basil
1½ pounds ground veal
3 or 4 strips of bacon

Cut crusts from bread and cut into cubes. Dissolve Beef Stock Base in hot water. Pour ½ cup of beef stock over bread cubes. Add tomato sauce, egg, Onion Powder, and Poultry Seasoning. Mix thoroughly. Crush Sweet Basil and add along with ground veal. Mix until completely blended. Shape into loaf and let stand for an hour before baking. Top loaf with strips of bacon. Pour remaining beef stock around loaf and bake in a 325° oven for 1½ hours or until done. Serve hot or cold. Makes 8 servings.

LAMB

The seasoning techniques of many foreign lands are represented in these lamb recipes. Economical cuts of lamb receive luxurious treatment here.

Broiled Leg of Lamb

🌿 An excellent choice for a small dinner party—easy to carve and serve. Wheat or Rice Pilaff goes well with lamb.

3½ to 4-pound leg of lamb, boned
½ teaspoon Oregano
¼ teaspoon Garlic Powder
½ teaspoon Lemon Peel

1 teaspoon Beau Monde Seasoning
1 teaspoon Parsley
⅛ teaspoon Cracked Bay Leaf
¼ cup olive oil

Have leg of lamb boned, but not tied, at the market. Spread lamb out flat and cut off excess fat and gristly pieces. Crush Oregano and combine with Garlic Powder, Lemon Peel, Beau Monde, Parsley, and Bay Leaf. Rub well into lamb. Place lamb in a glass baking pan. Pour olive oil over meat and turn until thoroughly coated with oil. Let marinate for about an hour at room temperature. Place lamb on broiler pan 7 or 8 inches from unit, fat side of lamb toward source of heat; broil for about 40 minutes. Turn and broil for 10 to 15 minutes. Carve into ¼-inch slices. Serve hot. Makes 6 servings.

Roast Shoulder of Lamb in White Wine

4 to 4½-pound lamb shoulder roast, boned and rolled
1 teaspoon Bouquet Garni for Lamb
2 cups dry white wine
2 tablespoons salad oil
½ teaspoon Garlic Powder
2 tablespoons butter
¼ cup finely chopped walnuts
4 or 5 chicken livers

1 can (4 oz.) sliced mushrooms
1½ cups hot water
1 tablespoon Arrowroot
1 tablespoon cold water
½ teaspoon salt
½ teaspoon Mei Yen Seasoning
⅛ teaspoon Fine Grind Black Pepper

Place roast in large bowl. Crush Bouquet Garni and add to wine along with salad oil and Garlic Powder. Pour over roast; let marinate in refrigerator several hours or overnight, turning occasionally. Place roast on a rack in a shallow pan. Do not cover. Roast in a 325° oven for about 2½ hours (35 to 40 minutes per pound). Baste frequently with marinade. Meanwhile, melt butter in small frying pan; add chopped walnuts and cook until nuts are toasted and crisp. Set toasted nuts aside. Cook chicken livers until done; chop coarsely. Combine with toasted nuts; add mushrooms, including liquid, and any remaining marinade; simmer for 5 minutes. Arrange roast on hot platter. Skim off excess fat from drippings in roasting pan. Pour in hot water and cook, stirring constantly, until drippings are dissolved. Add mixture of toasted nuts, chicken livers, and mushrooms. Mix Arrowroot with cold water and stir into sauce. Stir constantly, and cook until sauce is thickened and bubbling. Season with salt, Mei Yen, and Pepper. Carve lamb and spoon sauce over slices of hot lamb. Makes 6 servings.

Lamb Shanks Sicilian

4 lamb shanks
2 tablespoons Instant Minced Onions
2 tablespoons water
¼ teaspoon Garlic Powder
2 teaspoons Spaghetti Sauce Seasoning

1 teaspoon salt
2 tablespoons brown sugar
1 can (8 oz.) tomato sauce
1 cup dry white wine

Wipe shanks with damp cloth. Arrange in baking dish. Rehydrate Onions in water. Combine with Garlic Powder, Spaghetti Sauce Seasoning, salt, brown sugar, tomato sauce, and wine. Pour over lamb shanks. Cover and bake in a 400° oven for 1 hour. Turn oven down to 350°. Uncover and continue baking for another 1½ hours or until shanks are tender. Baste frequently with sauce. Makes 4 servings.

Lamb Chops in Sherried Orange Sauce

Serve with steamed rice, spooning the sauce over the rice and chops.

4 shoulder lamb chops, cut about ¾ inch thick
½ teaspoon salt
1 teaspoon Mei Yen Seasoning
⅛ teaspoon Medium Grind Black Pepper
2 teaspoons Chicken Seasoned Stock Base

1 cup hot water
1 tablespoon currant jelly
¼ teaspoon Orange Peel
¼ teaspoon Garlic Powder
½ teaspoon Bouquet Garni for Lamb
½ cup sherry

Brown chops thoroughly in a heavy frying pan. When brown, arrange chops in casserole or baking dish. Sprinkle with salt, Mei Yen, and Pepper. Pour off excess fat from frying pan. Dissolve Chicken Seasoned Stock Base in hot water and add to drippings in pan. Stir in currant jelly, Orange Peel, and Garlic Powder. Simmer until jelly is dissolved. Crush Bouquet Garni and add along with sherry; pour over lamb chops. Cover and bake in a 350° oven for about 1 hour or until chops are tender. Makes 4 servings.

Ground Lamb en Palla

This same mixture can be made into a loaf instead of lamb balls. Bake the loaf for 45 minutes at 350°.

1 tablespoon Instant Minced Onions
1 tablespoon Green Bell Peppers
2 teaspoons Parsley
½ cup milk
¼ cup fine dry bread crumbs
¼ teaspoon Bouquet Garni for Lamb
1 teaspoon salt

¼ teaspoon Garlic Powder
1 egg
1 pound lean ground lamb
1 tablespoon shortening or salad oil
2 cups hot water
1 tablespoon Arrowroot
1 tablespoon cold water

Combine Onions, Green Peppers, Parsley, and milk in a large bowl. Let stand for 2 or 3 minutes. Mix in bread crumbs. Crush Bouquet Garni and add to soaked crumbs along with salt and Garlic Powder; beat in egg. Add ground lamb and mix thoroughly. Form into small balls; brown in hot shortening or oil. Pour hot water over browned lamb balls; cover and simmer for 30 to 40 minutes. Mix Arrowroot with cold water and stir into gravy. Cook, stirring constantly, until gravy is thickened. Serve hot. Makes 4 servings.

Rogan Jaush

The name means "Color-Passion Curry" and is from the classic cuisine of India. Pungently seasoned, but proving that curry doesn't have to be hot, this is considered one of the epicurean Indian curries.

2 pounds lean boneless lamb	½ teaspoon Ground Cumin
¼ cup butter	¼ teaspoon Ground Ginger
¼ cup Instant Minced Onions	½ teaspoon Paprika
¼ cup water	2 teaspoons salt
½ teaspoon Turmeric	½ cup yoghurt
2 teaspoons Ground Coriander	3 medium-size tomatoes

Trim any excess fat from lamb; cut into 2-inch cubes. Melt butter in heavy kettle or Dutch oven. Meanwhile, rehydrate Onions in water. Add to butter and cook until golden brown. Add lamb, Turmeric, Coriander, Cumin, and Ginger. Cook for 12 to 15 minutes or until meat is browned. Add Paprika, salt, and yoghurt. Peel tomatoes, cut into chunks, and remove seeds. Add to meat and cook for 4 or 5 minutes, stirring well. Cover and simmer gently for about 1½ hours or until meat is tender. If sauce is too thin, cook uncovered for the last 5 to 10 minutes. Serve hot with steamed rice. Makes 6 servings.

Lamb Stew Italian Country-Style

Different seasonings than those usually used with lamb; serve with buttered noodles or spaghetti. Anchovies and Beef Stock Base provide plenty of salt, so take care in adding any more.

2 pounds lean lamb shoulder	2 tablespoons Red Wine Vinegar
2 tablespoons olive oil	½ teaspoon Fine Grind Black Pepper
1 tin (2 oz.) anchovy filets	2 teaspoons Beef Stock Base
½ teaspoon Fennel Seed	1 cup hot water
½ teaspoon Lemon Peel	2 teaspoons Arrowroot
¼ teaspoon Garlic Powder	1 tablespoon cold water

Trim excess fat from lamb and cut into 1½-inch cubes. Brown slowly in olive oil in heavy frying pan or Dutch oven. Chop anchovy filets; crush Fennel Seed. Combine anchovies, Fennel Seed, Lemon Peel, Garlic Powder, and Vinegar. When meat is well browned, pour off excess fat. Sprinkle with Pepper and stir in anchovy mixture. Dissolve Beef Stock Base in hot water. Pour over meat; cover and simmer slowly for about 1 hour or until meat is tender. Mix Arrowroot with cold water. Mix into stew and cook, stirring constantly, until sauce is thickened. Serve hot. Makes 6 servings.

Braised Lamb with Sour Cream

An economical meat dish with plenty of flavor. Serve with buttered noodles, mashed potatoes, or steamed rice.

2 pounds lamb neck slices or other lamb stew meat
2 tablespoons flour
¼ teaspoon Garlic Powder
⅛ teaspoon Fine Grind Black Pepper
1 teaspoon salt
4 teaspoons Beef Stock Base

2 cups hot water
2 tablespoons Instant Minced Onions
½ teaspoon Bouquet Garni for Lamb
1 tablespoon Garlic Wine Vinegar
1 cup dairy sour cream

Trim excess fat from meat. Render a piece of fat in a heavy frying pan. Combine flour, Garlic Powder, Pepper, and salt. Coat each piece of meat in flour mixture; brown slowly in hot fat. Remove meat from pan; skim off excess fat. Stir remaining flour into drippings; brown lightly. Dissolve Beef Stock Base in hot water; add Onions to stock. Pour into browned flour. Cook, stirring constantly, until gravy is thickened. Return browned meat to pan. Crush Bouquet Garni and sprinkle over lamb; stir in Vinegar. Cover and cook over low heat until meat is very tender, about 1½ hours. Stir in sour cream; heat just to boiling and serve at once. Makes 4 servings.

Lamb Casserole Bouquet Garni

3 tablespoons salad oil
2 cups pared, diced eggplant (1 medium-size)
2 tablespoons Instant Minced Onions
1 tablespoon Green Bell Peppers
¼ cup water
1½ to 2 cups cooked lamb, cut into ½-inch cubes
¼ teaspoon Garlic Powder
2 teaspoons Beau Monde Seasoning

1 teaspoon salt
⅛ teaspoon Fine Grind Black Pepper
1 can (1 lb.) tomatoes
½ teaspoon Bouquet Garni for Lamb
⅛ teaspoon Lemon Peel
1 cup cooked brown rice or cracked wheat
¼ cup grated Parmesan or Romano cheese

Heat oil in heavy frying pan; add eggplant, cover and cook slowly until eggplant is almost tender. Rehydrate Onions and Green Peppers in water. Add to eggplant along with diced lamb. Cook until Onions and meat are lightly browned. Season with Garlic Powder, Beau Monde, salt, and Pepper. Stir in tomatoes. Crush Bouquet Garni and add along with Lemon Peel. Simmer slowly for about 20 minutes. Spoon cooked rice or wheat into 1½-quart casserole. Top with lamb and eggplant mixture. Sprinkle with grated cheese. Bake in a 375° oven until brown and bubbling hot. Serve hot. Makes 6 servings.

PORK

The knowing use of seasonings enhances the distinctive flavor of pork. Give this meat long, slow cooking for highly gratifying results.

Old Hickory Spareribs

Real barbecue flavor done in the oven. So simple and easy, a recipe is almost unnecessary. The secret is the long, slow roasting and the constant draining off of fat.

3 to 3½ pounds spareribs
1 teaspoon Mei Yen Seasoning

1 to 2 teaspoons Old Hickory Smoked Salt

Cut spareribs into serving-size pieces. Spread out in a large baking pan. Sprinkle with Mei Yen. Roast in a 300° oven for about 2 hours or until spareribs are done and brown. Drain off fat frequently. Just before serving, sprinkle generously with Old Hickory. Serve hot as an entrée or as hors d'oeuvres. Makes 4 servings.

Spiced Spareribs, German-Style

Serve potato pancakes or baked or mashed sweet potatoes with these flavorful, spicy ribs.

4 to 5 pounds spareribs
2 teaspoons salt
2 cups boiling water
1 tablespoon Beef Stock Base
2 tablespoons tomato catsup
2 teaspoons brown sugar
2 tablespoons Red Wine Vinegar

3 Whole Allspice
¼ teaspoon Caraway Seed
2 tablespoons Worcestershire sauce
1/16 teaspoon Cayenne Pepper
½ teaspoon Lemon Peel
2 teaspoons Arrowroot
1 tablespoon cold water

Have ribs cracked through the center; trim off excess fat and cut into serving-size pieces. Sprinkle with 1 teaspoon salt. Arrange in flat baking pan; bake in a 350° oven for 1 to 1½ hours, turning several times. Drain off excess fat and sprinkle with remaining teaspoon of salt. Combine boiling water, Beef Stock Base, tomato catsup, brown sugar, Vinegar, Allspice, Caraway Seed, Worcestershire sauce, Cayenne, and Lemon Peel. Pour over ribs and continue baking for another hour, turning ribs frequently. When ribs are done, arrange on large platter. Skim off fat from liquid in baking pan. Mix Arrowroot with cold water and stir into liquid in pan. Cook, stirring constantly, until sauce is thickened. Pour over spareribs. Serve hot. Makes 6 servings.

Loin of Pork Rotisserie

Of course, loin of pork can be roasted, too, but it is far better done on a rotisserie—in the oven, a portable rotisserie, or a barbecue rotisserie.

4-pound loin of pork	¼ cup Red Wine Vinegar
2 teaspoons Mei Yen Seasoning	1 tablespoon Worcestershire sauce
½ teaspoon Garlic Powder	½ teaspoon Ground Ginger
1 cup hot water	½ teaspoon Hot Mustard
1 tablespoon tomato paste	⅛ teaspoon Fine Grind Black Pepper
1 tablespoon honey	⅛ teaspoon Cracked Bay Leaf

Have backbone cut from loin so it will balance better on spit. Dissolve Mei Yen and Garlic Powder in hot water. Add tomato paste, honey, Vinegar, Worcestershire sauce, Ginger, Mustard, Pepper, and Bay Leaf. Bring marinade to a boil. Pour over pork loin and marinate for an hour or two at room temperature or 8 to 10 hours in refrigerator. Secure meat on spit and roast slowly for about 2 hours or until pork is done. Brush meat frequently with marinade while roasting. Carve meat into chops; serve hot. Makes 6 servings.

Baked Spiced Pork Chops

Serve with mashed sweet potatoes, spooning the spicy sauce over the potatoes. Steamed rice is a good accompaniment, too.

4 loin or shoulder pork chops, cut 1 inch thick	¼ teaspoon Thyme
1½ teaspoons Mei Yen Seasoning	¼ teaspoon Ground Cinnamon
1 tablespoon Chicken Seasoned Stock Base	¼ teaspoon Ground Allspice
	⅛ teaspoon Fine Grind Black Pepper
1½ cups hot water	1 tablespoon Instant Minced Onions
¼ teaspoon Orange Peel	

Brown pork chops in heavy frying pan. Season with Mei Yen. Arrange chops in casserole or baking dish. Dissolve Chicken Seasoned Stock Base in hot water. Add Orange Peel. Crush Thyme and add to stock with Cinnamon, Allspice, Pepper, and Onions. Pour over chops. Cover and bake in a 300° oven for 1½ hours or until chops are tender. Skim off any excess fat. Serve hot from casserole or baking dish, using the sauce as gravy. Makes 4 servings.

Pork Sauté

 Pork cooked in a gourmet sauce is a delicious entrée. If cut thin, pork will cook quickly.

1 to 1½ pounds tenderloin or lean pork steak, sliced thin
1 tablespoon butter
¼ teaspoon Garlic Powder
1 teaspoon Beau Monde Seasoning

1 teaspoon Powdered Mushrooms
½ cup dry white wine
⅛ teaspoon Spice Parisienne

Cut pork into 1½-inch squares. Melt butter in heavy frying pan. Add pork; sprinkle with Garlic Powder. Sauté until brown, turning pork frequently. Sprinkle with Beau Monde and Powdered Mushrooms. Cook for 10 to 15 minutes. Add wine and Spice Parisienne. Continue cooking, covered, for 10 to 15 minutes, stirring occasionally, until pork is tender. Serve hot. Makes 4 servings.

Caribbean Pork and Bean Stew

 From the West Indies comes this full-meal stew with its unusual seasonings and interesting combination of vegetables.

1 pound dry pink beans
1½ quarts warm water
1½-pound piece lean pork shoulder or 3 fresh pork hocks
2 tablespoons Instant Minced Onions
1 tablespoon Green Bell Peppers
½ teaspoon Ground Coriander
¼ teaspoon Garlic Powder

¼ teaspoon Fine Grind Black Pepper
2 teaspoons salt
¼ teaspoon Oregano
1 medium-size tomato
1 medium-size potato
1 cup cubed yellow squash or pumpkin

Wash beans; cover with 1 quart warm water. Bring to a boil and boil for 5 minutes. Turn off heat; cover beans and let soak for 1 hour. Meanwhile, cut pork shoulder into 6 pieces. (If using pork hocks, have them cut in two when purchasing.) Add meat along with remaining warm water to beans. Stir in Onions, Green Peppers, Coriander, Garlic Powder, Pepper, and 1 teaspoon salt. Crush Oregano and add to beans. Simmer until beans are almost tender. Add the remaining 1 teaspoon salt. Peel tomato and potato; cut into cubes and add to stew along with cubed squash or pumpkin. Continue simmering for 30 to 40 minutes, or until vegetables and meat are tender. Serve in bowls with hot French bread. Makes 6 servings.

HAM

Spicy flavors do wonderful things to ham, and fruit glazes and garnishes are a decorative and compatible finishing touch.

Baked Ham with Orange-Wine Sauce

❦ Another good way to pep up the flavor of a canned ham. Garnish the ham with a favorite canned fruit, using the fruit syrup as part of the fruit juice.

1 canned ham (8 to 10 pounds)
¾ cup fruit juice or syrup (pineapple, apricot, pear, or peach)
¾ cup Port wine
2 teaspoons Orange Peel
1½ cups brown sugar
1 teaspoon Hot Mustard
¼ teaspoon Ground Cloves

The day before the ham is to be served, open ham and scrape off jellied coating. Score ham, if desired. Place in large bowl; stick prongs of kitchen fork deep into ham. Combine fruit juice, Port wine, Orange Peel, 1 cup brown sugar, Mustard, and Cloves. Pour over ham. Marinate for about 24 hours in a cool place but not in the refrigerator. Turn ham several times. Bake ham in open baking pan the length of time suggested on can. Baste frequently with marinade. About 40 minutes before ham is to be served, pour off fat in pan. Cover top of ham with remaining brown sugar. Pour rest of marinade around ham. Continue baking until ham is glazed and marinade thickens slightly to form sauce. Carve ham and serve with sauce in pan. Makes 8 to 10 servings with leftovers.

Sweet-Sour Baked Ham

❦ Those who think canned ham needs a flavor lift will like this.

1 canned ham (8 to 10 pounds)
½ cup Tarragon Red Wine Vinegar
½ cup brown sugar
½ teaspoon Mild Mustard
½ teaspoon Ground Cloves

Place ham and the jellied meat juices coating it in a roasting pan with cover. Score ham; pour Vinegar over ham. Mix together brown sugar, Mustard, and Cloves. Pat on top of ham to form coating. Cover ham and roast in a 350° oven for 2 to 2½ hours or about 15 to 20 minutes per pound. Baste frequently with juices in bottom of pan. Carve, and spoon the sweet-sour sauce over ham slices or serve with Spiced Raisin Sauce (page 119). Makes 8 to 10 servings with leftovers.

Ham Slice with Curried Cherry Sauce

2½ to 3 pounds center-cut ham slice
1 jar (1 lb. 1 oz.) dark, sweet cherries
⅛ teaspoon Ground Allspice

1 teaspoon Curry Powder
2 teaspoons Lemon Peel
1 tablespoon Red Wine Vinegar

Score fat edge of ham slice every 2 or 3 inches. Place in flat baking pan or dish. Drain juice from cherries. Combine juice with Allspice, Curry Powder, Lemon Peel, and Vinegar. Simmer for 2 or 3 minutes; pour over ham. Bake in 350° oven, basting frequently with sauce, for about 1 hour. Cover ham slice with drained cherries; continue baking for another 30 minutes, basting occasionally, until ham is tender and well glazed. To serve, cut ham into serving-size portions. Spoon cherries and sauce over ham. Serve hot. Makes 6 servings.

VARIETY MEATS

Herbs and spices contribute refreshing overtones to the delicious delicacies that fall into this category.

Sweetbreads in Mushroom Sauce

Powdered Mushrooms make a delicious sauce that blends perfectly with the flavor of sweetbreads.

2 pairs sweetbreads
1 tablespoon White Wine Vinegar
1 teaspoon salt
4 tablespoons butter
1 teaspoon Arrowroot
2 teaspoons Powdered Mushrooms
1 teaspoon tomato paste

1 teaspoon Chicken Seasoned
   Stock Base
½ cup hot water
¼ cup sherry
½ teaspoon Beau Monde Seasoning
1/16 teaspoon Cracked Bay Leaf

Wash sweetbreads and soak in cold water for 30 to 40 minutes. Drain; cover with cold water. Add Vinegar and salt. Bring to a boil; simmer, covered, for 15 minutes; drain and cover with ice water. When cool enough to handle, remove membrane and tubes. Cut into cubes. Melt butter; brown sweetbreads lightly in butter. Remove from heat. Remove sweetbreads from pan; stir Arrowroot into butter. Combine Powdered Mushrooms, tomato paste, Chicken Seasoned Stock Base, and hot water. Add to butter and Arrowroot. Cook over low heat, stirring constantly, until sauce thickens slightly and is smooth. Add sherry, Beau Monde, Bay Leaf, and sweetbreads. Simmer slowly for 15 minutes. Serve on triangles of crisp toast. Makes 4 servings.

Chicken Livers Stroganoff

❀ Delicious served at a supper party with buttered noodles or at a hearty brunch with hominy grits.

1 pound chicken livers
¼ cup butter
2 tablespoons Instant Minced Onions
2 tablespoons water
1 teaspoon Arrowroot
1 tablespoon Powdered Mushrooms
1 teaspoon Chicken Seasoned
    Stock Base

½ cup hot water
1 cup sour cream
1 teaspoon Beau Monde Seasoning
⅛ teaspoon Fines Herbes
1 tablespoon sherry
1 teaspoon Parsley or Chervil

Wash livers and cut in two. Brown in butter in heavy frying pan for about 5 minutes, turning frequently. Meanwhile, rehydrate the Onions in water. Remove livers from pan; add Onions and cook for 3 or 4 minutes, but do not let brown. Stir in Arrowroot. Combine Powdered Mushrooms, Chicken Seasoned Stock Base, and hot water. Add to Onions. Stir in sour cream, Beau Monde, and Fines Herbes. Add chicken livers and sherry. Heat thoroughly but do not boil. Sprinkle with Parsley or Chervil. Makes 4 servings.

Kidney Sauté Montmartre

❀ An excellent "quickie" for the chafing dish or electric frying pan.

6 or 8 lamb kidneys
3 tablespoons White Wine Vinegar
2 tablespoons Instant Minced Onions
2 tablespoons water
2 tablespoons butter
1 teaspoon Powdered Mushrooms
1 teaspoon Chicken Seasoned Stock
    Base

½ cup hot water
⅛ teaspoon Thyme
½ teaspoon Beau Monde Seasoning
⅛ teaspoon Spice Parisienne
2 teaspoons sherry

Split kidneys; remove membrane and center gristle. Cut each kidney half into 2 or 3 pieces. Wash in cold water. Soak for about 30 minutes in Vinegar. Drain and dry on paper towels. Rehydrate Onions in water. Melt butter in frying pan. Add Onions and cook until lightly browned. Add kidneys and cook for about 5 minutes. Dissolve Powdered Mushrooms and Chicken Seasoned Stock Base in hot water. Pour over kidneys. Crush Thyme and add along with Beau Monde and Spice Parisienne. Simmer for about 20 minutes or until kidneys are tender. Stir in sherry. Serve on crisp buttered toast or steamed rice. Makes 4 servings.

Sautéed Liver with Fines Herbes

🌱 Cook liver quickly and it will be tender and juicy.

1 pound calves' liver, thinly sliced	½ teaspoon salt
2 tablespoons flour	3 tablespoons butter
1 teaspoon Mei Yen Seasoning	½ teaspoon Fines Herbes
⅛ teaspoon Fine Grind Black Pepper	½ cup sherry

Cut liver into serving-size pieces. Combine flour, Mei Yen, Pepper, and salt. Dip liver in seasoned flour. Melt butter in heavy frying pan. When hot, sauté liver quickly, turning once. Arrange on heated platter. Crush Fines Herbes and add to drippings in frying pan; add sherry. Bring to a boil and simmer for 2 or 3 minutes. Pour over liver and serve at once. Makes 4 servings.

Calves' Liver à la Johnnie May

🌱 Johnnie May was a cook for a family in the Deep South. Her way of cooking liver rates "superb" even with those who don't usually care for this nutritious meat.

1 pound calves' liver, thinly sliced	6 tablespoons Garlic Wine Vinegar
5 tablespoons butter	

Cut liver into serving-size pieces. Melt 1 tablespoon butter in heavy frying pan. Sauté liver quickly, turning to brown both sides (liver should be slightly pink inside). Keep warm. Add rest of butter and Vinegar to drippings in pan. Heat to boiling, stirring constantly. Pour over liver and serve at once. Makes 3 or 4 servings.

Western-Style Franks

🌱 Serve franks on toasted buns with a spoonful or two of sauce, or with steamed rice, beans, or macaroni.

1 cup pineapple juice	½ teaspoon Garlic Salt
½ cup chili sauce	2 tablespoons Soy Sauce
1 tablespoon Green Bell Peppers	1 tablespoon molasses
½ teaspoon Hot Mustard	1 pound frankfurters
2 tablespoons Garlic Wine Vinegar	1 tablespoon Instant Toasted Onions

Combine pineapple juice, chili sauce, Green Peppers, Hot Mustard, Vinegar, Garlic Salt, Soy Sauce, and molasses in large frying pan. Simmer for about 15 minutes, stirring frequently. Add frankfurters and cook until thoroughly heated; stir in Toasted Onions and serve at once. Makes 5 servings.

POULTRY

POULTRY IS inexpensive, economical, and one of the most versatile of foods, and it is no wonder that it has long been a favorite of cooks throughout the world.

Turkey, once reserved for the special holiday table, now is served all year round — as a whole roasted bird, or in slices on the buffet table; in a delicate sauce, or with the robust flavor of the barbecue; in a hearty casserole, or in a light luncheon salad.

Chicken, too, appears in many forms; and as a result of its long popularity in various parts of the world, it has taken on many accents. Browned in olive oil and simmered in a tomato sauce, the accent is Italian. In Chicken Valenciana, the overtones are decidedly Spanish. The fine hand of the French chef shows itself in Poulet Bercy.

The delicate flavor of poultry makes it especially suited to herb cookery; and a change in the herb that is used in a poultry recipe can transform the dish completely. In these recipes, poultry is herbed with Chervil, Bay Leaf, Rosemary, Saffron, Parsley, and Sweet Basil. These are a few of the possibilities; you are certain to find others.

Use herbs, spices, and other seasonings, too, to give character and personality to poultry stuffings, marinades, and basting sauces.

Chicken Chasseur

1½ to 2-pound broiling chicken, cut into quarters
2 tablespoons butter
1 teaspoon Mei Yen Seasoning
¼ teaspoon Fine Grind Black Pepper
¼ teaspoon Onion Powder

2 teaspoons Chicken Seasoned Stock Base
½ cup dry white wine
½ cup tomato sauce
½ cup sliced fresh mushrooms
2 teaspoons Chervil

Brown chicken in butter in heavy frying pan or casserole; season with Mei Yen and Pepper. Combine Onion Powder, Chicken Seasoned Stock Base, wine, tomato sauce, sliced mushrooms, and 1 teaspoon Chervil. Pour over chicken. Cover and bake for about 30 minutes in a 350° oven or until chicken is tender. Uncover and bake for about 10 minutes longer to brown well. Just before serving, sprinkle with remaining Chervil. Serve with steamed browned or wild rice. Makes 4 servings.

Savory Oven-Fried Chicken

1 egg
½ cup milk
½ teaspoon Cracked Black Pepper
1½ cups cornflake crumbs
¼ teaspoon Garlic Powder

2 teaspoons Beau Monde Seasoning
1 teaspoon Shredded Green Onions
2 pounds chicken parts, or 3-pound frying chicken, disjointed
¼ cup melted butter

Beat together egg, milk, and Cracked Pepper. Combine cornflake crumbs, Garlic Powder, Beau Monde, and Shredded Green Onions. Dip pieces of chicken in egg-milk mixture and then coat thoroughly with seasoned cornflake crumbs. Arrange crumbed chicken in shallow baking pan or flat baking dish. Pour melted butter over chicken. Bake in a 400° oven for 45 to 50 minutes or until chicken is done and brown. Serve hot. Makes 4 servings.

Chicken Cacciatora

2 to 2½-pound frying chicken, disjointed
3 tablespoons olive oil
1 teaspoon Beau Monde Seasoning
½ teaspoon salt

1 can (6 oz.) tomato paste
1 can (6 oz.) water
1 tablespoon Spaghetti Sauce Seasoning
½ cup dry white wine

Brown pieces of chicken in olive oil; sprinkle with Beau Monde and salt. Blend together tomato paste, water, Spaghetti Sauce Seasoning, and white wine. Pour over chicken. Cover and simmer for about 30 minutes or until chicken is tender. Serve chicken and sauce with spaghetti, polenta, or steamed rice. Makes 4 servings.

Chicken Sauté with Rosemary

Rosemary adds a pleasing herb accent to Chicken Sauté. For 4 servings, use a large broiler-fryer, cut into quarters.

1½ to 2-pound broiling chicken, cut into halves
2 teaspoons Chicken Seasoned Stock Base
½ cup hot water
2 tablespoons sherry
1 teaspoon Garlic Salt
⅛ teaspoon Cracked Bay Leaf
3 tablespoons melted butter
⅛ teaspoon Medium Grind Black Pepper
¼ teaspoon Rosemary

Arrange chicken in flat baking pan. Combine Chicken Seasoned Stock Base, hot water, sherry, ½ teaspoon Garlic Salt, Cracked Bay Leaf, melted butter, and Pepper. Pour over chicken. Marinate for about 1 hour, turning chicken several times. Bake uncovered in a 400° oven for 45 to 50 minutes, turning chicken occasionally so that it browns evenly. When chicken is about half done, crush Rosemary and sprinkle over chicken along with remaining Garlic Salt. Arrange chicken on serving plates; spoon sauce in pan over chicken. Serve hot. Makes 2 servings.

Poulet Bercy

Herbs, wine, and mushrooms make a gourmet sauce for chicken.

2 to 2½-pound frying chicken, cut into quarters
1 tablespoon Instant Minced Onions
1 tablespoon water
3 tablespoons butter
¼ teaspoon Garlic Powder
2 teaspoons Powdered Mushrooms
2 teaspoons Chicken Seasoned Stock Base
½ teaspoon Mei Yen Seasoning
½ cup dry white wine
½ teaspoon Fines Herbes
1/16 teaspoon Cracked Bay Leaf
1 teaspoon Chervil
1 egg yolk
1 cup light cream

Arrange chicken in flat pan. Rehydrate Onions in water. Melt butter; add Onions and Garlic Powder and cook gently for about 5 minutes. Combine Powdered Mushrooms, Chicken Seasoned Stock Base, Mei Yen Seasoning, and white wine. Add to Onions. Crush Fines Herbes and add along with Cracked Bay Leaf and Chervil. Heat just to simmering. Pour over chicken; marinate for 1 hour, turning pieces of chicken occasionally. Bake in a 400° oven for 30 to 40 minutes, or until chicken is done and brown. Baste frequently. When chicken is done, arrange on hot plates. In a small saucepan, beat egg yolk and cream together slightly. Add liquid from chicken. Cook over low heat, stirring constantly, until sauce is thickened slightly and thoroughly heated. Do not allow to boil. Pour over chicken and serve at once. Makes 4 servings.

Chicken Coriander

3 tablespoons Instant Minced
   Onions
3 tablespoons water
2 to 2½-pound frying chicken,
   disjointed or cut into quarters
3 tablespoons butter

½ teaspoon Turmeric
1 tablespoon Ground Coriander
½ teaspoon Chili Powder
1 teaspoon salt
¼ cup hot water
1 tablespoon lime juice

Rehydrate Onions in water. Sprinkle Onions over chicken; toss to mix thoroughly and let stand for 15 to 20 minutes. Melt butter in heavy frying pan or casserole. Stir in Turmeric, Ground Coriander, and Chili Powder. Cook gently for about 1 minute. Add chicken and Onions; brown chicken. Sprinkle with salt. Add hot water; cover tightly and simmer for 30 to 40 minutes or until chicken is tender; or bake in a 300° oven for 30 to 40 minutes or until chicken is done. Stir in lime juice. Serve at once. Makes 3 or 4 servings.

Chicken Valenciana

8 chicken breasts
8 chicken thighs or drumsticks
¼ teaspoon Garlic Powder
¼ cup olive oil
1 teaspoon salt
¼ teaspoon Medium Grind Black
   Pepper
¼ cup slivered almonds
3 tablespoons Instant Minced Onions
3 tablespoons water
1 can (4 oz.) pimientos
1 tablespoon Paprika

⅛ teaspoon Powdered Saffron
1 tablespoon Parsley
2 teaspoons Beau Monde Seasoning
2 cups rice
1 can (8 oz.) tomato sauce
4 teaspoons Chicken Seasoned Stock
   Base
2 cups hot water
½ cup dry white wine
1 package (10 oz.) frozen peas
1 cup cubed smoked ham

Remove bones from chicken breasts; cut in two, if large. Add Garlic Powder to olive oil and heat in large frying pan or Dutch oven. Brown chicken in olive oil; season with salt and Pepper while browning. Remove chicken from oil; brown almonds lightly in oil and set aside with chicken. Rehydrate Onions in water. Cut pimientos into strips. Add Onions and pimientos to drippings along with Paprika, Saffron, Parsley, Beau Monde, and rice. Stir until rice is coated with seasonings. Combine tomato sauce, Chicken Seasoned Stock Base, hot water, and wine. Add to rice. Bring to a boil. Mix in almonds, peas, and ham. Arrange pieces of chicken on top. Cover tightly and bake at 350° for about 45 minutes or until rice has absorbed all liquid and each grain stands out separately. To serve, spoon out onto large platter or chop plate. Arrange pieces of chicken around edge of rice. Serve hot. Makes 8 servings.

Chicken Limone

1 cup sliced fresh mushrooms	¼ cup dry white wine
¼ cup butter	1 cup water
3 to 3½-pound frying chicken, disjointed	½ teaspoon Tarragon
	1 lemon, thinly sliced
2½ teaspoons Mei Yen Seasoning	1 teaspoon Arrowroot

Sauté mushrooms in 2 tablespoons butter until lightly browned. Remove from pan and reserve. Brown chicken in remaining butter. Sprinkle Mei Yen over chicken during browning. Blend wine, ½ cup water, and Tarragon, into pan juices; add half the lemon slices (reserve remaining lemon for garnish). Cover and simmer for 35 minutes or until tender. Remove chicken pieces to heated serving platter. Blend Arrowroot with remaining ½ cup water. Add to pan juices with mushrooms. Cook, stirring constantly, until the mixture boils and thickens. Spoon over chicken. Garnish with reserved lemon slices. Makes 2 generous servings.

Caneton à l'Orange

4 to 4½-pound duck	1 tablespoon honey
3 cups hot water	1 teaspoon Orange Peel
3 teaspoons Beau Monde Seasoning	¼ teaspoon Fine Grind Black Pepper
½ teaspoon Parsley	1 tablespoon Arrowroot
½ teaspoon Ground Ginger	1 tablespoon water
1½ cups apricot nectar	1 tablespoon Orange Curacao or brandy
1 tablespoon Soy Sauce	
1 teaspoon Onion Powder	

Wash duck thoroughly; cut off excess skin at neck and wing tips. Place heart and gizzard, neck and wing tips in saucepan. Add hot water, 1 teaspoon Beau Monde, and Parsley. Cover and simmer while duck is roasting. Prick duck on breast and back with sharp fork. Rub inside with 1 teaspoon Beau Monde and Ground Ginger. Place on rack in open roasting pan and roast in a 450° oven for 45 minutes. Drain off fat and lower temperature to 400°. Mix together apricot nectar, Soy Sauce, Onion Powder, and honey. Baste duck frequently with mixture and continue roasting until duck is tender and well glazed, about 1 hour. When duck is done, arrange on hot platter. Pour excess fat from drippings; add remainder of basting sauce to drippings along with 2 cups stock from giblets. Simmer for 5 or 6 minutes or until browned drippings in pan are dissolved in stock. Stir in Orange Peel, remaining 1 teaspoon Beau Monde, and Pepper. Mix Arrowroot with water and stir into sauce. Cook, stirring constantly, until sauce has thickened slightly and is smooth. Just before serving add Orange Curacao or brandy. Carve duck and spoon sauce over slices of duck. Makes 3 or 4 servings.

Breast of Turkey Cacciatora

1½ to 2 pounds breast of turkey, fresh or frozen
2 tablespoons olive oil
½ teaspoon Garlic Powder
2 tablespoons Instant Minced Onions
2 tablespoons water

2 teaspoons Powdered Mushrooms
1½ teaspoons Mei Yen Seasoning
1 can (8 oz.) tomato sauce
½ cup dry white wine
½ cup hot water
½ teaspoon Sweet Basil

With a sharp knife cut turkey breast from bone; cut into ½-inch-thick slices. Pour oil into frying pan; stir in Garlic Powder. Heat oil; brown turkey slices in hot oil. Set aside while making sauce. Rehydrate Onions in water; add to oil and cook gently for about 5 minutes. Combine Powdered Mushrooms, Mei Yen, tomato sauce, wine, and hot water. Add to Onions; crush Sweet Basil and stir into sauce. Add browned turkey slices to sauce. Cover and simmer gently for about 1 hour or until tender. Serve over hot cooked spaghetti or noodles. Makes 5 or 6 servings.

Roast Rock Cornish Game Hens with Orange Stuffing

6 Rock Cornish game hens
2 cups boiling water
2 teaspoons Beau Monde Seasoning
6 cups small cubes of dry bread
1 tablespoon Poultry Seasoning
1 teaspoon Orange Peel
¾ cup butter

¾ cup finely chopped celery and celery leaves
1 can (11 oz.) Mandarin oranges
1 tablespoon Instant Toasted Onions
1 tablespoon Arrowroot
1 tablespoon water

Thaw birds if frozen; remove giblets and necks. Simmer necks and giblets in boiling water seasoned with Beau Monde; add liver for the last 15 or 20 minutes. Wash hens thoroughly; drain. Combine bread cubes, Poultry Seasoning, and Orange Peel. Melt ½ cup butter in frying pan; add celery and cook until tender but not brown. Drain oranges; add orange sections to bread cubes with celery and butter and Toasted Onions. Toss to combine. Stuff hens and tie with string or fasten with skewers. Rub with remaining ¼ cup butter. Roast in a 400° oven for 1 hour or until tender and well browned; turn once during roasting. Remove string or skewers and arrange hens on serving platter or individual plates. When giblets are tender, discard necks and chop giblets. Add stock and chopped giblets to drippings in roasting pan. Simmer until drippings are well dissolved in stock. Mix Arrowroot with water; add to gravy. Simmer gravy for 2 or 3 minutes, stirring constantly, until thickened and smooth. Serve hot from gravy boat. Makes 6 servings.

Basic Poultry Stuffing

3 cups fresh bread crumbs
1 tablespoon Instant Minced Onions
1 tablespoon water

1 tablespoon Poultry Seasoning
2 tablespoons melted butter

Tear bread, including crusts, into crumbs. Rehydrate Onions in water. Add to bread crumbs; sprinkle with Poultry Seasoning. Pour melted butter over crumbs; toss to combine thoroughly. Makes enough for a 4-pound roasting chicken; double the recipe for a small turkey and triple it for a 12 to 15-pound bird.

Sesame Seed Stuffing

½ cup Sesame Seed
3 tablespoons Instant Minced Onions
3 tablespoons water
3 quarts toasted bread cubes
1 cup chopped celery
1 tablespoon Parsley
1 tablespoon Poultry Seasoning

1 tablespoon Sage
1 teaspoon salt
½ teaspoon Medium Grind Black Pepper
½ cup melted butter
¾ cup turkey giblet stock

Spread Sesame Seed in large shallow pan and toast in a 350° oven for 30 to 40 minutes or until golden brown. Stir occasionally so seeds will brown evenly. Rehydrate Onions in water. Combine Sesame Seed and Onions with toasted bread cubes, chopped celery, Parsley, Poultry Seasoning, Sage, salt, and Pepper. Mix thoroughly. Pour butter and stock over stuffing and toss lightly. Stuff crop and body cavity of turkey. Makes 12 cups stuffing.

Sweet Potato-Sausage Stuffing

6 slices bread
1 cup mashed sweet potatoes
½ cup finely chopped celery
½ pound pork sausage links
2 tablespoons Instant Minced Onions

2 tablespoons water
1 teaspoon salt
¼ teaspoon Fine Grind Black Pepper
1 teaspoon Poultry Seasoning

Toast bread and cut into cubes. Combine with mashed sweet potatoes and celery. Cut each sausage link into 4 or 5 pieces. Fry slowly in heavy frying pan until well browned. Pour off all but 2 tablespoons fat. Rehydrate Onions in water. Add to browned sausage and fat and cook until Onions are golden, stirring frequently. Stir in salt, Pepper, and Poultry Seasoning. Pour over bread cubes and sweet potatoes. Toss to combine thoroughly. Makes 5 cups stuffing—enough to stuff a large capon or a small turkey.

SEAFOOD

FLAVORFUL AND interestingly different, the seafood recipes in this chapter will bring bounteous compliments to the cook.

Fish here are not overpowered by highly seasoned sauces. They are, however, given that necessary seasoning touch that effectively brings out their delicate flavor and provides that extra "zip" that is called for.

Simple fried oysters are delicious, but add the taste of Old Hickory Smoked Salt and they are outstanding. Fish filets are good when they are baked in a hot oven, but bake them in sour cream seasoned with Ground Ginger, Mild Mustard, and Salad Herbs and they are superb. The secret is the artful selection of seasoning ingredients that do not in any way detract from the goodness of the fish itself.

Seafood deserves a place on the guest menu as well as on the family dinner table. For an impressive dinner for special guests, what could be more festive that Fish Flambe, flamed at the table and served with finesse by host or hostess! For an unusual entree, serve marinated cubes of swordfish that have been broiled just to the right degree of doneness.

The way seafood is presented is highly important. Many fish are rather colorless, and the addition of a sprinkling of Parsley, or Chervil, or Paprika does a lot to pique the appetite.

Clams Genovese

Especially good when made with fresh clams, but whether made from fresh or canned, Clams Genovese is an excellent entrée for a small supper party.

4 tablespoons butter
2 cups ground or minced clams or 2 cans (7 oz. each) minced clams
½ teaspoon Garlic Powder
1 teaspoon Spaghetti Sauce Seasoning

½ cup dry white wine
½ pound spaghetti
2 cups boiling salted water
2 teaspoons Parsley
⅓ cup grated Parmesan cheese

Melt butter in frying pan; add undrained ground or minced clams. Stir in Garlic Powder and Spaghetti Sauce Seasoning. Add wine and simmer for 20 minutes. Meanwhile, cook spaghetti in boiling salted water until done. Drain and rinse in hot water. Arrange on heated platter or individual plates. Pour clams over spaghetti. Sprinkle with Parsley and Parmesan cheese. Serve hot. Makes 6 servings.

Crab Casserole Amandine

An elegant casserole to serve for a supper or luncheon party. Bake in individual ramekins or shells, if desired. Use two 6-ounce cans of canned crab if fresh isn't available.

1 tablespoon Green Bell Pepper
1 tablespoon water
¼ cup butter
4 teaspoons Arrowroot
1 cup undiluted evaporated milk
⅓ cup water
½ teaspoon Mei Yen Seasoning
½ teaspoon Chervil

1 cup thinly sliced celery
2 tablespoons chopped pimiento
1 pound fresh crab meat
2 hard-cooked eggs
½ cup toasted slivered almonds
½ cup buttered bread crumbs
½ cup shredded Cheddar cheese

Crush Green Peppers and rehydrate in the 1 tablespoon water. Melt butter; add Green Peppers and cook for 4 or 5 minutes or until crisp-tender. Remove from heat and stir in Arrowroot. Combine evaporated milk and ⅓ cup water. Add to butter and Arrowroot. Return to heat; cook over low heat, stirring constantly, until thick and smooth. Stir in Mei Yen, Chervil, celery, pimiento, and crab meat. Chop eggs coarsely and add to crab with toasted slivered almonds. Pour into a buttered 1½-quart casserole. Top with buttered crumbs and shredded cheese. Bake in a 350° oven for 30 to 35 minutes or until bubbling hot and cheese is melted. Serve hot. Makes 6 servings.

Broiled Lobster with Lemon Butter

1½ to 2-pound lobster or 2 one-pound
   lobsters
⅓ cup sweet or unsalted butter
1 teaspoon Mei Yen Seasoning

1 tablespoon lemon juice
⅛ teaspoon Lemon Peel
½ teaspoon Parsley
⅛ teaspoon Tarragon

Split lobsters and remove somach sac and sand vein. Loosen lobster meat from shell. Melt butter; add Mei Yen, lemon juice, Lemon Peel, and Parsley. Crush Tarragon and add to butter sauce. Stir well and spoon onto lobster. Broil lobster for 15 to 20 minutes or until done and brown, basting frequently. Pour any remaining butter over lobster just before serving. Or pour sauce into small cup and serve with lobster for dunking. Serve hot. Makes 2 servings.

Oysters Bordelaise

¼ cup butter
¼ teaspoon Garlic Powder
½ teaspoon Onion Powder
½ teaspoon Tarragon

1 teaspoon Parsley
1 pint or 1 jar (12 oz.) medium-size
   oysters
1 tablespoon fine cracker crumbs

Soften butter to room temperature. Cream Garlic Powder and Onion Powder into butter. Crush Tarragon and cream into butter along with Parsley. Arrange oysters in baking dish or shells for baking. Dot with one-half of the herb butter. Roast in a 400° oven until edges begin to curl. Turn oysters and dot with rest of butter. Sprinkle with cracker crumbs and roast for 10 minutes or until crumbs are brown. Makes 2 or 3 servings.

Old Hickory Fried Oysters

Old Hickory Smoked Salt is a new and interesting seasoning for fried oysters. Serve with Special Cocktail Sauce (page 125).

1 pint or 1 jar (12 oz.) medium-size
   oysters
1 egg

¾ teaspoon Old Hickory Smoked Salt
2 tablespoons water
½ cup fine dry bread crumbs

Drain oysters and remove any bits of shell. With fork, beat together lightly egg, Old Hickory, and water. Dip oysters in mixture, then in bread crumbs. Fry in generous amount of hot shortening or oil. Sprinkle with additional Old Hickory, if desired. Makes 3 or 4 servings.

Shrimp Supreme

🌱 Here's a casserole that can be made ahead of time and then baked just before serving.

1 pound large raw shrimp, fresh or frozen
1 tablespoon Chicken Seasoned Stock Base
1 cup hot water
½ cup rice
¼ cup butter
1 tablespoon Arrowroot

1½ cups milk
½ teaspoon Dill Weed
1 tablespoon Eschalot Wine Vinegar
1 teaspoon Beau Monde Seasoning
½ teaspoon salt
1½ cups shredded Cheddar cheese
Paprika

Shell and devein shrimp. Dissolve Chicken Seasoned Stock Base in hot water; bring to a boil, add rice. Turn down heat, cover and steam until rice is done. Melt butter; remove from heat and stir in Arrowroot. Add milk; return to heat and cook, stirring constantly, until thickened and smooth. Stir in Dill Weed, Vinegar, Beau Monde, and salt. Add cleaned shrimp and simmer gently for about 10 minutes or until shrimp turn red. Spoon rice into a buttered 1½-quart baking dish. Pour shrimp over rice; top with shredded cheese and sprinkle with Paprika. Bake in a 350° oven for 25 to 30 minutes or until cheese is melted and rice and shrimp are hot. Serve hot. Makes 6 servings.

Bombay Shrimp Curry

🌱 Apples and Onions simmered and then puréed give this curry sauce its interesting flavor and consistency. Serve with steamed or boiled rice.

1 pound large raw shrimp
¼ cup butter
1 tablespoon Curry Powder
4 tablespoons Instant Minced Onions
4 tablespoons water
3 medium-size apples, peeled and sliced, or 1½ cups drained canned apples

2 cups hot water
1 tablespoon Chicken Seasoned Stock Base
1 tablespoon Beau Monde Seasoning
2 teaspoons Arrowroot
1 tablespoon cold water
3 hard-cooked eggs
¼ cup undiluted evaporated milk

Shell and devein shrimp. Melt butter; stir in Curry Powder and cook for 3 or 4 minutes over low heat. Meanwhile, rehydrate Onions in water; add to Curry and simmer for 2 or 3 minutes. Add apples, hot water, Chicken Seasoned Stock Base, and Beau Monde. Simmer gently for about 40 minutes, stirring occasionally. Put through food mill or wire sieve. Add shrimp to Curry Sauce and simmer for 30 minutes. Mix Arrowroot and cold water and stir into sauce. Cook until thickened. Slice hard-cooked eggs; add to Curry along with milk. Serve hot. Makes 6 servings.

Shrimp Espanol

This exotic Latin dish is a wonderful one to cook for a party. The sauce simmers a long time, but there's no hurried last minute preparation. Serve over steamed or boiled rice.

1 tablespoon Green Bell Peppers	⅛ teaspoon Cracked Bay Leaf
1 teaspoon Onion Powder	⅛ teaspoon Garlic Powder
2 tablespoons water	¼ teaspoon Oregano
3 tablespoons olive oil	1 tablespoon Parsley
2 cups cooked or canned tomatoes	2 teaspoons Mei Yen Seasoning
1 can (8 oz.) tomato sauce	2 pounds cleaned, cooked shrimp
¼ teaspoon Celery Seed	

Crush Green Peppers; rehydrate with Onion Powder in water. Sauté for 3 or 4 minutes in olive oil. Add tomatoes, tomato sauce, Celery Seed, Bay Leaf, and Garlic Powder. Crush Oregano and stir into sauce along with Parsley and Mei Yen. Simmer over very low heat for about 2 hours. Just before serving, add cleaned shrimp. Heat thoroughly. Serve hot. Makes 8 servings.

Meurette

A Meurette is a classic fish stew from the province of Burgundy in France. Though usually made with Burgundy wine, it can be made with other red wines.

3 pounds fresh or frozen fish (bass, perch, lake trout, etc.)	3 medium-size carrots
2 cups water	2 leeks
2 cups Burgundy or other dry red wine	¼ teaspoon Thyme
2 tablespoons Instant Minced Onions	⅛ teaspoon Cracked Bay Leaf
¼ teaspoon Garlic Powder	⅛ teaspoon Spice Parisienne
2 tablespoons Chicken Seasoned Stock Base	2 teaspoons Beau Monde Seasoning
	¼ cup brandy
	1 tablespoon butter

Thaw frozen fish or wash fresh fish and cut into thick slices or chunks. Meanwhile, combine water, wine, Onions, Garlic Powder, and Chicken Seasoned Stock Base. Heat to simmering. Scrape carrots and slice thinly; clean leeks and slice thinly, using white portion only. Add vegetables to simmering stock. Crush Thyme and add to stock along with Bay Leaf, Spice Parisienne, and Beau Monde. Simmer for 40 to 45 minutes or until vegetables are tender. Force through a wire sieve or food mill. Add brandy. Place fish in large casserole or Dutch oven. Pour stock over fish and cook in a 325° oven for 45 minutes to 1 hour. Stir butter into stew. Ladle stew into bowls or soup plates over slices of Garlic French bread. Serve at once. Makes 6 servings.

Fish Filets Baked in Sour Cream

1 pound fresh or frozen fish filets
(cod, haddock, halibut, sole,
etc.)
1 cup dairy sour cream
1½ teaspoons Beau Monde Seasoning

⅛ teaspoon Mild Mustard
⅛ teaspoon Ground Ginger
¼ teaspoon Salad Herbs
Paprika

Let frozen fish thaw until filets can be separated. Arrange fish filets in flat baking dish. Mix together sour cream, Beau Monde, Mustard, and Ginger. Crush Salad Herbs and blend into sour cream. Spread over fish. Sprinkle with Paprika. Bake in a 400° oven for 25 to 30 minutes or until fish is done and sauce bubbling. Serve at once. Makes 3 or 4 servings.

Savory Broiled Fish

1½ to 2 pounds fresh or frozen fish
filets (halibut, haddock, cod, or
other firm white fish)
½ cup dry white wine
2 tablespoons Soy Sauce

¼ teaspoon Horseradish
1½ teaspoons Mei Yen Seasoning
½ teaspoon Onion Powder
2 tablespoons salad oil

Arrange fish on oven-proof platter or in shallow baking dish. Combine wine, Soy Sauce, Horseradish, Mei Yen, Onion Powder, and salad oil. Pour over fish. Broil for 20 to 30 minutes, basting frequently with sauce in baking dish. Serve hot. Makes 4 servings.

Fish Flambé

An easy way to crush Fennel Seed is to put it in an electric blender for a minute or two.

2 pounds fish filets or a whole fish,
split (such as butterfish, bluefish,
or weakfish)
2 teaspoons Beau Monde Seasoning
1 teaspoon Fennel Seed

¼ teaspoon Thyme
1 teaspoon Parsley
⅛ teaspoon Ground White Pepper
1 tablespoon lemon juice
½ cup brandy

Arrange fish in oiled metal baking pan or platter. Sprinkle both sides of fish with Beau Monde. Broil without turning until fish is done. If broiled in pan, remove to heatproof platter. Crush Fennel Seed and Thyme; combine with Parsley and Pepper. Sprinkle over fish. Spoon lemon juice over fish. Warm brandy and pour over hot fish. Set brandy aflame. As soon as flame dies down, serve at once. Makes 4 servings.

Filets of Mackerel Vénitienne

3 fresh mackerel (about 1 pound each)
2 teaspoons Mei Yen Seasoning
¼ teaspoon Ground White Pepper
1 cup dry white wine
4 tablespoons butter

1½ tablespoons Arrowroot
1 cup light cream
¼ teaspoon Tarragon
2 teaspoons Chervil
12 small new potatoes

Clean mackerel; pull out bones and split fish. Arrange filets in a large frying pan. Combine 1 teaspoon Mei Yen, Pepper, and wine; pour over fish. Simmer very gently for 20 minutes or until fish is done. Lift filets out gently with spatula turner and arrange on oven-proof platter. Melt 2 tablespoons butter in saucepan; remove from heat and stir in Arrowroot. Add cream and the wine mixture in which fish was poached. Cook sauce, stirring constantly, until thickened and smooth. Add remaining 1 teaspoon Mei Yen; crush Tarragon and stir into sauce along with 1 teaspoon Chervil; pour over fish. Bake in a 350° oven for 15 minutes or until sauce is bubbling. Meanwhile, cook potatoes until done; peel while hot. Add remaining 2 tablespoons butter and 1 teaspoon Chervil to potatoes. As butter melts, spoon over potatoes until thoroughly coated with butter and Chervil. Arrange on platter with fish. Serve at once. Makes 6 servings.

Fresh Salmon Tarragon

When fresh salmon is at its best, try a whole fish or large piece. Frozen fish responds well to this way of cooking, too.

2½ to 3 pounds fresh salmon, whole or large piece
2 cups water
½ cup Tarragon White Wine Vinegar

1 tablespoon Beau Monde Seasoning
1 tablespoon Instant Minced Onions
3 or 4 whole Black Peppercorns

Place salmon on rack in large kettle. Combine water, Vinegar, Beau Monde, Onions, and Peppercorns; pour over fish. Cover and simmer over very low heat until done, about 45 minutes. Lift fish out carefully; remove skin. Serve hot or well chilled. Arrange salmon on platter; garnish with cucumbers and watercress. Top servings of salmon with spoonfuls of Tarragon Sauce. Makes 6 servings.

TARRAGON SAUCE

1 cup dairy sour cream
2 tablespoons Tarragon White Wine Vinegar

2 teaspoons Beau Monde Seasoning
1 tablespoon Shredded Green Onions
½ teaspoon sugar

Combine sour cream, Vinegar, Beau Monde, Shredded Green Onions, and sugar.

Filet of Sole l'Indienne

A classic recipe from India, using whole seeds rather than ground. Crush the seeds in a mortar and pestle or put them in the electric blender. Let blender whirl for a time and the seeds will crush beautifully.

1 pound fresh or frozen filet of sole
1 tablespoon Arrowroot
4 tablespoons salad oil
½ teaspoon Turmeric
⅛ teaspoon Ground Ginger
1 Whole Cardamom
⅛ teaspoon Anise Seed

¼ teaspoon Cumin
2 tablespoons Instant Minced Onions
2 tablespoons water
½ cup dry white wine
½ cup dairy sour cream
1 teaspoon salt
¼ teaspoon Lemon Peel

Coat fish with Arrowroot. Arrange filets in flat baking dish. Combine 2 tablespoons salad oil with Turmeric and Ginger. Pour over fish, turning the fish several times to coat with the seasoned oil. Let stand at room temperature for about an hour. Crack the Whole Cardamom and remove the seeds. Combine the Cardamom Seeds with Anise Seed and Cumin. Crush thoroughly. Rehydrate Onions in water. Cook in remaining 2 tablespoons oil for 4 or 5 minutes or until golden. Add crushed seeds, wine, sour cream, salt, and Lemon Peel. Spoon over fish. Bake in a 350° oven for about 30 minutes or until fish is done. Spoon sauce over fish two or three times while fish is baking. Serve with steamed or boiled rice. Makes 4 servings.

Filet of Sole au Raisin Blanc

¼ cup butter
1 pound small filets of sole
½ teaspoon salt
1 tablespoon lemon juice
Dash Cayenne Pepper
½ cup dry white wine

¼ teaspoon M.S.G.
Paprika
½ cup white seedless grapes, cut in half
⅛ teaspoon Lemon Peel
1 teaspoon Chervil

Melt butter in heavy frying pan. Add filets and cook for about 5 minutes or until very lightly browned. Turn carefully with spatula. Sprinkle filets with salt, lemon juice, and Cayenne. Combine wine and M.S.G. Pour over fish and cook until fish is done, about 5 minutes. With spatula lift fish out to heated serving plates or small platter. Sprinkle with Paprika. To sauce in pan add grapes, Lemon Peel, and Chervil. Bring sauce to boil and simmer for a few minutes until grapes are hot. Pour over filets and serve at once. Makes 4 servings.

Skewered Swordfish

🌿 The original of this recipe comes from a Turkish cook book.

2 pounds swordfish, cut 1 inch thick
1 teaspoon Paprika
½ teaspoon Lemon Peel
2 tablespoons White Wine Vinegar
4 tablespoons olive oil

½ teaspoon Onion Powder
½ teaspoon Cracked Bay Leaf
1 teaspoon Mei Yen Seasoning
1 to 2 teaspoons Parsley

Cut swordfish into 1-inch cubes. Arrange in glass baking pan. Combine Paprika, Lemon Peel, Vinegar, olive oil, Onion Powder, Cracked Bay Leaf, and Mei Yen. Mix well and pour over fish. Let fish marinate for 1 to 2 hours. Arrange cubes on skewers. Broil for 20 to 30 minutes, turning frequently and brushing liberally with marinade. Just before serving brush again with marinade and sprinkle with parsley. Makes 6 servings.

Creamed Eggs and Tuna

1 tablespoon Green Bell Pepper
1 tablespoon Instant Minced Onions
2 tablespoons water
2 tablespoons butter
1½ tablespoons Arrowroot
2 cups milk
1 teaspoon Spaghetti Sauce Seasoning

1 teaspoon Beau Monde Seasoning
½ teaspoon salt
6 hard-cooked eggs
1 can (7 oz.) solid pack tuna
1 tablespoon sherry
Paprika

Crush Green Peppers; rehydrate Peppers and Onions in water. Melt butter; sauté Peppers and Onions in butter for 4 or 5 minutes. Remove from heat and stir in Arrowroot. Add milk and Spaghetti Sauce Seasoning. Return to heat and cook, stirring constantly, until thickened and smooth. Season with Beau Monde and salt. Cut eggs into quarters; separate tuna into chunks and add to sauce. Heat thoroughly. Add sherry and spoon over crisp toast. Sprinkle with Paprika. Serve hot. Makes 6 servings.

Baked Finnan Haddie

1½ to 2 pounds Finnan Haddie
2 cups cold milk
¼ teaspoon Ground White Pepper

1 piece (½-inch) whole Ginger
1 tablespoon butter

Arrange Finnan Haddie in baking dish. Combine milk, Pepper, and Whole Ginger. Pour over fish. Bake uncovered in a 325° oven for 45 minutes. Just before serving spread butter over top of fish. Serve hot. Makes 6 servings.

BARBECUE
SPECIALTIES

ALL FOODS seem to become more exciting and flavorful when they are served out-of-doors, and nothing piques the appetite quite like the sight and the tantalizing aroma of a succulent roast turning on the spit or a luscious steak sizzling on the grill.

It is in the realm of outdoor cookery that marinades and basting sauces come into their own. These wonderful mixtures help to tenderize meats and keep them moist as they cook over the coals. They also impart their own good flavors to barbecued foods. You'll find some special barbecue marinades and sauces here. These are robust sauces to go with outdoor appetites and outdoor flavors.

There are simple recipes here and a few rather elegant ones. You can barbecue a whole leg of lamb to impress special guests, or you can transform an ordinary hamburger into a very special Pepperburger to intrigue the men in your family.

Appetites are hearty out-of-doors. Keep the food simple—but be generous in the amounts. Casseroles are wonderful companions to the entrées that come from the barbecue. Glance through the chapters on Vegetables, Rice and Pasta, Eggs and Cheese; you'll find many substantial and tasty casserole combinations to include in your barbecue menu.

Barbecued Steak, Family Style

2½ to 3 pounds chuck or round steak
    (6 steaks, cut about 1 inch thick)
½ cup dry red wine
1 teaspoon Seasoned Meat
    Tenderizer
¼ teaspoon Ground Cardamom
⅛ teaspoon Garlic Powder
⅓ cup salad oil
3 tablespoons Soy Sauce

Arrange steaks in glass baking pan. Combine wine, Meat Tenderizer, Cardamom, Garlic Powder, oil, and Soy Sauce. Pour over steaks. Marinate for 1 hour at room temperature, turning meat several times. Drain steaks. Barbecue steaks, turning once, for about 20 minutes or until done as desired. Brush frequently with marinade while steaks are barbecuing. Makes 6 servings.

Barbecued London Broil

Use this marinade, too, on chuck or other budget steaks. It will help to tenderize less expensive meats. Leave meat in the marinade overnight.

1½-pound flank steak
1 tablespoon tomato paste
1 cup hot water
1½ teaspoons Garlic Salt
¼ cup Red Wine Vinegar
¼ teaspoon Cracked Black Pepper
⅛ teaspoon Cracked Bay Leaf
¼ teaspoon Bouquet Garni for Beef
2 tablespoons salad oil

Score flank steak well and place in glass baking pan. Combine tomato paste with hot water; add Garlic Salt, Vinegar, Pepper, and Bay Leaf. Crush Bouquet Garni and stir into marinade along with salad oil. Pour over steak. Let marinate overnight in refrigerator or several hours at room temperature. Barbecue quickly, about 5 to 7 minutes on each side. Spoon marinade over meat while barbecuing. Cut flank steak into thin slices diagonally across the grain. Heat any remaining marinade and serve with steak. Makes 4 servings.

Barbecued Pepperburgers

2 pounds lean ground beef
½ cup hot water
1 teaspoon Mei Yen Seasoning
½ teaspoon Old Hickory Smoked Salt
2 teaspoons Soy Sauce
½ teaspoon Cracked Black Pepper
Instant Toasted Onions

Place ground beef in mixing bowl. Combine water, Mei Yen, Old Hickory, Soy Sauce, and Cracked Pepper. Pour over ground beef. Mix carefully and thoroughly so Pepper is evenly distributed through meat. Form into 6 thick patties. Refrigerate until ready to barbecue. Grill slowly over glowing coals, about 10 minutes on each side or until done. Just before serving, sprinkle with Toasted Onions and additional Old Hickory if desired. Makes 6 servings.

Lamb Ribs Teriyaki

3 to 4 pounds breast of lamb
3 tablespoons Soy Sauce
1 teaspoon Ground Ginger
1 teaspoon Mei Yen Seasoning

1 teaspoon Garlic Salt
2 teaspoons sugar
½ cup sherry

Have breast of lamb cut into serving-size pieces of 2 or 3 ribs. Arrange ribs in glass baking pan or mixing bowl. Combine Soy Sauce, Ginger, Mei Yen, Garlic Salt, sugar, and wine. Stir until well blended. Pour over ribs. Marinate for several hours at room temperature or overnight in refrigerator. Drain ribs and barbecue very slowly over glowing coals, turning frequently and brushing occasionally with marinade. Barbecue for about 1 hour or until ribs are crisp and brown and meat is done as desired. Makes 4 servings.

Barbecued Lamb Kebabs

2 to 2½ pounds leg or shoulder of
   lamb, cut into 1-inch cubes
⅛ teaspoon Garlic Chips
¼ cup Tarragon White Wine Vinegar

½ cup sherry
2 tablespoons salad oil
2 teaspoons Mixed Pickling Spice
¼ teaspoon Bouquet Garni for Lamb

Arrange lamb cubes in glass baking pan or mixing bowl. Combine Garlic Chips, Vinegar, sherry, and salad oil. Crush Pickling Spice and Bouquet Garni and stir into marinade. Pour over lamb. Marinate in the refrigerator for 6 to 8 hours or overnight. Thread meat on skewers and barbecue over glowing coals for 20 to 30 minutes or until done as desired. Turn meat frequently and brush with marinade as it barbecues. Makes 6 servings.

Barbecued Leg of Lamb

3½ to 4-pound leg of lamb
½ teaspoon Garlic Powder
1 teaspoon Bouquet Garni for Lamb

2 teaspoons Mei Yen Seasoning
⅓ cup olive oil
3 tablespoons Red Wine Vinegar

Have leg of lamb boned. Spread meat out flat and cut off excess fat and gristly pieces. Combine Garlic Powder, Bouquet Garni, and Mei Yen. Rub well into meat. Place in glass baking pan or large bowl. Combine olive oil and Vinegar; pour over lamb and turn until thoroughly coated. Marinate several hours at room temperature or overnight in the refrigerator. Barbecue over glowing coals for 45 to 50 minutes, turning every 10 to 15 minutes and brushing with marinade. Place meat on platter or cutting board and cut into ¼-inch slices. Spoon any remaining marinade and meat juices over slices of lamb and serve at once. Makes 6 servings.

Barbecued Lamb Chops

6 large loin lamb chops, cut 1 inch thick
¼ cup melted butter
½ cup dry white wine

¼ teaspoon Bouquet Garni for Lamb
Salt
Medium Grind Black Pepper

Arrange lamb chops in large glass baking pan. Combine melted butter and wine; crush Bouquet Garni and add to butter and wine. Pour over lamb chops and marinate at room temperature for several hours. Drain chops and barbecue for about 30 minutes, turning several times and basting frequently with remaining marinade. Season to taste with salt and Pepper. Makes 6 servings.

Spiced Barbecued Pork

This spicy barbecue sauce is good not only on pork chops but on pork steaks or on a thick slice of ham.

4 large pork chops or steaks
½ cup dry white wine
¼ cup Soy Sauce
2 tablespoons salad oil

½ teaspoon Pumpkin Pie Spice
½ teaspoon Hot Mustard
1 teaspoon sugar

Arrange pork chops or steaks in glass baking pan. Combine wine, Soy Sauce, salad oil, Pumpkin Pie Spice, Mustard, and sugar. Pour over pork chops; let marinate for an hour or so. Barbecue pork chops very slowly, basting frequently with sauce and turning occasionally, for 45 to 50 minutes. Just before serving, bring marinade to boiling and pour a spoonful over each chop. Makes 4 servings.

Sweet and Sour Barbecued Fish

2 to 3 pounds fresh fish steaks or filets such as salmon, halibut, or bass
½ cup salad oil
¼ cup Tarragon Red Wine Vinegar
½ teaspoon Ground Ginger

1 tablespoon sugar
1 teaspoon Mei Yen Seasoning
2 tablespoons sherry
3 tablespoons Soy Sauce
¼ teaspoon Garlic Powder

Arrange fish steaks or filets in glass baking pan. Combine salad oil, Vinegar, Ginger, sugar, Mei Yen, sherry, Soy Sauce, and Garlic Powder. Pour over fish; marinate for 1 hour. Place fish on well-oiled grill over glowing coals. Or place in a well-oiled hinged grill. Barbecue for 10 to 15 minutes, brushing frequently with marinade. Turn carefully with spatula or turn the hinged grill. Continue barbecuing for 10 to 15 minutes or until fish is done. Lift carefully with spatula onto hot platter. Brush well with remaining marinade. Serve at once. Makes 5 servings.

Barbecued Carrots

1 pound small young carrots
Boiling salted water
½ cup salad oil

1 teaspoon Garlic Salt
¼ teaspoon Rosemary or Summer Savory

Scrape carrots. Cook in boiling salted water until almost done; drain. Combine salad oil, Garlic Salt, and Rosemary or Summer Savory. Pour over carrots; let marinate. Grill for 10 to 15 minutes, turning frequently and brushing with seasoned oil. Makes 4 servings.

Barbecued New Potatoes

6 whole new potatoes
½ cup salad oil
1 teaspoon Onion Salt

¼ teaspoon Oregano
Old Hickory Smoked Salt

Boil potatoes in their jackets until barely tender. Peel. Combine salad oil, Onion Salt, and Oregano. Pour over potatoes; let marinate. Grill for 10 to 15 minutes, turning frequently and brushing with seasoned oil. Sprinkle with Old Hickory Smoked Salt just before serving. Makes 6 servings.

Cheesed Potatoes in Foil

4 large baking potatoes
Old Hickory Smoked Salt

8 thin slices process American cheese

Boil or bake potatoes in their jackets until tender. Peel, and cut each potato into 3 slices lengthwise. Sprinkle potatoes generously with Old Hickory Smoked Salt. Place a cheese slice between each potato slice. Wrap each potato in a double thickness of heavy foil. Barbecue slowly over glowing coals for 20 to 30 minutes, turning packages frequently. Makes 4 servings.

Barbecued Zucchini

1 to 1½ pounds zucchini
Boiling salted water
½ cup salad oil

¼ teaspoon Garlic Powder
¼ teaspoon Sweet Basil

Scrub zucchini and cut off ends. Cook in salted water until almost done; drain. Combine salad oil, Garlic Powder, and Sweet Basil. Pour over zucchini; let marinate for an hour or so. Grill over glowing coals for 10 to 15 minutes, turning frequently and brushing with seasoned oil. Makes 4 servings.

All-Purpose Barbecue Marinade

Use this marinade on steaks, chops, hamburgers, chicken, game — almost any kind of meat or fowl you wish to barbecue. It has a tenderizing effect on those less expensive steaks, too.

2 teaspoons sugar
1 teaspoon Cracked Black Pepper
4 Whole Cloves
1 teaspoon Parsley
¼ teaspoon Garlic Powder
1 teaspoon Onion Powder

2 teaspoons Mei Yen Seasoning
¼ teaspoon Cracked Bay Leaf
½ cup Red Wine Vinegar
1½ cups dry red wine
2 tablespoons salad oil

Combine sugar, Pepper, Cloves, Parsley, Garlic Powder, Onion Powder, Mei Yen, Bay Leaf, Vinegar, wine, and salad oil. Stir until well blended. Pour marinade over meat in large pottery, glass, or enamelware bowl or pan. Marinate for 8 to 12 hours in the refrigerator. Less tender meat should marinate longer than tender cuts. Drain meat and barbecue slowly to desired doneness, basting frequently with marinade. Makes 2 cups marinade.

Basic Marinade for Chicken

½ cup salad oil
3 tablespoons White Wine Vinegar
1 teaspoon Mei Yen Seasoning
1 teaspoon Garlic Salt

½ teaspoon Cracked Black Pepper
1 teaspoon Parsley
½ teaspoon Rosemary, Tarragon, Oregano, or Sweet Basil

Combine oil, Vinegar, Mei Yen, Garlic Salt, Pepper, and Parsley. Crush Rosemary or other herb and stir into marinade. Pour over chicken quarters or halves; marinate for an hour or two at room temperature. Barbecue over glowing coals, turning frequently and brushing with marinade. Barbecue for 40 minutes or until chicken is done. Serve hot. Makes ¾ cup marinade.

Soy Marinade for Seafood

Good for uncooked large-size shrimp, lobster, crab; excellent for salmon.

⅓ cup Soy Sauce
⅓ cup salad oil
⅓ cup sherry

½ teaspoon Onion Powder
¼ teaspoon Ground Ginger

Combine Soy Sauce, salad oil, sherry, Onion Powder, and Ground Ginger. Marinate seafood for about ½ hour at room temperature, salmon for several hours. Arrange on skewers, in a hinged broiler, or on grill, or barbecue a whole salmon on a spit. Barbecue over glowing coals. Makes 1 cup marinade.

VEGETABLES

SEASONINGS ARE essential if you wish to make vegetable dishes interesting. All of us get into a menu rut at times, and vegetables seem to suffer from a lack of imaginative cookery more than most other items in the menu. Although it is simpler to serve a vegetable with butter than it is to try out other seasonings and sauces, a little experimentation can bring forth surprise flavors that will make ordinary vegetables extraordinary.

If treated with the respect they deserve, vegetables take on new stature and become a distinguished addition to the meal. A bit of Lemon Peel, a pinch of Dill Weed, or a hint of Thyme or Tarragon will change the flavor of some vegetables so subtly that they become a completely new taste adventure.

The sauce you mix with or pour over vegetables transforms them, too. Vinaigrette Sauce, for example, dresses up asparagus or broccoli. Squash is a taste treat when tossed with Dill Weed, sour cream, and Toasted Onions.

The toppings you use—bubbling hot cheese, buttered toast cubes, a sprinkling of Parsley or Chervil—provide eye appeal and give a finishing touch to vegetable dishes.

Vegetable casseroles are wonderful side dishes—especially good to serve with barbecued meats. And here again, spices and herbs step in to lift them out of the ordinary.

Artichokes with Sour Cream Soy Dip

❧ Not only is Sour Cream Soy Dip good with artichokes, but it is also delicious as a dip for celery or carrot sticks, cooked whole shrimp, lobster tails, or potato chips.

6 artichokes	1 tablespoon Beau Monde Seasoning
1 to 2 quarts boiling water	

Trim artichokes. Cook in boiling water seasoned with Beau Monde for 30 to 40 minutes or until artichokes are tender. Drain and serve hot or chilled with Sour Cream Soy Dip. Makes 6 servings.

SOUR CREAM SOY DIP

1 cup dairy sour cream	1 tablespoon Garlic Wine Vinegar
2 tablespoons Soy Sauce	½ teaspoon Curry Powder

Combine sour cream, Soy Sauce, Vinegar, and Curry Powder. Chill in refrigerator for about an hour for flavors to blend.

Asparagus Vinaigrette

❧ Vinaigrette Sauce is good, too, on other vegetables such as broccoli, green beans, spinach, and cauliflower.

1 pound fresh asparagus	2 tablespoons Tarragon White Wine Vinegar
½ cup water	
2 teaspoons Beau Monde Seasoning	5 tablespoons olive oil
½ teaspoon Cracked Black Pepper	1 tablespoon sour cream
⅛ teaspoon Garlic Powder	1 hard-cooked egg, finely chopped
¼ teaspoon Mild Mustard	1 teaspoon Parsley

Trim and wash asparagus and scrape off scales. Cover asparagus with water; add 1 teaspoon Beau Monde. Cook until barely tender. Meanwhile, combine in a bowl 1 teaspoon Beau Monde, Pepper, Garlic Powder, Mustard, Vinegar, olive oil, and sour cream. Beat well to combine thoroughly. Stir in finely chopped hard-cooked egg and Parsley. Drain asparagus and cover with sauce. Heat thoroughly and serve at once. Or chill asparagus and sauce and serve cold. Makes 4 servings.

Navy Beans Indienne

🌿 Here's a vegetable dish that can be served as an entrée; it has some of the same seasonings as Curry. Omit the bacon, if desired, or use the end of a roast or a ham hock instead.

1 pound navy or pea beans
1½ quarts warm water
¼ to ½-pound piece bacon
2 tablespoons Red or Green Bell Peppers
2 tablespoons Instant Minced Onions
¼ cup water
2 tablespoons butter
¼ teaspoon Garlic Powder
¼ teaspoon Ground Ginger

¼ teaspoon Turmeric
1 teaspoon Ground Coriander
2 teaspoons Beau Monde Seasoning
½ teaspoon Cracked Black Pepper
1 large fresh tomato
1 to 2 teaspoons salt
1 tablespoon lemon juice
1 tablespoon Chervil

Wash beans and add 1 quart warm water. Bring to a boil and boil for 5 minutes. Cover and soak for 1 hour. Add remaining warm water and bacon. Simmer for about an hour or until beans are almost tender. Meanwhile, rehydrate Peppers and Onions in water. Sauté gently in butter for 5 to 10 minutes. Stir in Garlic Powder, Ginger, Turmeric, Coriander, Beau Monde, and Pepper. Add to beans. Peel tomato and cut into chunks. Add to beans and continue cooking for another hour or until beans are tender. Add salt to taste. Just before serving, stir in lemon juice and sprinkle with Chervil. Serve hot. Makes 8 servings.

Lima Bean Pot Paesano

🌿 Rich in flavor and hearty enough for a main course.

1 pound small dry lima beans
5 to 6 cups water
2 teaspoons Beef Stock Base
½ teaspoon salt
1 teaspoon Beau Monde Seasoning
1 tablespoon Instant Minced Onions

2 teaspoons Green Bell Peppers
¼ teaspoon Garlic Powder
¼ cup chopped celery
¼ teaspoon Oregano
1/16 teaspoon Ground Cumin Seed
½ cup shredded Cheddar cheese

Wash beans and combine in large kettle with 4 cups water. Bring to a boil and boil for 5 minutes. Turn off heat and soak beans for 1 hour. Add enough more water to cover beans (1 to 2 cups), Beef Stock Base, salt, Beau Monde, Onions, Green Peppers, Garlic Powder, and celery. Crush Oregano and stir into beans along with Ground Cumin. Cover and cook slowly until beans are tender, 1 to 1½ hours. Pour beans into bean pot or casserole. Sprinkle with shredded cheese. Bake in a 350° oven for 20 to 30 minutes or until bubbling hot and cheese is melted. Serve hot. Makes 6 servings.

Hawaiian Bean Pot

🌺 A good casserole to go along with barbecued meats; it can be put together while the fire is getting ready.

1 can (1 lb. 13 oz.) pork and beans
1 can (8 oz.) pineapple tidbits, drained
1 tablespoon Soy Sauce
2 tablespoons Instant Toasted Onions

½ teaspoon Old Hickory Smoked Salt
3 or 4 slices bacon or Canadian bacon

Mix together pork and beans, pineapple tidbits, Soy Sauce, Toasted Onions, and Old Hickory Smoked Salt. Pour into 1½-quart casserole. Top with bacon slices or Canadian bacon. Bake in a 350° oven for about 30 minutes or until beans are hot and bacon is crisp and brown. Makes 6 servings.

Cabbage à la King

2 quarts water
2 teaspoons salt
4 cups shredded cabbage
1 teaspoon Arrowroot

1 tablespoon Chicken Seasoned Stock Base
1 cup dairy sour cream
1 teaspoon Dill Weed

Combine water and salt and bring to a boil. When boiling rapidly, add cabbage. When water again comes to a boil, boil for 1 minute, uncovered. Drain cabbage and sprinkle with Arrowroot and Chicken Seasoned Stock Base. Add sour cream. Cook gently over low heat, stirring carefully, until slightly thickened. Blend in Dill Weed and serve at once. Makes 6 servings.

Panned Cabbage and Celery

🌺 For best flavor and texture, do not overcook.

1 tablespoon salad oil
4 cups shredded cabbage
1 cup sliced celery
1 tablespoon Chicken Seasoned Stock Base

½ cup hot water
2 tablespoons Soy Sauce
1 tablespoon Instant Toasted Onions

Heat salad oil in heavy frying pan. Add cabbage and sliced celery. Stir Chicken Seasoned Stock Base into hot water; add Soy Sauce and pour over vegetables. Cook over high heat for 5 minutes, turning vegetables frequently with pancake turner. Cook until vegetables are barely tender but still crisp. Add Toasted Onions and serve at once. Makes 6 servings.

Cauliflower Sauté

2 tablespoons butter
4 cups thinly sliced cauliflower
1 cup thinly sliced celery
1 tablespoon Instant Toasted Onions
1 tablespoon Chicken Seasoned Stock Base

½ cup dry white wine
1 teaspoon Mei Yen Seasoning
½ teaspoon salt
⅛ teaspoon Medium Grind Black Pepper

Melt butter in large, heavy frying pan. Add cauliflower, celery, and Toasted Onions. Combine Chicken Seasoned Stock Base with wine, Mei Yen, salt, and Pepper. Pour over vegetables. Cook quickly over high heat, turning constantly with wide spatula or pancake turner. Cook until vegetables are barely tender and still crisp, about 7 or 8 minutes. Serve at once. Makes 6 servings.

Celery Amandine

4 cups diagonally-sliced celery
2 tablespoons butter
½ cup slivered, blanched almonds
1 tablespoon Chicken Seasoned Stock Base

⅛ teaspoon Garlic Powder
2 teaspoons Instant Minced Onions
2 tablespoons dry white wine
1 teaspoon Mei Yen Seasoning
1 teaspoon Parsley

Use the large, green outer stalks of celery. Slice about ¼ inch thick diagonally. Rinse in cold water. Melt 1 tablespoon butter in frying pan; add almonds and cook until brown. Stir frequently. (Be careful not to burn almonds.) In a saucepan or large frying pan, melt the remaining butter. Add celery; sprinkle with Chicken Seasoned Stock Base, Garlic Powder, and Onions. Cover and cook over low heat, turning celery several times with a pancake turner. Cook just until celery is crisp-tender, about 10 minutes. Add the white wine, Mei Yen, and toasted almonds. Cook for 2 or 3 minutes longer. Sprinkle with Parsley and serve at once. Makes 6 servings.

Gingered Carrots

3 or 4 medium-size carrots (about 1 pound)
½ cup water
½ teaspoon Mei Yen Seasoning

½ teaspoon Ground Ginger
½ teaspoon sugar
2 tablespoons butter

Scrape carrots. Cut into julienne strips. Add water and Mei Yen. Simmer over low heat for about 10 minutes or just until tender. Add Ginger, sugar, and butter. Cook for about 2 or 3 minutes longer, turning carrots carefully several times. Serve hot. Makes 4 servings.

Corn Fritters

Corn Fritters are delicious for breakfast served with crisp bacon and maple syrup. Or they are an excellent accompaniment to broiled chicken or chops.

2 cups fresh, frozen, or canned
    whole kernel corn
4 tablespoons flour
¼ teaspoon baking powder
1 teaspoon Beau Monde Seasoning
½ teaspoon Mild Mustard
1 teaspoon salt
¼ teaspoon Fine Grind Black Pepper

½ teaspoon Thyme
½ teaspoon sugar
1 cup dairy sour cream
¼ cup milk
2 eggs
2 tablespoons melted butter

If using fresh corn, cut from the cob. (Thaw frozen whole kernel corn; drain canned corn well.) Add flour, baking powder, Beau Monde, Mustard, salt, and Pepper. Crush Thyme and blend into corn along with sugar, sour cream, and milk. Mix thoroughly. Separate eggs; beat yolks into fritter batter along with melted butter. Beat egg whites until stiff but not dry. Fold into fritter batter. Heat a heavy frying pan until very hot. Melt a small amount of butter or shortening in frying pan. Drop batter by teaspoonfuls. Brown on one side, turn and brown on the other side. Serve at once. Makes 4 servings.

Eggplant en Casserole

An excellent casserole to serve out-of-doors along with barbecued meats.

1 large eggplant (about 1½ lbs.)
2 tablespoons butter
½ cup hot water
2 teaspoons Beef Stock Base
1½ teaspoons Spaghetti Sauce
    Seasoning
1 cup dairy sour cream

1 tablespoon Instant Toasted Onions
½ teaspoon salt
¼ teaspoon Medium Grind Black
    Pepper
¼ cup fine dry French bread crumbs
2 tablespoons grated Parmesan
    cheese

Pare eggplant and cut into cubes. Melt butter in large frying pan and sauté eggplant for about 5 minutes or until slightly soft. Combine hot water, Beef Stock Base, and Spaghetti Sauce Seasoning. Pour over eggplant; cover and simmer until eggplant is tender and liquid absorbed. Spoon eggplant into flat baking dish. Combine sour cream, Toasted Onions, salt, and Pepper. Pour over eggplant; cover with crumbs and sprinkle with cheese. Bake in a 350° oven for 20 to 25 minutes or until bubbling hot and brown. Makes 6 servings.

Creamed Peas and Water Chestnuts

🌱 This combination of vegetables is particularly good as an accompaniment to rice casserole dishes. Add a few toasted slivered almonds as a variation.

1 package (10 oz.) frozen peas
½ cup hot water
2 teaspoons Chicken Seasoned Stock Base
1 cup light cream (approximately)

3 tablespoons butter
1 tablespoon Arrowroot
1 can (5 oz.) water chestnuts
1 teaspoon Mei Yen Seasoning
⅛ teaspoon Fine Grind Black Pepper

Cook peas in hot water and Chicken Seasoned Stock Base until tender. Drain; to the liquid add enough light cream (approximately 1 cup) to make 1½ cups liquid. Melt butter in saucepan. Remove from heat and stir in Arrowroot. Add liquid; cook over low heat, stirring constantly, until thickened and smooth. Drain and slice water chestnuts. Add to cream sauce along with cooked peas. Season with Mei Yen and Pepper. Heat thoroughly and serve hot. Makes 6 servings.

Stuffed Peppers Ricci

🌱 A deft hand with seasonings makes this old favorite especially flavorful.

3 large green peppers
Boiling salted water
3 tablespoons Instant Minced Onions
3 tablespoons water
1 pound lean ground beef
½ cup quick-cooking rice
½ teaspoon salt

1 teaspoon Mei Yen Seasoning
¼ teaspoon Spice Parisienne
2 cans (8 oz. each) tomato sauce
½ cup hot water
½ cup dry white wine
1 cup shredded sharp Cheddar cheese

Split green peppers in half lengthwise. Remove seeds and stems; wash peppers, drop into a large pot of boiling salted water. Turn off heat and let stand for 5 minutes. Drain and arrange peppers in casserole. Rehydrate Onions in water. Mix with ground beef, rice, salt, Mei Yen, Spice Parisienne, and 1 can tomato sauce. Fill peppers with meat mixture. Combine 1 can tomato sauce with hot water and wine. Pour over stuffed peppers. Cover and bake in a 350° oven for 40 minutes. Uncover; sprinkle with shredded cheese and continue baking for 20 minutes longer or until the cheese is melted. Serve hot. Makes 6 servings.

Herbed New Potatoes and Peas

🌿 Be careful not to let the cream boil or it will separate.

1 pound small new potatoes	½ teaspoon Salad Herbs
1½ to 2 pounds fresh peas	½ teaspoon salt, or to taste
Lightly salted boiling water	1 tablespoon butter
½ cup light cream	⅛ teaspoon Cracked Black Pepper

Scrape new potatoes; shell peas. Cook potatoes and peas separately in very lightly salted boiling water. Drain and combine potatoes and peas. Heat cream just to simmering; crush Salad Herbs and add to cream along with salt and butter. Pour over peas and potatoes; let stand for 3 or 4 minutes. Taste and add additional salt if desired. Mix again carefully. Sprinkle with Pepper and serve at once. Makes 6 servings.

Sweet Potatoes with Orange and Ginger

1 can (1 lb. 7 oz.) syrup-pack sweet potatoes	1 teaspoon finely chopped Crystallized Ginger
¼ cup honey	1 tablespoon butter
2 teaspoons Orange Peel	

Drain and reserve liquid from sweet potatoes. Arrange sweet potatoes in flat baking dish. Combine liquid with honey, Orange Peel, and chopped Ginger. Pour over sweet potatoes. Dot with butter. Bake in a 375° oven for 20 to 30 minutes or until sweet potatoes are well glazed. Serve hot. Makes 4 servings.

Baked Onions

4 very large dry yellow onions	2 teaspoons honey
1 cup hot water	¼ teaspoon Lemon Peel
2 teaspoons Chicken Seasoned Stock Base	¼ teaspoon Paprika
1 tablespoon butter	2 tablespoons buttered bread crumbs or finely chopped walnuts
1 teaspoon salt	

Peel onions; cut in half and arrange in large casserole. Combine hot water, Chicken Seasoned Stock Base, butter, salt, honey, Lemon Peel, and Paprika. Pour over onions. Cover and bake in a 350° oven for 1 hour or until onions are tender. Uncover and spoon bread crumbs or chopped nuts over onions. Continue baking for 10 to 15 minutes or until crumbs or nuts are crisp and brown. Makes 6 to 8 servings.

Winter Squash with Dill and Sour Cream

2 to 2½ pounds banana or
    Hubbard squash
½ cup water
1 teaspoon salt

½ cup dairy sour cream
½ teaspoon Dill Weed
1 tablespoon Instant Toasted Onions
¼ teaspoon Cracked Black Pepper

Cut squash into 1½-inch cubes. Pare off tough rind. Combine in saucepan with water and salt and cook until tender. Drain and toss gently with sour cream, Dill Weed, and Toasted Onions. Sprinkle with Cracked Black Pepper. Serve at once. Makes 6 servings.

Savory Zucchini

Serve these thin match-like sticks of zucchini the instant they are done. You'll need a sharp knife for the slicing.

1 pound zucchini
2 tablespoons butter
1 tablespoon Instant Minced Onions

4 teaspoons Beef Stock Base
⅓ cup water

Wash zucchini and cut in half. Slice thinly lengthwise; then cut each thin slice into match-like sticks. Heat butter in large, heavy frying pan. Add Onions, Beef Stock Base, and water. Stir to mix and add zucchini. Cook quickly over high heat, turning constantly with pancake turner. Cook only until zucchini is crisp-tender and liquid absorbed, not more than 5 minutes. Serve immediately. Makes 4 servings.

Scalloped Tomatoes

1 can (1 lb. 13 oz.) tomatoes
2 tablespoons Instant Toasted
    Onions
1 tablespoon brown sugar
1 tablespoon Chicken Seasoned
    Stock Base

¼ teaspoon Fine Grind Black Pepper
¼ teaspoon Sweet Basil
1½ cups toasted bread cubes (about
    3 slices bread)
1 tablespoon butter

Combine tomatoes, Toasted Onions, brown sugar, Chicken Seasoned Stock Base, and Pepper. Crush Basil and add to tomatoes. Arrange 1 cup of toasted bread cubes in 1½-quart casserole. Pour tomatoes over toast cubes. Melt butter in small frying pan; add remaining ½ cup toast cubes and toss in butter. Spread over top of tomatoes. Bake in a 350° oven for about 30 minutes or until hot and top is browned. Makes 6 servings.

RICE & PASTA

RICE AND PASTA have a special affinity for seasonings. Rather bland alone, these foods welcome added flavor touches. Sometimes, as in Lasagne, interest is added by means of a savory sauce. In others cases—Macaroni Parmesan, for example—seasonings are tossed with the rice or pasta just before serving. Frequently, particularly in the rice dishes, the seasonings are added to the cooking water; our Rice Pilaff, for example, cooks in water that has been seasoned with Beef Stock Base and flavored with Onions and Orange Peel.

Both main dishes and side dishes receive favored treatment here. Mingled with the flavorful goodness of a perfectly blended sauce and combined with other ingredients, rice and pasta become enticing entrées. Gently sauced or buttered and judiciously seasoned with herbs or spices, they become light but tasty supporting dishes.

Midway between the rice or pasta entrée and the light side dish are the fairly substantial casserole accompaniments. Many of these are the favorites of the barbecue chef. Although they do not compete in heartiness with the entrée that is served up from the barbecue grill or spit, they are filling enough to satisfy outdoor appetites. They are in demand, too, because they can be prepared in advance and because they hold up well while the main course is being barbecued and served.

Spanish Rice

2 tablespoons Green Bell Peppers
2 tablespoons Instant Minced Onions
¼ cup water
3 tablespoons olive oil
2 tablespoons Spaghetti Sauce
   Seasoning

1 teaspoon Beau Monde Seasoning
1 can (1 lb. 13 oz.) tomatoes
¾ cup rice
½ teaspoon salt
1 cup shredded Cheddar cheese

Crush Green Peppers. Combine with Onions and rehydrate in water. Cook Peppers and Onions slowly in olive oil until Onions are lightly browned. Stir in Spaghetti Seasoning, Beau Monde, tomatoes, and rice. Heat to boiling, add salt and pour into 1½-quart casserole. Cover and bake in a 350° oven for 35 minutes. Uncover and fluff with a fork. Sprinkle with cheese and return to oven until cheese is melted. Serve hot. Makes 6 servings.

Saffron Rice

Measure the Saffron carefully — it's better to have too little than too much.

2 tablespoons Instant Minced
   Onions
2 tablespoons water
6 tablespoons butter
1 cup rice

1/32 teaspoon Powdered Saffron
2 tablespoons Chicken Seasoned
   Stock Base
2 cups hot water

Rehydrate Onions in water. Melt butter in saucepan with tight-fitting lid. Add Onions and cook over low heat for about 5 minutes or until Onions are golden. Stir in rice. Dissolve Saffron and Chicken Seasoned Stock Base in hot water. Pour over rice. Cover and cook over low heat until rice is done and stock absorbed, about 30 minutes. Fluff rice with a fork and serve at once. Makes 6 servings.

Green Rice

2 tablespoons Chicken Seasoned
   Stock Base
1 teaspoon Onion Powder
1½ cups hot water

1½ cups quick-cooking rice
1 tablespoon butter
1 tablespoon Chervil

Add Chicken Seasoned Stock Base and Onion Powder to hot water. Bring to a boil. Add rice. Cover and remove from heat. Let stand for about 5 minutes. Add butter and Chervil. Fluff with a fork so Chervil is well mixed and butter is melted. Serve at once. Makes 6 servings.

Rice with Ripe Olives and Dill

🌿 Double or triple this family-size recipe for a party — an excellent choice to serve with cold turkey, roast beef, broiled chops, or chicken.

2 teaspoons Chicken Seasoned
  Stock Base
1 teaspoon Beau Monde Seasoning
1¼ cups hot water
½ cup rice

½ cup sliced ripe olives
1 cup dairy sour cream
½ teaspoon Dill Weed
2 tablespoons toasted, slivered
  almonds

Add Chicken Seasoned Stock Base and Beau Monde to hot water. Bring to a boil and add rice. Cover and steam for 25 to 30 minutes or until rice is done. Fluff with a fork and add olives, sour cream, and Dill Weed. Mix thoroughly with fork. Spoon into serving dish or onto plates and sprinkle with toasted almonds. If you wish to prepare this dish in advance, turn rice into buttered casserole and sprinkle with almonds; reheat casserole in a 300° oven for about 20 minutes or until thoroughly heated. Makes 4 servings.

Curried Rice

🌿 Serve Curried Rice with a sprinkling of shredded coconut and chopped peanuts, if desired. For a hot curry use 2 teaspoons Curry Powder; for a milder curry, use less.

1 tablespoon Chicken Seasoned
  Stock Base
1 teaspoon Powdered Mushrooms
1⅓ cups hot water
1⅓ cups quick-cooking rice
4 tablespoons butter

2 tablespoons Instant Minced Onions
2 tablespoons water
1 to 2 teaspoons Curry Powder
2 medium-size tomatoes
½ teaspoon salt

Add Chicken Seasoned Stock Base and Powdered Mushrooms to hot water. Prepare rice according to directions on package, using stock for liquid. Meanwhile melt 2 tablespoons butter in large frying pan. Rehydrate Onions in water. Add to melted butter and cook gently for about 5 minutes. Add remaining 2 tablespoons butter; stir in Curry Powder. Scald and peel tomatoes; cut into wedges. Add to curry mixture and cook for about 10 minutes or until tomatoes are soft. Add rice and mix thoroughly. Season with salt. Serve at once. Makes 4 to 6 servings.

Rice Pilaff

4 tablespoons butter	2 tablespoons Instant Minced Onions
¾ cup rice	½ teaspoon Orange Peel
2 tablespoons Beef Stock Base	2 tablespoons toasted slivered
2 cups hot water	almonds or pine nuts

Melt butter in flame-proof casserole. Add rice and brown lightly. Dissolve Beef Stock Base in hot water; add Onions and Orange Peel and pour over rice. Cover and bake in a 350° oven for about 30 minutes or until rice is done and stock absorbed. Fluff rice with a fork and sprinkle with nuts. Serve hot. Makes 6 servings.

Rice Pilaff Noroian

🌱 If pilaff is served with highly seasoned meats, no further seasoning is necessary. Otherwise, add a dash of salt and Black Pepper.

¼ cup butter	2 tablespoons Chicken Seasoned
½ cup finely broken vermicelli	Stock Base
1 cup rice	2½ cups boiling water

Melt butter over low heat. Add finely broken vermicelli; cook until golden brown, stirring constantly. Stir in rice. Dissolve Chicken Seasoned Stock Base in boiling water and pour over rice and vermicelli. Cover and steam for 25 minutes or until all stock is absorbed. Fluff with fork. Cover and let stand for 10 minutes before serving. Serve hot. Makes 6 servings.

Barley Pilaff

2 tablespoons Instant Minced Onions	4 teaspoons Beef Stock Base
2 tablespoons water	1 cup barley
2 tablespoons butter	1½ teaspoons Beau Monde Seasoning
2 cups hot water	1 teaspoon Parsley
1 teaspoon Powdered Mushrooms	

Rehydrate Onions in water. Melt butter in saucepan with tight-fitting lid. Add Onions and simmer gently until golden, about 4 minutes. Add hot water, Powdered Mushrooms, and Beef Stock Base. Bring to a boil. Add barley, Beau Monde, and Parsley. Cover tightly. Turn heat down and cook over low heat for 45 to 50 minutes or until barley is done and all liquid is absorbed. Fluff with a fork and serve hot. Makes 6 servings.

Lasagne

An authentic Italian recipe, yet much simplified because it's so easy to make the sauce.

2 cans (6 oz. each) tomato paste
2 cans water
4 tablespoons olive oil
2 tablespoons Spaghetti Sauce Seasoning
½ cup dry red wine
½ pound lasagne
2 quarts boiling salted water

½ pound Italian sausage, salami, or ground beef
1 pound ricotta or cottage cheese
4 to 6 ounces Mozzarella or process American cheese, sliced thin
⅓ cup grated Parmesan or Romano cheese

Combine tomato paste, water, olive oil, Spaghetti Sauce Seasoning, and wine. Simmer for 20 minutes. Cook lasagne in boiling salted water for 20 minutes or until barely tender. Drain and rinse in cold water. Skin sausage and slice thin. Fry sausage until brown or ground beef until crumbly and lightly browned. Arrange a layer of lasagne in a 7 x 11-inch baking pan. Spoon on 4 or 5 spoonfuls of ricotta cheese and one-third of the meat. Cover with sauce and thin slices of Mozzarella cheese, using about one-fourth of each. Repeat layers, topping with sauce and cheese slices. Sprinkle with grated Parmesan cheese. Bake in a 350° oven for 20 minutes or until bubbling hot and cheese is melted. Cut into squares and spoon out onto plates. Serve hot. Makes 6 servings.

Noodles Romanoff

An old favorite that's good as a meatless main dish or to go along with sliced cold meats or barbecued meats.

4 ounces wide egg noodles
1 quart boiling salted water
2 tablespoons Instant Minced Onions
2 tablespoons water
1 cup cream-style cottage cheese
1 cup dairy sour cream
¼ teaspoon Garlic Powder

2 teaspoons Beau Monde Seasoning
1 teaspoon Worcestershire sauce
Dash Tabasco
¼ cup fine dry bread crumbs
¼ cup grated Parmesan cheese
Paprika

Cook noodles in boiling salted water. Drain and rinse in hot water. Meanwhile, rehydrate Onions in water. Combine noodles with Onions, cottage cheese, sour cream, Garlic Powder, Beau Monde, Worcestershire sauce, and Tabasco. Mix thoroughly and pour into greased 1½-quart casserole. Sprinkle with bread crumbs and cheese. Bake in a 350° oven until hot and top is brown, 20 to 25 minutes. Sprinkle with Paprika. Serve hot. Makes 6 servings.

Sesame Seed Noodles

 Sesame Seed Noodles or one of the variations is a delicious accompaniment to pot roasts, stews, goulashes, braised meats of all kinds. Cut the recipe in half for a small family meal.

1 package (12 oz.) egg noodles
2 to 3 quarts boiling water
2 tablespoons salt
3 tablespoons butter

4 tablespoons Sesame Seed
3 tablespoons Chicken Seasoned Stock Base

Cook noodles in boiling salted water until tender. Drain and rinse in hot water. Melt butter; add Sesame Seed and cook, stirring constantly, until seeds are brown. Pour over noodles. Add Chicken Seasoned Stock Base. Toss until thoroughly mixed. Serve at once. Makes 8 servings.

POPPY SEED NOODLES
Substitute 2 tablespoons Poppy Seed for Sesame Seed. Add seeds to melted butter but do not toast.

TOASTED ALMOND NOODLES

Substitute 3 to 4 tablespoons slivered almonds for Sesame Seed. Toast in melted butter.

PAPRIKA NOODLES

Add 3 teaspoons Paprika to melted butter instead of seeds.

Macaroni Parmesan

 To make a ring, pack Macaroni Parmesan into a well-buttered 5-cup ring mold. Set in a 300° oven for 15 to 20 minutes. Unmold on a heated platter and fill with braised beef or stew.

½ pound macaroni
1 quart boiling water
1 tablespoon salt
¼ cup butter
½ cup grated Parmesan cheese

1 teaspoon Parsley
¼ teaspoon Spice Parisienne
1 teaspoon Beau Monde Seasoning
¼ teaspoon Fine Grind Black Pepper

Cook macaroni in boiling salted water until tender. Drain and rinse in hot water. Add butter, cheese, Parsley, Spice Parisienne, Beau Monde, and Pepper. Toss until butter is melted and cheese and seasonings are mixed throughout. Serve at once. Makes 6 servings.

EGGS & CHEESE

EGGS AND CHEESE are among the most versatile of foods. They may be served simply and alone, or they may be combined with each other or with other ingredients in delectable casseroles, salads, puffy soufflés, and tender, golden omelets. They fit easily into almost any type of meal and can be varied in many ways to become an hors d'oeuvres, a main dish, a complement to a meal, or a decorative garnish.

At breakfast or brunch, eggs may appear with ham and a smooth Hollandaise Sauce in Eggs Benedict. At luncheon, they may be glamorized with wine and herbs in Ham and Eggs Vegas. Hangtown Fry brings eggs to the supper table. And the zesty seasonings of Fried Eggs Soubise are appropriate for a late evening snack.

Cheese, too, is adaptable. Serve it at a luncheon in a Roquefort Mousse to accompany a fresh fruit salad, at supper in a Chili Cheese Soufflé, as a midnight snack in a Tomato Rarebit or a Swiss Cheese Fondue.

A change in seasonings brings a change in character to eggs and cheese. The simple omelet, for example, has almost limitless possibilities for flavor variations; and the cheese soufflé that has a smoky flavor when one of its ingredients is Old Hickory Smoked Salt can be given a Mexican character if the Old Hickory is replaced by Chili Con Carne Seasoning Powder.

Bacon and Eggs Cebolla

3 slices bacon

2 tablespoons Instant Minced Onions

2 tablespoons water

1 teaspoon Parsley

½ teaspoon salt

⅛ teaspoon Spice Parisienne

4 eggs

⅛ teaspoon Fine Grind Black Pepper

½ cup shredded Swiss cheese

Cut bacon into pieces with kitchen scissors. Fry until brown but not crisp. Pour off all but 1 tablespoon of fat. Meanwhile, rehydrate Onions in water. Add to bacon along with Parsley and sauté until Onions are lightly browned. Season with ¼ teaspoon salt and Spice Parisienne. Spread out evenly in frying pan. Break eggs into pan. Season with remaining ¼ teaspoon salt and Pepper. Sprinkle with cheese. Cover and cook slowly until eggs are set and cheese is melted. Serve at once. Makes 2 servings.

Ham and Eggs Vegas

¼-pound slice ham

⅛ teaspoon Garlic Powder

1½ teaspoons Arrowroot

2 teaspoons Beef Stock Base

1 teaspoon Powdered Mushrooms

1 cup hot water

¼ cup dry red wine

2 teaspoons Instant Minced Onions

⅛ teaspoon Medium Grind Black Pepper

¼ teaspoon Spice Parisienne

6 hard-cooked eggs

Cut ham into thin strips. Sauté ham lightly in frying pan. Stir in Garlic Powder and Arrowroot. Dissolve Beef Stock Base and Powdered Mushrooms in hot water. Add wine and Onions. Pour over ham. Cook over low heat, stirring constantly, until thickened and smooth. Season with Pepper. Add Spice Parisienne. Cut hard-cooked eggs into quarters. Add to sauce; when thoroughly heated serve over toast triangles or steamed rice. Makes 4 servings.

Fried Eggs Soubise

2 tablespoons butter

½ teaspoon Beau Monde Seasoning

½ teaspoon Paprika

⅛ teaspoon Cracked Black Pepper

4 eggs

2 tablespoons dry red wine

2 teaspoons Instant Toasted Onions

½ teaspoon Chervil

Melt butter in medium-size frying pan. Add Beau Monde, Paprika, and Pepper. Break eggs into pan. Cook slowly, basting frequently with the seasoned butter, until eggs are done as desired. Place eggs on hot serving plates. Add wine and Onions to butter. Heat to simmering. Spoon over eggs. Sprinkle Chervil over eggs. Serve at once. Makes 2 servings.

Hangtown Fry

🌱 A popular dish in the Gold Rush days in the Far West, Hangtown Fry is now served coast to coast. Good for a late Sunday breakfast or a midnight supper.

1 tablespoon Green Bell Peppers
2 tablespoons water
2 tablespoons butter
1 tablespoon Instant Toasted Onions
6 oysters, fresh, frozen, or canned

4 eggs
½ teaspoon Old Hickory Smoked Salt
⅛ teaspoon Medium Grind Black Pepper
¼ teaspoon Paprika

Rehydrate Green Peppers in water. Melt butter in frying pan. Add Green Peppers and cook until crisp-tender but not brown. Add Toasted Onions and oysters. Cook until edges of oysters curl. Beat eggs slightly with Old Hickory, Pepper, and Paprika. Pour into frying pan. Cook slowly, lifting mixture from bottom of pan occasionally, until eggs are cooked but not dry. Serve at once. Makes 2 servings.

Eggs in Ramekins with Chicken Livers and Mushrooms

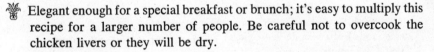

🌱 Elegant enough for a special breakfast or brunch; it's easy to multiply this recipe for a larger number of people. Be careful not to overcook the chicken livers or they will be dry.

¼ cup light cream
½ teaspoon Chervil

1 teaspoon Beau Monde Seasoning
8 eggs

Combine cream, Chervil, and Beau Monde. Spoon into four buttered ramekins. Heat for about 5 minutes in a 300° oven. Break 2 eggs into each ramekin. Bake for 5 to 10 minutes or until eggs are done as desired. Serve with Chicken Livers and Mushrooms. Makes 4 servings.

CHICKEN LIVERS AND MUSHROOMS

3 tablespoons butter
½ pound chicken livers
1 cup sliced fresh mushrooms
¼ teaspoon Fines Herbes

½ teaspoon Beau Monde Seasoning
⅛ teaspoon Fine Grind Black Pepper
½ cup Madeira wine
Chervil

Melt butter in frying pan. Add chicken livers and mushrooms and cook until livers are done. Crush Fines Herbes and stir into chicken livers and mushrooms along with Beau Monde and Pepper. Add wine. Heat to simmering and spoon over eggs in ramekins. Garnish with Chervil and serve at once.

Eggs Benedict

 If you haven't time to make Hollandaise Sauce, try one of the excellent canned ones on the market. Or make a Mock Hollandaise by blending a tablespoon cream and 2 teaspoons lemon juice with ¼ cup mayonnaise.

1 English muffin
2 thin slices ham or Canadian bacon
2 poached eggs
Beau Monde Seasoning
Medium Grind Black Pepper

2 tablespoons Hollandaise Sauce (page 124)
⅛ teaspoon Chervil
Paprika

Split English muffin and toast. Fry ham or Canadian bacon until lightly browned. Arrange on muffin halves. Top with poached egg; sprinkle with Beau Monde and Pepper. Heat Hollandaise Sauce and mix with Chervil. Spoon a tablespoon of sauce over each egg; sprinkle with Paprika. Serve at once, or keep hot in a 300° oven for a few minutes until ready to serve. Makes 1 serving.

Eggs Florentine

 When eggs are to make the meal, try this flavorful spinach and egg dish. For heartier servings, increase the number of eggs.

1 package (10 oz.) frozen chopped spinach
2 teaspoons Beau Monde Seasoning
1 tablespoon melted butter
6 eggs
2 tablespoons butter
2 teaspoons Arrowroot

2 cups milk
1 egg yolk
½ cup shredded Swiss cheese
½ teaspoon Chervil
⅛ teaspoon Rosemary
Paprika

Thaw frozen spinach. Mix with ½ teaspoon Beau Monde and melted butter. Arrange in flat casserole or baking dish. Carefully break eggs into spinach. Melt butter in saucepan; remove from heat and stir in Arrowroot. Add milk and 1½ teaspoons Beau Monde. Return to heat and cook over low heat, stirring constantly, until thickened and smooth. Beat egg yolk slightly; stir in a spoonful or two of the hot sauce. Mix well and then add egg to sauce in pan. Stir in shredded cheese. Crush Chervil and Rosemary and add to sauce. Spoon carefully over eggs. Bake in a 350° oven for about 20 minutes or until sauce is bubbling hot. Sprinkle with Paprika and serve at once. Makes 6 servings.

Eggs in Aspic

6 eggs
1 envelope unflavored gelatin
½ cup cold water
4 teaspoons Chicken Seasoned
   Stock Base

1½ cups boiling water
1 teaspoon Chervil
6 slices cold roast turkey or ham

Poach eggs. (An easy way to poach several eggs at a time is to break eggs into well-oiled muffin pans. Place muffin pan on a rack in a large roaster. Fill with one inch of hot water. Cover roaster and set on unit on top of the range. Cook eggs until done as desired.) Remove eggs to platter and chill. Soften gelatin in cold water. Dissolve Chicken Seasoned Stock Base in boiling water; add softened gelatin and stir until gelatin is dissolved. Crush Chervil and add to aspic. Spoon some of the hot chicken aspic into 6 individual molds or ramekins. Chill molds until aspic begins to set. Cool remaining aspic. Arrange chilled eggs, upside-down, on aspic in molds. Spoon remaining aspic over eggs. Place slices of cold turkey or ham on aspic. Chill until firm. Unmold; spoon Sour Cream and Onion Sauce over eggs. Sprinkle with Paprika. Makes 6 servings.

SOUR CREAM AND ONION SAUCE

1 cup dairy sour cream
1½ teaspoons Beau Monde Seasoning
1 teaspoon sugar

1 tablespoon White Wine Vinegar
1 tablespoon Instant Toasted Onions
Paprika

Mix together sour cream, Beau Monde, sugar, and Vinegar. Just before serving, stir in Toasted Onions.

French Omelet with Fines Herbes and Onions

4 eggs
1 teaspoon Beau Monde Seasoning
⅛ teaspoon Fine Grind Black Pepper
2 tablespoons water, milk, or cream

⅛ teaspoon Fines Herbes
1 tablespoon butter
1 tablespoon Instant Toasted Onions
Paprika

Break eggs into bowl; add Beau Monde, Pepper, and water (or milk or cream). Beat with fork until blended. Crush Fines Herbes and add to eggs. Melt butter in small frying pan or omelet pan. Pour eggs into pan. As omelet sets at edges, lift with spatula to let uncooked omelet flow to bottom. When omelet is cooked but still soft, sprinkle Toasted Onions over top. Tilt pan and roll up omelet starting from handle and rolling toward opposite side. Turn out onto platter. Sprinkle with Paprika. Serve at once. Makes 2 servings.

Welsh Omelet

🌿 A modern version of an old, old Welsh recipe, this omelet is perfect for a late Sunday breakfast or a late evening snack.

4 slices bacon	4 eggs
2 tablespoons Instant Minced Onions	½ cup light cream
2 tablespoons water	⅛ teaspoon Fine Grind Black Pepper
1 teaspoon Parsley	1 cup shredded Swiss cheese
1½ teaspoons Beau Monde Seasoning	Paprika

Cut bacon slices in two. Fry until partially cooked but not crisp. Remove from pan. Meanwhile, rehydrate Onions in water. Add to bacon drippings along with Parsley and sauté until Onions are lightly browned. Season with ½ teaspoon Beau Monde. Spoon into 8-inch pie pan and spread out evenly. Beat eggs slightly with cream. Season with remaining 1 teaspoon Beau Monde and Pepper. Pour over Onions; sprinkle with cheese. Arrange bacon slices on top; sprinkle with Paprika. Bake in a 350° oven for 15 minutes or until eggs are set and cheese is melted. Cut into wedges and serve at once. Makes 4 servings.

Old Hickory Cheese Soufflé

🌿 High and light, with a robust smoky flavor. Rush this soufflé to the table the minute it comes from the oven.

2 tablespoons butter	1 cup (¼ pound) shredded Cheddar cheese
2 tablespoons Arrowroot	
1 cup rich milk	½ teaspoon Old Hickory Smoked Salt
	3 eggs

Melt butter in saucepan. Remove from heat and stir in Arrowroot. Add milk to butter and Arrowroot. Return to heat; cook over low heat, stirring constantly, until very thick. Blend in shredded cheese and Old Hickory. Separate eggs; beat egg yolks into sauce, one at a time. Beat eggs whites until stiff but not dry and fold into cheese mixture. Pour into 1½-quart ungreased casserole. Bake in a 325° oven for 45 to 50 minutes or until soufflé is puffed and brown and a sharp knife inserted in the center comes out clean. Serve immediately. Makes 4 servings.

CHILI CHEESE SOUFFLÉ

Omit Old Hickory Smoked Salt. Add 2 teaspoons Chicken Seasoned Stock Base to milk. Season with 1 teaspoon Chili Con Carne Seasoning Powder, ½ teaspoon Beau Monde Seasoning, and ½ cup sliced ripe olives.

Chervil Soufflé

The delicate flavor of Chervil is perfect for a high, light soufflé. Be sure to serve the soufflé the minute it comes out of the oven or it will fall.

3 tablespoons butter
2 tablespoons fine dry bread crumbs
2 tablespoons Arrowroot
½ teaspoon Onion Powder
1 teaspoon Chicken Seasoned Stock Base
1 cup milk

½ cup shredded mild Cheddar cheese
4 eggs
⅛ teaspoon Medium Grind Black Pepper
2 teaspoons Chervil
¼ teaspoon salt

Soften 1 tablespoon butter and butter bottom and one inch up the sides of a 1½-quart casserole. Coat with bread crumbs. Melt remaining 2 tablespoons butter in saucepan. Remove from heat and stir in Arrowroot. Combine Onion Powder, Chicken Seasoned Stock Base, and milk; add to blended butter and Arrowroot. Return to heat and cook, stirring constantly, until thick and smooth. Add cheese and stir until melted. Separate eggs; beat yolks until lemon-colored. Pour hot sauce slowly over egg yolks. Return sauce to pan and cook over low heat, stirring constantly, until sauce just begins to bubble and is thickened again. Stir in Pepper and Chervil. Add salt to egg whites; beat until stiff but not dry. Fold carefully into sauce. Pour into casserole and bake in a 375° oven for 30 minutes or until soufflé is brown and done. Serve hot. Makes 4 servings.

Swiss Cheese Fondue

Use Gruyère cheese if you can, but otherwise a good domestic or imported Swiss cheese.

3 cups shredded Swiss cheese (¾ pound)
¼ teaspoon Garlic Powder
2 tablespoons flour
½ teaspoon salt

⅛ teaspoon Cracked Black Pepper
1½ cups dry white wine
2 tablespoons kirsch or cognac, if desired

Toss together shredded cheese, Garlic Powder, flour, salt, and Pepper. Heat wine in chafing dish, earthenware casserole on candlewarmer or small electric heater, or in an electric frying pan with temperature control set at "low." When wine is hot, add cheese mixture, a little at a time. As cheese melts, add additional cheese; stir constantly. When cheese is melted and smooth, stir in kirsch or cognac. Serve warm, stirring occasionally as each person dips into fondue with cubes of crusty French bread. Makes 3 or 4 servings as an entrée or 12 servings as an appetizer.

Chili Rarebit

🌿 Process cheese makes a smooth, creamy rarebit. If rarebit is a bit thin at first, it will thicken on standing. Be sure to keep the heat low.

½ pound process American cheese
1 tablespoon butter
¼ teaspoon salt

1 teaspoon Chili Con Carne Seasoning Powder
¾ cup beer

Cut cheese into cubes. Melt butter in double boiler over hot water or in an electric frying pan with temperature control set at "low." Add cheese, salt, and Chili Con Carne Seasoning. Stir occasionally as cheese melts. When cheese is melted, add beer slowly; stir until smooth. Serve hot on crisp toast. Makes 3 or 4 servings.

Tomato Rarebit

½ pound process cheese or cheese food
1 cup undiluted evaporated milk
1 can (10½ oz.) undiluted condensed tomato soup

½ teaspoon Onion Powder
⅛ teaspoon Medium Grind Black Pepper
¼ teaspoon Sweet Basil

Shred cheese or cut into cubes. Combine in top of double boiler with evaporated milk. Heat over hot water until cheese is melted, stirring occasionally. Stir in tomato soup, Onion Powder, and Pepper. Crush Basil and mix into rarebit. Serve hot on crisp toast, crackers, rusks. Makes 6 servings.

Roquefort Mousse

🌿 For an outstanding luncheon menu serve Roquefort Mousse with a fresh fruit salad and hot rolls.

¼ pound Roquefort cheese
2 tablespoons White Wine Vinegar
2 teaspoons Parsley
2 teaspoons Onion Salt
⅛ teaspoon Ground White Pepper

2 tablespoons chopped pimiento
1 cup well-drained grated cucumber
1 cup heavy cream
1 envelope unflavored gelatin
¼ cup cold water

Mash cheese and mix thoroughly with Vinegar, Parsley, Onion Salt, White Pepper, and pimiento. Add grated cucumber and mix well. Whip cream and fold into cheese mixture. Soften gelatin in cold water in cup. Place cup in pan of hot water and dissolve gelatin. Stir into cheese mixture. Pour into oiled 3-cup mold and chill until firm. Unmold and serve. Makes 6 servings.

SAUCES

A GOOD SAUCE is a culinary triumph, a crowning achievement that can lift a simple recipe into the realm of perfection. But a sauce is also an essential part of a recipe; it should contribute flavorful overtones, but it should not dominate.

The seasoning shelf offers many shortcuts in the making of smooth, savory sauces. Beef Stock Base and Chicken Seasoned Stock Base simplify the making of such classics as Sauce Espagnole, Madeira Sauce, Sauce Diable, or Sauce Robert. Basic Brown Sauce can be varied to make Onion Gravy, Mushroom Herb Sauce, Wine Herb Sauce, or Mushroom Gravy. The knowing cook can change a basic Cream Sauce to complement many different foods. It becomes a Curry Sauce that does wonderful things for leftover chicken or turkey, or a Paprika Sauce to flatter veal steak, or an Onion Cream Sauce to give a refreshing tang to vegetables.

Garlic butter is well known to most cooks—but have you considered how many other savory butters can be made in the same way? Try the herb butters on page 126; then look over the other herbs and spices on your shelf and think of the foods that can be seasoned with them. You'll discover many possibilities for compound butters that can be stored in the freezer and used to dress up hamburgers, fish, broiled steaks, roast corn, potatoes, onions.

Basic Cream Sauce

🌱 Arrowroot used as a thickening in cream sauces gives a smooth, delicate sauce. Be careful not to overheat Arrowroot when adding it to the butter; too high heat may make the sauce elastic rather than smooth and creamy.

2 tablespoons butter	2 cups milk
4 teaspoons Arrowroot	Dash Ground White Pepper or
2 teaspoons Mei Yen Seasoning	Fine Grind Black Pepper

Melt butter in saucepan over low heat. Remove from heat and stir in Arrowroot. Add Mei Yen to milk. Add milk to butter and Arrowroot. Return to heat and cook slowly, stirring constantly, until thickened and smooth. Add Pepper. For a richer sauce, use light cream instead of milk. Makes 2 cups.

DELUXE CREAM SAUCE

Make as for Basic Cream Sauce, except add 1 teaspoon of Mei Yen Seasoning and 1 teaspoon Chicken Seasoned Stock Base to 2 cups rich milk or light cream before adding to butter and Arrowroot. Use with cooked vegetables, meats, fish or poultry; or wherever Velouté Sauce is called for.

GOURMET CREAM SAUCE

Make as for Basic Cream Sauce, except stir 1 tablespoon Onion Powder, ½ teaspoon Curry Powder, and 2 teaspoons Arrowroot into melted butter. Add 2 teaspoons Mei Yen Seasoning to 2 cups rich milk before adding to butter and seasonings. After sauce has thickened, stir in 2 tablespoons sherry wine. Use combined with seafood, poultry, or vegetables, or as a sauce for cutlets, croquettes, meat or fish loafs.

QUICK CURRY SAUCE

Make as for Gourmet Cream Sauce, but add 1 tablespoon Curry Powder. Omit sherry. Add 1½ cups cooked, cleaned shrimp, cooked chicken or turkey, or 6 sliced hard-cooked eggs to sauce. Serve over hot cooked rice.

QUICK PAPRIKA SAUCE

Make as for Gourmet Cream Sauce except add 1 tablespoon Paprika instead of Curry Powder. Serve as a sauce for veal steak or chops, chicken, or left-over roast veal, beef, or lamb.

CHEESE SAUCE

Make Basic Cream Sauce. Just before serving stir in 1 cup shredded or diced Cheddar or process cheese and ¼ teaspoon Paprika. Stir until cheese is melted.

MORNAY SAUCE

Make Basic Cream Sauce. Just before serving stir in ½ cup shredded Swiss cheese and 2 tablespoons cream. Stir until cheese is melted.

TOASTED ONION CREAM SAUCE

Make DeLuxe Cream Sauce. When sauce is done, add 2 tablespoons Instant Toasted Onions. Combine sauce with 1½ to 2 cups of cooked vegetables or diced cooked meat, fish, or poultry; or use as a sauce for cooked cauliflower, potatoes, carrots, or string beans.

Chili Cream Sauce

1 tablespoon Instant Minced Onions
1 tablespoon Red Bell Peppers
2 tablespoons water
2 tablespoons butter
2 teaspoons Arrowroot

2 teaspoons Chicken Seasoned Stock Base
1½ cups milk
⅛ teaspoon Fine Grind Black Pepper
½ teaspoon Chili Powder

Rehydrate Onions and Peppers in water. Melt butter in saucepan. Add Onions and Peppers and cook over low heat for about 5 minutes. Remove from heat and stir in Arrowroot. Combine Chicken Seasoned Stock Base and milk and stir into Onions and Peppers. Cook over low heat, stirring constantly, until sauce is thickened and bubbling. Add Pepper and Chili Powder and mix thoroughly. Serve hot with cooked vegetables or as a sauce for meat. Makes 1½ cups.

Vendôme Sauce

Top asparagus spears, broccoli, artichoke hearts, or steamed wild or brown rice with sliced turkey or chicken, or seafood. Spoon on Vendôme Sauce and sprinkle with buttered crumbs or grated cheese and brown in oven or broiler.

4 tablespoons butter
2 tablespoons Arrowroot
2 cups rich milk
1 egg yolk

1 teaspoon Old Hickory Smoked Salt
¼ teaspoon Rosemary
2 tablespoons sherry

Melt butter in saucepan over low heat. Remove from heat and stir in Arrowroot. Add milk and cook over low heat, stirring constantly, until thickened and smooth. Beat egg yolk slightly; stir in a spoonful or two of hot sauce, then stir back into sauce in pan. Season with Old Hickory Smoked Salt. Crush Rosemary and add to sauce along with sherry. Makes 2 cups.

Basic Brown Sauce

Use this basic sauce as a base for countless other sauces—the classics such as Sauce Espagnole or Robert, Madeira Sauce, Ravigote or Piquante Sauce; or use wherever a recipe calls for Brown Sauce. It's good with roast beef—indispensable when there are not enough drippings to make gravy, or to serve with leftover slices when the gravy is all gone.

2 tablespoons butter
4 teaspoons Arrowroot
2 tablespoons Beef Stock Base

2 cups hot water
⅛ teaspoon Fine Grind Black Pepper

Melt butter. Remove from heat and stir in Arrowroot. Add Beef Stock Base to water and add to butter and Arrowroot. Cook over low heat, stirring constantly, until thickened and smooth. Add Pepper. Serve hot as gravy or use as a base for other sauces. Makes 2 cups.

ONION GRAVY OR SAUCE

Make as for Basic Brown Sauce except rehydrate 2 tablespoons Instant Minced Onions in 2 tablespoons water. Add to melted butter and cook for about 5 minutes or until Onions are slightly yellow. Complete sauce as for Basic Brown Sauce. Serve with broiled hamburgers or liver, or as a sauce for leftover pot roast or meat loaf.

MUSHROOM HERB SAUCE

Make as for Basic Brown Sauce except add 1 teaspoon Powdered Mushrooms along with Beef Stock Base to hot water. Complete as for Basic Brown Sauce; then crush ⅛ teaspoon Bouquet Garni for Beef and add to sauce instead of Pepper.

WINE HERB SAUCE

Make as for Basic Brown Sauce except reduce hot water to 1½ cups and add ½ cup dry red wine. Complete as for Basic Brown Sauce; crush ¼ teaspoon Oregano and stir into sauce. Serve with wild duck or venison, broiled liver or kidneys.

MUSHROOM GRAVY OR SAUCE

Make as for Basic Brown Sauce except drain liquid from a 2-ounce can sliced or button mushrooms; add enough water to make 2 cups liquid. Complete as for Basic Brown Sauce. When thickened and smooth, stir in 3 tablespoons evaporated milk or cream and drained mushrooms. Heat thoroughly and serve hot over mashed potatoes or steamed rice, or as a sauce for croquettes, cutlets, hamburgers, or steak.

Antigua Onion Sauce

❦ Antigua Instant Coffee gives this Onion Sauce a distinctively different flavor. It's good to dress up ground beef patties, lamb chops, or slices of leftover roast beef, lamb, or pork.

3 tablespoons Instant Minced Onion
3 tablespoons water
2 tablespoons butter
1 teaspoon Antigua Instant Coffee

2 teaspoons Beef Stock Base
½ cup boiling water
⅛ teaspoon Fine Grind Black Pepper

Rehydrate Onions in water. Melt butter in saucepan; stir in Onions and cook until golden, about 5 minutes. Add Instant Coffee and Beef Stock Base to boiling water. Stir into Onions and cook until Onions are tender, about 5 minutes. Season with Pepper. Serve hot. Makes 1½ cups.

Basil Mint Sauce

❦ Excellent to serve with roast lamb or broiled lamb chops, this sauce will keep indefinitely in the refrigerator.

1 cup Basil White Wine Vinegar
¼ cup sugar

1/16 teaspoon salt
¼ cup Spearmint

Combine Vinegar, sugar, and salt. Bring to a boil; stir in Spearmint. Remove from heat and let cool. Serve cold. Makes 1½ cups.

Spiced Raisin Sauce

❦ Baked ham, especially canned ham, is doubly good when served with Spiced Raisin Sauce. Try this sauce, too, on a slice of fried ham. Keep any leftover sauce in refrigerator; reheat as much at a time as you need.

1 cup brown sugar
1½ tablespoons Arrowroot
⅛ teaspoon Mild Mustard
⅛ teaspoon Ground Cloves
¼ teaspoon Ground Allspice
¼ teaspoon Ground Cinnamon

½ cup Tarragon Red or White Wine Vinegar
2 cups water
1 cup seedless raisins
2 tablespoons butter or salad oil

Combine brown sugar, Arrowroot, Mustard, Cloves, Allspice, and Cinnamon in top of double boiler. Mix in Vinegar and water. Cook over low heat, stirring constantly, until sauce comes to a boil and is thickened and smooth. Rinse raisins and add to sauce. Set top of double boiler over hot water. Cook sauce over boiling water until raisins are plump, about 30 minutes. Stir in butter or salad oil. Serve hot. Makes 4 cups.

Horseradish Cream Sauce

🌱 Those who like Horseradish Sauce with roast beef will enjoy this.

3 teaspoons Horseradish
2 tablespoons water

½ cup heavy cream
¼ teaspoon salt

Combine Horseradish and water. Let stand while whipping cream. Stir Horseradish and salt into whipped cream. Chill for 20 to 30 minutes for flavors to develop. Makes 1 cup.

Old Hickory Tomato Sauce

🌱 Excellent with cold sliced meat, hamburgers, or frankfurters, this sauce will keep for two or three weeks in the refrigerator.

3 tablespoons Instant Minced Onions
1 cup chopped celery
2 cups cooked or canned tomatoes
1 tablespoon Old Hickory Smoked Salt

¼ teaspoon Hot Mustard
1 teaspoon Arrowroot
¼ teaspoon Chili Powder
¼ cup brown sugar
1 tablespoon Red Wine Vinegar

Combine Onions, chopped celery, and tomatoes in a 1½-quart saucepan. Simmer for about 10 minutes or until Onions and celery are tender but still crisp. Blend thoroughly Old Hickory, Mustard, Arrowroot, Chili Powder, and brown sugar. Stir into tomatoes and cook for 5 minutes longer or until sauce has thickened slightly. Add Vinegar. Chill thoroughly. Makes 3½ cups.

Smokehouse Mustard Sauce

🌱 Nippy with Mustard and the outdoorsy flavor of Old Hickory, this sauce goes with almost any kind of meat.

2 teaspoons Arrowroot
2 tablespoons Hot Mustard
1 tablespoon sugar
1 egg yolk
¾ cup cold milk

5 tablespoons White Wine Vinegar
1½ teaspoons Old Hickory Smoked Salt
½ cup dairy sour cream

Mix Arrowroot, Mustard, and sugar in saucepan. Beat egg yolk and cold milk together. Blend into dry ingredients. Cook over low heat, stirring constantly, until thickened and smooth. (If sauce should curdle slightly, beat hard with rotary beater or electric mixer.) Remove from heat; stir in Vinegar. Cool and blend in Old Hickory Smoked Salt and sour cream. Chill. Serve cold. Makes 1½ cups.

Bearnaise Sauce

A favorite sauce to go with steak, Bearnaise Sauce is equally good with lamb or fish. It is made similarly to Hollandaise but is sharper in flavor.

1 tablespoon Eschalot Wine
    Vinegar
1/16 teaspoon Garlic Powder
⅛ teaspoon Cracked Black Pepper
¼ teaspoon Tarragon

1 teaspoon Chervil
¼ teaspoon salt
3 egg yolks
¼ pound butter

Combine Vinegar, Garlic Powder, and Pepper in small heat-proof casserole or in top of double boiler. Crush Tarragon and add to Vinegar along with Chervil and salt. Place on range unit turned to "warm" or over hot but not boiling water. Beat egg yolks slightly; stir into Vinegar and seasonings. Melt butter; add a tablespoon or two at a time, beating with a wire whip after each addition. Just before serving, garnish with a sprinkling of Chervil. Serve warm. If sauce is to be held, be sure it does not become too warm or it will separate. Makes 1 cup.

Epicurean Sauce

An excellent sauce for an omelet, it's good, too, with broiled young turkey or chicken. Another time try it as a sauce for spaghetti.

¼ cup butter
1 package (8 oz.) frozen chicken
    livers or ½ pound fresh
    chicken livers
2 tablespoons Powdered Mushrooms
1 teaspoon Beau Monde Seasoning

1 teaspoon Chicken Seasoned
    Stock Base
1½ cups hot water
⅛ teaspoon Spice Parisienne
1 tablespoon sherry

Melt butter in medium-size frying pan. Add chicken livers. Cook over low heat, separating the livers with a spoon. When livers are completely thawed and have lightened in color, stir in Powdered Mushrooms and Beau Monde. Dissolve Chicken Seasoned Stock Base in hot water and add to chicken livers. Simmer gently until livers are tender, about 1 hour. Cool slightly and pour into electric blender. Blend for about 1 minute or until smooth. (Or force livers through a food mill or wire sieve.) Return sauce to pan; add Spice Parisienne. If sauce seems too thick, add a little more hot water. Heat thoroughly. Stir in sherry. Serve hot. Makes 1¾ cups.

Cumberland Sauce

Sweet and peppery, Cumberland Sauce is a perfect accompaniment to wild game, or to goose, duck, turkey, or ham.

1 teaspoon Instant Minced Onions
½ teaspoon unflavored gelatin
1 tablespoon cold water
4 tablespoons red currant jelly
¾ cup Port wine
2 tablespoons Red Wine Vinegar

1 teaspoon Orange Peel
1 teaspoon Lemon Peel
1 teaspoon Mild Mustard
⅛ teaspoon Cayenne Pepper
¼ teaspoon Ground Ginger

Combine Onions, gelatin, and cold water in small saucepan. Let stand for 5 minutes. Add jelly, Port wine, and Vinegar. Heat until jelly is melted. Add Orange and Lemon Peel to sauce along with Mustard, Cayenne, and Ginger. Simmer for 2 or 3 minutes. Serve hot or cold. Makes 1½ cups.

Pizza or Spaghetti Sauce

Long cooking is not required for this delicious sauce.

2 tablespoons olive oil
1 tablespoon Spaghetti Sauce Seasoning

1 can (6 oz.) tomato paste
1 can (6 oz.) water

Heat olive oil in small saucepan with cover. Add Spaghetti Sauce Seasoning and cook about 5 minutes or until lightly browned. Add tomato paste and water and simmer, covered, for 20 minutes. Stir occasionally. Makes 1½ cups.

FOR SPAGHETTI

Serve hot over cooked spaghetti; sprinkle with grated Romano or Parmesan cheese. Add cooked ground beef or pork, cooked chicken livers or Italian sausage to sauce if desired.

FOR PIZZAS

Make pizza dough from hot roll mix or any preferred recipe. Roll out to fit pizza pan or roll into 9 or 10-inch circle and place on cooky sheet. Brush generously with olive oil. Spoon sauce onto pizza; there is enough sauce for 2 pizzas. Arrange on sauce any preferred topping such as anchovy filets, sliced ripe olives or mushrooms, sliced Italian sausage or salami, browned and drained ground beef or sausage or cooked and cut-up link sausage. Arrange slices of Mozzarella, Monterey Jack, or Cheddar or process cheese over sauce and topping. Sprinkle generously with grated Romano or Parmesan cheese. Bake in 400° oven for 20 minutes or until done. Cut into wedges to serve.

Hollandaise Sauce

🌱 Nepal Pepper gives Hollandaise Sauce added flavor, but Cayenne can be used instead. If your range has a unit that can be turned down to "warm," you won't have to use a double boiler.

3 egg yolks	1/16 teaspoon Nepal Pepper
1 teaspoon White Wine Vinegar	¼ pound butter
¼ teaspoon salt	2 or 3 tablespoons light cream
¼ teaspoon Lemon Peel	

Fill bottom part of a double boiler half full with hot water. Water should steam but not boil. Or use a heavy pan or heat-proof casserole on unit turned to "warm:" In top of double boiler, beat egg yolks and combine with Vinegar, salt, Lemon Peel and Nepal Pepper. Melt butter and add a tablespoon or two at a time. Whip with a wire whip after each addition. If sauce is thicker than desired, thin with cream until of desired consistency. Serve at once. Or if sauce is to be served later, remove from heat. Just before serving, re-heat just slightly, stirring in a little more cream if sauce is thicker than desired. Serve warm. Makes 1 cup.

Dilled Sour Cream

🌱 Always a hit, this sauce is delicious with poached or broiled salmon, halibut, cod, or bass. Use as a change from Tartar Sauce to go along with fried fish. It makes an unusually good topping for cooked broccoli or asparagus, or a garnish for hot or cold soups.

1 cup dairy sour cream	¼ teaspoon sugar
1 teaspoon Dill Weed	1 teaspoon salt
1 tablespoon Eschalot Wine Vinegar	

Mix together thoroughly sour cream, Dill Weed, Vinegar, sugar, and salt. Let chill for an hour or so for flavors to develop. Makes 1 cup.

Sauce Verte

🌱 Sauce Verte traditionally is served with cold seafood such as crab, lobster, or shrimp.

1 cup mayonnaise	1½ tablespoons Tarragon White Wine Vinegar
3 tablespoons baby food strained spinach	1 tablespoon Chervil
½ teaspoon Onion Powder	

Combine mayonnaise, strained spinach, Onion Powder, Vinegar, and Chervil. Chill for an hour or so for flavors to develop. Just before serving, garnish with a light sprinkling of Chervil. Makes 1½ cups.

Tartar Sauce with Dill Weed

1 cup mayonnaise
3 tablespoons finely chopped sweet pickles
1 tablespoon Basil White Wine Vinegar
1 tablespoon Dill Weed

1 teaspoon Parsley
½ teaspoon Worcestershire sauce
⅛ teaspoon salt
⅛ teaspoon Hot Mustard
Dash Cayenne Pepper

Mix together mayonnaise, chopped pickles, Vinegar, Dill Weed, Parsley, Worcestershire sauce, salt, Hot Mustard, and Cayenne. Makes 1 cup.

Special Cocktail Sauce

½ teaspoon Horseradish
1 teaspoon water
¾ cup catsup
1 teaspoon Shredded Green Onions
1 tablespoon White Wine Vinegar

1 teaspoon Worcestershire sauce
½ teaspoon Beau Monde Seasoning
¼ teaspoon Hot Mustard
⅛ teaspoon Cayenne Pepper
1 tablespoon finely chopped celery

Mix Horseradish with water then mix together with catsup, Shredded Green Onions, and Vinegar. Add Worcestershire sauce, Beau Monde, Hot Mustard, Cayenne, and chopped celery. Chill well before serving. Makes 1 cup.

Paprika Butter

6 tablespoons butter
1 teaspoon Onion Powder
1 teaspoon Paprika

In small saucepan melt 2 tablespoons butter. Stir in Onion Powder and cook until golden, stirring constantly. Cool and cream into remaining 4 tablespoons butter. Shape into molds or balls. Chill. Serve on broiled poultry or fish, or on baked potatoes or other cooked vegetables. Good, too, on hot muffins. Makes 6 servings.

Deluxe Steak Butter

¼ pound butter
¼ teaspoon Garlic Powder
1 teaspoon Shredded Green Onions
1 teaspoon Dill Weed

1 teaspoon lemon juice
¼ teaspoon Cracked Black Pepper
1 teaspoon Paprika

Let butter soften at room temperature. Blend in Garlic Power, Green Onions Dill Weed, lemon juice, Pepper, and Paprika. Spread on broiled steak, hamburgers, or chops. Makes 6 servings.

Onion Butter

6 tablespoons butter
1½ to 2 teaspoons Onion Powder
1 teaspoon Parsley

In small saucepan melt 2 tablespoons butter. Stir in Onion Powder and cook until golden, stirring constantly. Cool and cream into remaining 4 tablespoons butter. Shape into molds or balls. Chill. Serve on baked potatoes, hamburgers, chops, or steaks; or use as seasoning for vegetables. Makes 6 servings.

Buerre aux Fines Herbes

4 tablespoons butter   ½ teaspoon Fines Herbes
¼ teaspoon Beau Monde Seasoning

Cream together butter and Beau Monde. Crush Fines Herbes and mix into creamed butter. Store in refrigerator for several hours for flavor to develop. Makes 4 servings.

TARRAGON BUTTER

Cream butter; crush 1 teaspoon Tarragon and mix into creamed butter with 1 teaspoon Tarragon White Wine Vinegar. Serve on broiled chicken, steak, or fish.

SALAD HERB BUTTER

Cream butter; crush ¼ teaspoon Salad Herbs and blend into creamed butter with ¼ teaspoon lemon juice. Spread on thinly sliced French bread and toast lightly. Or use to season cooked vegetables.

OREGANO BUTTER

Cream butter; crush ⅛ teaspoon Oregano and blend into creamed butter with ¼ teaspoon White Wine Vinegar. Use as a spread for French bread or toast; or to season fish, steak, or chops.

DILL BUTTER

Cream butter. Blend in ¼ teaspoon Dill Weed and ½ teaspoon White Wine Vinegar. Spread on broiled fish; or use to season cooked cabbage, green beans, or broiled tomatoes.

CHERVIL BUTTER

Melt butter. Mix in ¼ teaspoon Lemon Peel and 2 teaspoons Chervil. Serve warm as sauce for broiled or poached fish, or as an accompaniment to broiled scallops, lobster, clams, or other seafood. Or use instead of Mâjtre d'Hôtel butter.

BREADS

BAKING IS a personal satisfaction—the creative experience of shaping dough, the delightful fragrance that fills the kitchen, the wonderful taste of fresh-from-the-oven products. It is not surprising that so many modern cooks cling to the practice of old-fashioned home baking in spite of the wide variety of factory-baked products obtainable in the market.

Even an inexperienced cook can enjoy these pleasures with today's easy-to-use packaged mixes and ready-to-bake rolls and biscuits—and these aids are a joy, too, to the cook who is short of time but who wants to treat her family or guests to a beautiful, oven-fresh luxury.

The imaginative cook will add her own variations to baked products, whether they are created from classic recipes or from quick-and-easy packaged mixtures. Look to the seasoning shelf for the indispensable little touches that can make an ordinary recipe your own. Experiment with adding seasonings to the dough or using them as toppings. The merest hint of Saffron in the dumplings makes them the perfect accompaniment to Chicken Fricassee; a change to Sage and Marjoram and they flatter Beef or Lamb Stew. Hot roll mix takes on distinction when a sprinkling of Celery Seed is added to the dough, and another time it can be varied to become Poppy Seed Herb Rolls or Quick Onion Rolls.

Herb Corn Bread

Bake in a square pan, or as muffins or cornsticks. Split and toast leftover bread and serve with creamed chicken or turkey.

1⅔ cups sifted all-purpose flour	¼ teaspoon Oregano
¾ cup yellow cornmeal	½ teaspoon Thyme
3 teaspoons baking powder	1 egg
½ teaspoon Beau Monde Seasoning	1½ cups milk
½ teaspoon salt	4 tablespoons melted butter
2 tablespoons sugar	

Sift flour with cornmeal, baking powder, Beau Monde, salt, and sugar. Crush Oregano and Thyme and stir into dry ingredients. Beat egg slightly; add milk and melted butter. Add all at once to dry ingredients; stir just until well moistened but still lumpy. Pour into well-greased 8-inch square baking pan, or into muffin or cornstick pans. Bake in a 425° oven for 25 minutes or until done and brown. Cut into squares. Serve hot. Makes 6 servings.

Onion Bread

Make Onion Bread early the day of your party; serve slightly warm as an accompaniment to spaghetti or casserole dishes. Any leftover bread is good toasted.

1 cake fresh yeast	1 teaspoon Celery Salt
¼ cup lukewarm water	½ teaspoon Sage
2 cups milk	6 cups sifted all-purpose flour
2 tablespoons shortening	4 tablespoons Instant Minced Onions
2 tablespoons sugar	4 tablespoons water
2 teaspoons salt	

Crumble yeast into lukewarm water in large bowl. Let stand 5 to 10 minutes; stir until dissolved. Meanwhile, heat milk just to simmering. Add shortening, sugar, and salt; stir until dissolved. Cool to lukewarm. Add lukewarm milk mixture to yeast. Add Celery Salt and Sage to two cups flour and sift into yeast mixture. Beat until smooth. Rehydrate Instant Onions in water. Add to dough. Add three more cups flour and mix well. Use enough of the remaining cup of flour to make a stiff dough. Turn dough out on floured board and knead until dough is smooth and satiny, about 10 minutes. Form into ball; lightly grease entire surface of dough; place in bowl. Cover with waxed paper. Let rise in warm place (80°) until doubled, about 1½ hours. Punch down; let dough rest 10 to 15 minutes. Divide into two loaves. Place in two greased 4 x 8-inch loaf pans. Brush top with oil or melted shortening. Cover and let rise until doubled, about 1 hour. Bake in 400° oven for about 45 minutes or until done and brown. Serve fresh while still slightly warm. Makes 2 loaves.

Herb Bread

🌱 For a fun way of serving Herb Bread at a buffet supper, place a fresh-baked loaf on a cutting board with a bread knife alongside. Let each guest cut his or her own slice.

1 cake fresh yeast	1 egg
¼ cup lukewarm water	½ teaspoon Beau Monde Seasoning
¾ cup milk	½ teaspoon Nutmeg
2 tablespoons sugar	½ teaspoon Sage
2 tablespoons shortening	2 teaspoons Caraway Seed
1 teaspoon salt	3½ to 4 cups sifted all-purpose flour

Crumble yeast into lukewarm water in mixing bowl. Let stand 5 to 10 minutes; stir until dissolved. Meanwhile, heat milk just to simmering. Add sugar, shortening, and salt; cool to lukewarm. Beat in egg, Beau Monde, Nutmeg, Sage, and Caraway Seed. Add to yeast. Add 2 cups of the flour and beat until smooth. Add enough of remaining flour to make a moderately soft dough. Turn out onto lightly floured board and knead until smooth and elastic, about 5 minutes. Shape into ball and place in greased bowl, turning dough to grease all over. Cover and let rise in warm place (80°) until doubled, about 1 hour. Punch down; let rest about 10 minutes. Shape into round loaf and place in greased 8-inch round pan. Cover and let rise again until doubled, about 1 hour. Bake in 400° oven for 40 to 45 minutes or until done and brown. Brush with melted shortening. Serve fresh-baked. Makes 1 large loaf.

Swedish Orange Rye Bread

🌱 This bread is perfect fare for smorgasbord or buffet supper, but it's just as delicious at any other meal.

1 cake fresh yeast	⅓ cup sugar
¼ cup warm water	1 teaspoon salt
2 tablespoons Orange Peel	2 tablespoons salad oil
1½ cups lukewarm water	2½ cups sifted rye flour
¼ cup molasses	2½ cups sifted all-purpose flour

In a large bowl crumble yeast into warm water. Let stand 5 minutes; stir until dissolved. Stir in Orange Peel, lukewarm water, molasses, sugar, salt, and salad oil. Gradually add rye and all-purpose flour to yeast mixture and beat until smooth. Turn out on board and knead about 5 minutes. Place in greased bowl and let rise in warm place (80°) until doubled, about 1 hour. Punch down and shape into two round loaves. Place in two greased 8-inch round pans. Let rise until doubled. Bake in a 375° oven for 45 minutes or until done. Brush top with salad oil. Let cool, but serve while still fresh. Makes 2 loaves.

Western Spoon Bread

An ideal side dish to accompany barbecued meats.

2 tablespoons Green Bell Peppers
1 tablespoon Instant Minced Onions
1 can (1 lb. 13 oz.) tomatoes
1 cup yellow cornmeal
1 egg

1½ teaspoons Chili Con Carne
  Seasoning Powder
½ teaspoon soda
1 teaspoon salt
1 cup shredded Cheddar cheese

Combine Green Peppers, Instant Onions, and tomatoes in mixing bowl. Let stand 4 or 5 minutes. Stir in cornmeal, egg, Chili Con Carne Seasoning Powder, soda, salt, and cheese. Mix thoroughly. Pour into a well-buttered 1½-quart casserole. Bake in 350° oven for 1 hour or until firm. Spoon out onto plates and serve hot, either plain or with butter. Makes 8 servings.

Lemon Twist

A delightful lemony hot bread. Try it for tea or a late-morning breakfast.

1 cup milk
2 tablespoons sugar
1½ teaspoons salt
2 tablespoons butter
1 cake fresh yeast

1 egg
1 tablespoon Lemon Peel
¼ teaspoon Ground Nutmeg
½ cup raisins
3½ cups sifted all-purpose flour

Heat milk to simmering. Combine sugar, salt, and butter in mixing bowl. Pour hot milk over mixture; cool to lukewarm. Crumble yeast into milk mixture; stir until dissolved. Beat in egg, Lemon Peel, Nutmeg, and raisins. Sift 3 cups of flour into yeast mixture; mix well. Sift remaining ½ cup flour onto board; turn dough onto board and knead until smooth, about 5 minutes. Shape dough into ball and place in clean, greased bowl. Let rise in a warm place (80°) until doubled, about 45 minutes. Punch down; let rest 4 or 5 minutes, then form into a "rope" about 18 inches long. Fold in two and twist the two strands to form a loaf. Place on a greased baking pan or sheet. Let rise 30 to 40 minutes until doubled. Bake in a 375° oven for 35 to 40 minutes or until done and lightly browned. Frost while hot. Makes 1 loaf.

FROSTING

1 cup powdered sugar
1 teaspoon Lemon Peel
2 or 3 tablespoons
  light cream

Mix together powdered sugar, Lemon Peel, and cream. Stir until smooth.

Southern Spoon Bread with Herbs

🌿 This recipe comes from a famous old hotel in the Shenandoah Valley. Vary the herb to suit your taste.

2½ cups milk
1 cup yellow cornmeal
3 eggs
2 tablespoons sugar
1¼ teaspoons salt

4 tablespoons melted butter
¼ teaspoon Summer Savory (or Rosemary, Thyme, or Marjoram)
1 teaspoon baking powder

Heat 2 cups milk to simmering; stir in cornmeal. (Mixture will be very thick.) Beat eggs well; mix in remaining ½ cup milk, sugar, salt, and melted butter. Combine with scalded cornmeal. Crush Summer Savory and stir into batter along with baking powder; mix thoroughly. Pour into well-buttered 1½-quart baking dish or casserole. Bake in a 400° oven for 45 minutes or until spoon bread is firm and lightly browned. Spoon out onto plates and serve at once with butter. Makes 6 servings.

Cardamom Coffee Braid

🌿 Delicious any time of the day but especially good for a midday brunch or late Sunday breakfast.

1 package (14½ oz.) hot roll mix
¾ cup warm water
2 tablespoons melted butter
1 egg, slightly beaten

2 teaspoons Ground Cardamom
¼ teaspoon Lemon Peel
¾ cup golden seedless raisins
¼ cup chopped walnuts

Soften yeast from package of roll mix in warm water. Stir in butter, egg, Cardamom, Lemon Peel, raisins, and nuts. Add roll mix and mix well. Cover with waxed paper and let rise in warm place (80°) until doubled, about 1 hour. Turn out on floured board and knead 2 or 3 minutes. Divide dough into thirds; shape each part into a roll about 12 inches long. Arrange on greased baking sheet about one inch apart. Braid loosely, from the middle. Pinch ends together. Cover and let rise again until doubled, about 40 minutes. Bake in 375° oven for 25 to 30 minutes or until done. Spread glaze over braid as it comes from oven. Serve hot. Makes 6 servings.

GLAZE

½ cup powdered sugar
¼ teaspoon Lemon Peel

1 tablespoon light cream

Combine powdered sugar, Lemon Peel, and cream.

Saffron Dumplings

🌿 Delicious served with Chicken Fricassee or Veal Stew. Try Herb Dumplings with Beef or Lamb Stew.

1/32 teaspoon Powdered Saffron
⅓ cup milk, plus 2 tablespoons
1 cup biscuit mix
⅛ teaspoon salt

½ teaspoon Parsley
⅛ teaspoon Ground Nutmeg
¼ teaspoon sugar

Dissolve Saffron in milk. Combine biscuit mix, salt, Parsley, Nutmeg, and sugar. Stir Saffron milk into biscuit mix to make a soft dough. Drop by spoonfuls onto fricassee or stew. Cover tightly and simmer for 20 minutes without lifting cover. Arrange stew on platter; surround with dumplings. Makes 8 medium-size dumplings.

HERB DUMPLINGS

Omit Powdered Saffron and Nutmeg. Crush ⅛ teaspoon each Sage and Marjoram or ⅛ teaspoon each Sage and Thyme. Stir into biscuit mix with salt, Parsley, and sugar. Or add ¼ teaspoon Bouquet Garni for Beef or Bouquet Garni for Lamb instead of other herbs.

CHICKEN DUMPLINGS

Increase Parsley to 1 teaspoon. Substitute 2 tablespoons hot water for 2 tablespoons milk. Dissolve 1½ teaspoons Chicken Seasoned Stock Base in hot water and combine with ⅓ cup milk.

Toasted Onion Muffins

🌿 A delicious quick bread to serve with casserole dishes. Toast any leftover muffins and top with creamed dried beef or tuna.

1¾ cups biscuit mix
2 tablespoons cornmeal
2 tablespoons Instant Toasted Onions
¼ teaspoon Fines Herbes

¼ teaspoon salt
1 egg
1 cup milk
2 tablespoons melted butter or salad oil

Combine biscuit mix, cornmeal, and Instant Toasted Onions. Crush Fines Herbes and mix in along with salt. Beat together slightly egg, milk, and melted butter or salad oil. Add to Toasted Onion mixture. Mix quickly, just enough to combine. Batter will be lumpy. Spoon into well-greased muffin pans. Bake in 400° oven for 25 minutes or until muffins are done and brown. Serve hot. Makes 8 medium-size muffins.

Celery Seed Rolls

Serve piping hot with your favorite casserole or luncheon salad.

1 package (14½ oz.) hot roll mix	1 teaspoon Whole Celery Seed
1 cup warm water	1 cup shredded sharp cheese

Soften yeast in warm water as directed on package of roll mix. Stir in Celery Seed, shredded cheese, and roll mix. Mix well; cover and let rise in warm place (80°) until doubled, about 1 hour. Turn out on floured board and knead 2 or 3 minutes. Shape into rolls; cover with waxed paper. Let rise until doubled in size, 40 to 50 minutes. Bake in a 375° oven for 15 to 20 minutes or until done and brown. Serve hot. Makes 1½ dozen rolls.

POPPY SEED HERB ROLLS

Omit Celery Seed and cheese. Crush ½ teaspoon Salad Herbs and add to yeast mixture along with ¼ teaspoon Beau Monde Seasoning and 1 teaspoon Poppy Seed.

QUICK ONION ROLLS

Omit the Celery Seed and cheese. Rehydrate 2 tablespoons Instant Minced Onions in 2 tablespoons of warm water. Soften yeast in remaining warm water. To the roll mix add ½ teaspoon Celery Salt and ¼ teaspoon Sage. Stir half into softened yeast; add Onions and remaining mix.

Swedish Cardamom Buns

Serve these delectable buns for tea, brunch, breakfast, or as a dessert.

1½ cups milk	4 cups sifted all-purpose flour
½ cup sugar	1 teaspoon Ground Cardamom
1 teaspoon salt	1 egg, beaten
1 teaspoon Orange Peel	Crushed cube sugar
½ cup butter	Chopped almonds
2 cakes fresh yeast	

Heat milk to simmering. Combine sugar, salt, Orange Peel, and butter in mixing bowl. Pour hot milk over mixture. Cool to lukewarm. Crumble yeast and add to warm mixture; stir until yeast is dissolved. Add 1 cup flour; beat until smooth. Sift remaining flour with Cardamom; add to dough. Mix thoroughly. Let rise in warm place (80°) until doubled. Turn out on floured board and knead until smooth. Roll about ½ inch thick; cut into ½-inch strips. Twist two strips together, and cut into 2-inch lengths. Arrange on greased baking sheet. Let rise again until doubled. Brush with beaten egg; sprinkle with crushed cube sugar and chopped almonds. Bake in 400° oven for 10 minutes or until done and brown. Serve warm. Makes 2 dozen buns.

Chervil Biscuits

¼ cup butter
⅛ teaspoon Garlic Powder
1 tablespoon Chervil

2 packages refrigerator biscuits
1 tablespoon grated Parmesan cheese

Melt butter in 7 x 11-inch baking pan. Stir in Garlic Powder and Chervil. Arrange biscuits in melted butter and Chervil mixture. Let stand in warm place about 20 to 30 minutes. Turn biscuits over carefully with spatula. Spoon some of melted butter and Chervil in bottom of pan on top of biscuits. Sprinkle with Parmesan cheese. Bake in a 425° oven for 15 to 20 minutes or until biscuits are done and brown. Serve at once. Makes 20 biscuits.

Gold Coast French Toast

1 egg
1 cup undiluted evaporated milk
1 tablespoon sugar
1 teaspoon Ground Cinnamon

¼ teaspoon Ground Nutmeg
¼ teaspoon salt
6 slices bread

Beat egg; add milk, sugar, Cinnamon, Nutmeg, and salt. Mix thoroughly. Cut bread into triangles, dip into egg and milk mixture. Brown on both sides on a well-greased griddle or frying pan. Serve with soft butter and maple syrup.

SESAME SEED FRENCH TOAST

Add 2 tablespoons Sesame Seed to dipping mixture. Mix well, so seeds are well distributed.

ORANGE FRENCH TOAST

Omit spices; add 1 tablespoon Orange Peel. Sprinkle with powdered sugar.

Cinnamon Toast

4 slices bread
2 tablespoons soft butter

4 tablespoons sugar
1 teaspoon Ground Cinnamon

Cream together the butter, sugar, and Cinnamon until mixture will spread easily. Toast bread in broiler on one side only. Spread Cinnamon mixture onto untoasted side of bread. Broil until sugar bubbles.

GINGER TOAST

Into the soft butter, cream 2 teaspoons finely chopped Crystallized Ginger and 1 teaspoon sugar.

PASTRIES & DESSERTS

THE DELECTABLE DESSERTS that we present here group themselves into several categories. There are the wonderfully refreshing fruit desserts and ice creams that provide just the proper light touch at the end of a heavy meal. We have given a few recipes for these, and the unusual dessert sauces and toppings at the end of the chapter offer many other combinations. Try fresh, whole strawberries, for example, with Orange Sour Cream Topping; or serve Antigua Rum Sauce over coffee ice cream.

Liqueurs, too, make delicious toppings for ice cream or sherbet and offer many wonderful flavor combinations. For a light but glamorous dessert, top Vanilla Mousse with Antigua Liqueur or Citrus Liqueur.

Our pies and cakes are special treats. Serve one of them to climax a light luncheon or supper; or invite friends to a "dessert and coffee" party where your fancy dessert will receive the attention it deserves. Variations are suggested for a number of these recipes. A few simple substitutions, for example, can change Turkish Coffee-Spice Cake to Nutmeg Cake or Orange Cake; and Antigua Angel Cake is a variation of Spiced Angel Cake. Glance over your spice shelf for other ideas.

Cookies, of course, are all-time favorites. Our recipes include some different ones. Keep plenty on hand; they'll disappear quickly!

Orange-Glazed Pears with Ginger Whipped Cream

1 can (1 lb. 14 oz.) pear halves
1 tablespoon Orange Peel
  Ginger Whipped Cream (page 144)

2 tablespoons toasted slivered almonds

Pour syrup from pears into a wide-bottomed saucepan. Stir in Orange Peel. Arrange pears carefully in syrup and simmer over low heat until pears are clear and syrup reduced by about one-half. Baste pears frequently with syrup while simmering. Chill thoroughly. Arrange two chilled pear haves in each sherbet glass or dessert bowl. Top with a spoonful of Ginger Whipped Cream. Sprinkle with toasted almonds. Serve at once. Makes 4 or 5 servings.

Midsummer Fruit Cup

¼ to ½ pound dark sweet cherries
3 or 4 large ripe peaches
  Sugar to taste

½ cup light sweet white wine
1 tablespoon finely chopped Crystallized Ginger

Pit cherries and cut in half. Peel peaches and slice. Combine fruits and sweeten to taste. Combine wine and Ginger and pour over fruit. Chill until very cold, at least 1 hour, for flavors to blend. Spoon into stemmed sherbet glasses or dessert bowls. Serve very cold. Makes 6 servings.

Mixed Fresh Fruits with Orange Rum Sauce

A delightful dessert for any time of year — the suggested fruits are delicious, but the dessert can be varied depending on which fruits are at their best. Canned or frozen fruits are good, too.

2 or 3 large, firm, ripe peaches
7 or 8 fresh, ripe apricots
1 cup seedless green grapes
1 cup sugar

1 cup water
2 teaspoons Orange Peel
⅛ teaspoon Ground Nutmeg
1 tablespoon Jamaica rum

Peel and slice peaches; cut apricots in quarters. Discard pits. Arrange peaches, apricots, and grapes in bowl. Combine sugar and water; bring to a boil. Stir in Orange Peel and Nutmeg. While still hot, pour over fruit. Cool and then refrigerate until very cold. Just before serving, add rum. Makes 6 servings.

Gingered Heavenly Hash

🌿 Serve this old favorite on slices of angel or chiffon cake or spoon into sherbet glasses and serve accompanied by crisp cookies.

1 can (1 lb.) fruit cocktail
1½ cups miniature marshmallows
1 cup dairy sour cream

2 tablespoons finely chopped Crystallized Ginger
2 tablespoons toasted slivered almonds

Drain fruit cocktail. Combine drained fruit with marshmallows, sour cream, and Ginger. Chill 3 or 4 hours. Just before serving, sprinkle with slivered almonds. Makes 6 servings.

Vanilla Mousse

🌿 A perfect ice cream to serve with fresh berries or fruit.

1 piece (3 inches) Vanilla Bean
2 cups heavy cream
½ cup sugar

2 egg whites
⅛ teaspoon salt

Split Vanilla Bean with kitchen scissors. Scrape out seeds and black pulp. Add pod, seeds, and pulp to ½ cup heavy cream. Heat to simmering; simmer for 2 minutes. Stir in sugar. Cool and remove Vanilla pod. Whip remaining 1½ cups cream just until very soft. Stir in cooled cream mixture. Combine egg whites and salt; beat until soft peaks form. Fold into whipped cream. Pour into refrigerator tray. Freeze until ice crystals form around edge, about 30 minutes. Scrape out into bowl; beat until smooth and creamy. Pour back into tray; continue freezing until firm. Makes 1 quart.

Bouquet of Spice Ice Cream

3 cups rich milk or light cream
2 tablespoons Bouquet of Spice Tea
4 eggs
¾ cup sugar

¼ teaspoon salt
½ cup orange blossom honey
2 cups heavy cream

Heat milk to simmering in top of double boiler; add Tea and let stand for 6 or 7 minutes. Separate eggs. Beat yolks slightly; add sugar and salt and beat until lemon-colored. Strain Tea leaves from milk and beat milk gradually into egg and sugar mixture. Return to double boiler and cook custard over hot water, stirring constantly, until thickened. Remove from heat; stir in honey. Cool. Beat egg whites until they stand in soft peaks. Whip cream. Fold beaten egg whites and whipped cream into custard. Pour into freezer can of ice cream freezer. Adjust dasher and lid. Freeze according to directions for your model ice cream freezer. Makes 2 quarts.

Ginger Apricot Ice Cream

1 cup heavy cream
1 can (12 oz.) apricot nectar
2 tablespoons lemon juice

¼ cup sugar
2 tablespoons finely chopped
Crystallized Ginger

Whip cream until stiff. Beat in apricot nectar, lemon juice, sugar, and Ginger. Pour into refrigerator tray. Freeze until mushy. Scoop out into bowl; beat until smooth. Return to tray; freeze until firm, about 1 hour. Makes 6 servings.

Molasses Clove Cookies

 These spicy cookies keep well; store them in a tightly covered container.

3 cups sifted all-purpose flour
2 teaspoons baking powder
1 teaspoon salt
1 teaspoon Ground Cloves
1 teaspoon Ground Ginger

2 cups sugar
1½ cups melted butter
2 eggs
½ cup molasses
1½ cups quick-cooking rolled oats

Sift together flour, baking powder, salt, Cloves, Ginger, and sugar into large mixing bowl. Stir in melted butter, eggs, and molasses. Mix until smooth with electric mixer, about 2 minutes. With a large spoon, stir in rolled oats. Drop by teaspoonfuls onto ungreased cooky sheet about 1-inch apart. Bake in a 375° oven for 10 minutes. Do not over-bake. Makes 3 dozen cookies.

Nutmeg Butter Cookies

1 cup butter
½ cup sugar
1 egg
1 teaspoon vanilla

3 cups sifted all-purpose flour
½ teaspoon baking powder
¼ teaspoon salt
1¼ teaspoons Ground Nutmeg

Cream together butter and sugar until light and fluffy. Beat in egg and vanilla. Sift together flour, baking powder, salt, and Nutmeg. Blend into creamed mixture. Shape into 2 or 3 rolls two inches in diameter. Wrap in foil or waxed paper. Chill thoroughly. Slice cookies about ¼ inch thick and bake on ungreased cooky sheet in a 425° oven for 5 to 7 minutes or until very lightly browned. Do not overbake. (Dough may be packed into cooky press to make desired shapes.) Makes about 6 dozen cookies.

LEMON BUTTER COOKIES

Substitute 2 teaspoons lemon extract for vanilla and 1 teaspoon Lemon Peel for Nutmeg.

Sesame Seed Cookies

½ cup Sesame Seed
¾ cup butter
1½ cups brown sugar
2 eggs
1 teaspoon vanilla

1¼ cups sifted all-purpose flour
¼ teaspoon salt
¼ teaspoon baking powder
½ teaspoon Ground Cinnamon

Toast Sesame Seed in heavy frying pan, stirring constantly so seeds will not burn. Cream butter and brown sugar together until light and fluffy. Beat in eggs, one at a time, along with vanilla. Sift together flour, salt, baking powder, and Cinnamon. Stir in toasted Sesame Seed. Add to creamed mixture; mix thoroughly. Line cooky sheet with waxed paper. Drop dough by teaspoonfuls onto waxed paper. Allow room for cookies to spread during baking. Bake in a 325° oven for 20 to 25 minutes or until cookies are done and lightly browned. While cookies are still hot, remove from waxed paper. For a change, replace the Cinnamon with ½ teaspoon Pumpkin Pie Spice or ¼ teaspoon Cardamom. Makes 6 dozen cookies.

Ginger Butterscotch Pie

5 tablespoons butter
¾ cup brown sugar
¾ cup boiling water
3 tablespoons Arrowroot
¼ teaspoon salt
1¼ cups milk
2 egg yolks
1 teaspoon vanilla
2 tablespoons finely chopped
   Crystallized Ginger

½ cup chopped walnuts
9-inch baked pie shell
1 cup heavy cream
4 tablespoons powdered sugar
2 teaspoons Vanilla Brandy
   (page 148)
Slivers of Ginger and chopped nuts
   for garnish

Melt butter in heavy frying pan over low heat. When butter is golden brown, add brown sugar and cook, stirring constantly, for 2 or 3 minutes or until sugar is foamy. Add boiling water and stir until sugar is dissolved. Remove from heat. In a saucepan, mix together Arrowroot, salt, and milk. Add butterscotch mixture; mix well. Cook over low heat, stirring constantly, until thickened and smooth and mixture comes to a boil. Beat egg yolks slightly. Stir about ½ cup of hot custard into egg yolks; stir egg yolks back into custard in saucepan and continue cooking until custard thickens again, about 1 minute. Stir in vanilla, Ginger, and walnuts. Cool for 5 to 10 minutes. Pour into pie shell. Cool thoroughly. Whip cream until almost stiff. Beat in powdered sugar and Vanilla Brandy. Spread on top of pie; garnish with slivers of Ginger and chopped nuts. Serve cold. Makes 8 servings.

Ginger Apple Pie

By using canned pie-sliced apples or frozen fruit, you can create a home-made pie in minutes. Crystallized Ginger adds a distinctive flavor touch. Serve garnished with a spoonful of Orange Sour Cream (page 144).

1 can (1 lb. 4 oz.) pie-sliced apples
1 tablespoon Arrowroot
⅔ cup brown sugar

1 to 2 tablespoons finely chopped Crystallized Ginger
Pastry for 8-inch double crust pie
1 tablespoon butter

Drain apples. Combine juice with Arrowroot and cook over low heat until juice starts to thicken. Stir in sugar, apples, and Crystallized Ginger. Line 8-inch pie pan with pastry. Fill with fruit. Dot with butter. Top with pastry. Bake in a 400° oven for 40 minutes or until crust is done and brown. Makes 6 servings.

GINGER PEACH PIE

Use two packages of frozen peaches instead of apples; omit sugar. Thaw peaches; drain. Measure ¼ cup of peach juice. Combine with Arrowroot. Arrange peaches and Ginger in pastry-lined pie pan. Pour juice over peaches. Dot with butter. Top with pastry. Bake in a 400° oven for 40 minutes or until crust is done and brown.·

Orange Parfait Pie

A delightfully refreshing end to a meal. Orange Peel enhances the flavor of the orange gelatin.

GRAHAM CRACKER CRUST

1⅓ cups graham cracker crumbs
1 teaspoon Orange Peel

2 tablespoons sugar
⅓ cup melted butter

Combine graham cracker crumbs, Orange Peel, and sugar; mix well. Add melted butter and blend into crumbs. Pack into a 9-inch pie pan; chill.

PARFAIT FILLING

1 package orange-flavored gelatin
1½ cups hot water
2 teaspoons Orange Peel

1 pint vanilla ice cream
1 teaspoon finely chopped Crystallized Ginger

Dissolve gelatin in hot water. Stir in Orange Peel. Spoon ice cream into dis-solved gelatin. When ice cream is melted, chill in refrigerator until partially set. Beat with rotary beater or electric mixer until fluffy. Stir in chopped Ginger. Pour into graham cracker crust and chill for several hours or until firm. Makes 8 servings.

Lemon-Filled Layer Cake

🌿 Lemon Peel and Nutmeg give extra flavor to this old favorite made with the help of mixes.

1 package white cake mix
2 teaspoons Lemon Peel
1 package lemon pudding or pie filling

1 cup heavy cream
¼ teaspoon Ground Nutmeg
Powdered sugar

Make cake according to package directions, adding 1 teaspoon Lemon Peel to the liquid called for. Bake in two 8-inch round cake pans. Cool. Split each layer in two. Make package of lemon pudding according to package directions; stir in remaining 1 teaspoon Lemon Peel. Cool. Whip cream; stir in Nutmeg. Fold cream into cooled filling. Spread filling between cake layers. Insert skewers or toothpicks to hold cake layers in place. Sift powdered sugar over top layer. Chill thoroughly; remove skewers or toothpicks. Cut into wedges to serve. Makes 12 servings.

Turkish Coffee-Spice Cake

🌿 More a confection than a cake, this delectable dessert finds its origin in the Middle Eastern countries.

2 cups brown sugar
2 cups sifted all-purpose flour
½ cup butter
½ teaspoon salt
2 tablespoons Turkish-type Coffee
1 teaspoon Ground Cinnamon

¼ teaspoon Ground Nutmeg
1 teaspoon soda
1 cup dairy sour cream
1 egg
½ cup chopped nuts (cashews, walnuts, or almonds)

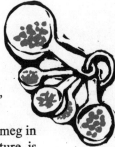

Combine brown sugar, flour, butter, salt, Coffee, Cinnamon, and Nutmeg in a medium-size mixing bowl. Blend with pastry blender until mixture is crumbly and completely blended. Butter a 9-inch square cake pan generously; spoon in half the crumb mixture. Stir soda into sour cream; mix into remaining crumbs along with egg. Pour batter over crumbs and sprinkle with chopped nuts. Bake in a 350° oven for 40 to 45 minutes or until done. Serve warm topped with Ginger or Orange Whipped Cream (page 144). Or cool and serve plain with fruit or ice cream. Makes 9 servings.

SYRIAN NUTMEG CAKE

Omit Coffee and Cinnamon. Increase Nutmeg to 1 teaspoon.

ARMENIAN ORANGE CAKE

Omit Coffee, Cinnamon, and Nutmeg. Add instead ½ teaspoon Allspice. To sour cream and egg mixture add 2 teaspoons Orange Peel.

Greek Walnut Cake

🌿 Serve this torte-like cake plain to go along with ice cream or top a square with whipped cream flavored with Vanilla Brandy and slivered Crystallized Ginger.

3 cups ground walnuts (about ½ pound shelled walnuts)
9 eggs
1 cup sugar
½ cup fine dry bread crumbs
1 tablespoon Orange Peel
1½ teaspoons Lemon Peel

½ teaspoon salt
1 teaspoon Ground Cinnamon
½ teaspoon Ground Cloves
2 teaspoons baking powder
¼ cup Vanilla Brandy (page 148)
3 tablespoons water

Grind walnuts through medium blade of food chopper. Separate eggs; beat egg yolks and sugar until thick and lemon-colored. Mix the ground nuts with bread crumbs, Orange and Lemon Peel, salt, Cinnamon, Cloves, and baking powder. Stir into egg yolk mixture. Mix in Vanilla Brandy and water. Beat egg whites until stiff but not dry. Fold gently, but thoroughly, into batter. Pour into greased 9 x 13-inch baking pan. Bake in 350° oven for 30 to 35 minutes or until a sharp knife inserted in center comes out clean. Cool in pan. Cut in squares to serve. Makes 12 servings.

Spiced Angel Cake

1 cup sifted cake flour
⅞ cup sugar
1 teaspoon Pumpkin Pie Spice
¼ teaspoon Ground Nutmeg
1½ cups egg whites (10-12 eggs)

1½ teaspoons Cream of Tartar
¼ teaspoon salt
2 teaspoons Vanilla Brandy (page 148)
¾ cup sugar

Combine the flour and ⅞ cup of sugar; sift together three times. Measure Pumpkin Pie Spice, Nutmeg, egg whites, Cream of Tartar, salt, and Vanilla Brandy into a large mixing bowl. Beat with an electric mixer or wire whip until foamy. Add the ¾ cup sugar, two tablespoons at a time, beating continuously. Continue to beat until meringue holds stiff peaks. Sift flour and sugar mixture gradually over meringue. Fold in gently until mixture disappears. Pour batter into 10-inch angel cake pan. Rap sharply to break any large air bubbles. Bake in a 350° oven for 40 to 45 minutes or until cake is done and lightly browned. Turn cake upside down; let hang until cold. Cut cake from pan. Serve plain or frosted. Makes 16 servings.

ANTIGUA ANGEL CAKE

Sift 1 tablespoon Antigua Instant Coffee with flour and sugar. Omit Pumpkin Pie Spice and Nutmeg. Increase Vanilla Brandy to 1 tablespoon.

Vanilla Butter Frosting

1 piece (1 inch) Vanilla Bean
2 tablespoons milk
½ cup butter

Dash of salt
1 package (1 lb.) powdered sugar
1 egg

Split Vanilla Bean; scrape out seeds. Add pod and seeds to milk and heat to simmering. Set aside to cool. Cream butter; add salt. Sift powdered sugar; cream into butter gradually, blending after each addition. Beat in egg; add Vanilla milk until frosting is the right consistency to spread. Makes 2½ cups frosting (enough to frost two 8-inch layers or a large sheet cake).

TURKISH COFFEE FROSTING
Blend 1 tablespoon Turkish-type Coffee into frosting along with egg and Vanilla milk.

ORANGE BUTTER FROSTING
Omit Vanilla Bean. Cream 1 tablespoon Orange Peel into butter along with salt. Use light cream or milk to replace Vanilla milk.

Sour Cream Ginger Frosting

1 package (1 lb.) powdered sugar
Dash of salt
¼ cup soft butter
⅓ cup dairy sour cream

1 tablespoon milk
1 tablespoon finely chopped Crystallized Ginger

Sift powdered sugar. Combine in bowl with salt, butter, sour cream, and milk. Beat until well blended and creamy. Mix in Crystallized Ginger. Makes 2½ cups frosting (enough to frost two 8-inch layers or a large sheet cake).

Antigua Rum Sauce

1 cup sugar
1½ cups hot water
2 tablespoons Antigua Instant Coffee
2 tablespoons Arrowroot

2 tablespoons cold water
2 tablespoons butter
¼ cup dark rum

Pour sugar into heavy frying pan. Melt sugar over low heat, stirring constantly, until melted and golden. Combine hot water and Antigua Coffee. Pour slowly and carefully over melted sugar. (Be very careful, melted sugar is very hot!) Stir frequently until sugar is completely dissolved in hot Coffee, about 15 minutes. Mix Arrowroot with cold water; stir into sauce. Continue cooking, stirring constantly, until sauce is thickened and smooth. Add butter and rum; stir until butter is melted. Serve warm over ice cream. Makes 2 cups.

Brandied Sour Cream Topping

🌿 A delicious topping for a plain cake, apple pie, or almost any fresh, frozen, or canned fruit.

1 cup dairy sour cream
2 tablespoons powdered sugar

1 tablespoon Vanilla Brandy
(page 148)
⅛ teaspoon Ground Nutmeg

Mix together thoroughly sour cream, powdered sugar, Vanilla Brandy, and Nutmeg. Chill thoroughly. Serve very cold. Makes 4 to 6 servings.

ORANGE SOUR CREAM TOPPING

Substitute 2 tablespoons brown sugar for powdered sugar. Omit Vanilla Brandy and Nutmeg and add ½ teaspoon Orange Peel. Serve on cooked or canned fruit, pumpkin pie or pudding, fruit pies.

Orange Whipped Cream

½ cup heavy cream
1 tablespoon powdered sugar

½ teaspoon Orange Peel
1 tablespoon Orange Curacao

Whip cream until smooth and glossy. Stir in powdered sugar, Orange Peel, and Orange Curacao. Let stand about an hour for flavors to blend. Serve on pumpkin pie, chiffon or angel food cake, custards, fresh or cooked fruit. Makes 4 servings.

GINGER WHIPPED CREAM

Make as for Orange Whipped Cream substituting 1 tablespoon slivered Crystallized Ginger for the Orange Peel. Use either Orange Curacao or 1 tablespoon Vanilla Brandy (page 148). Serve on pumpkin pie, coconut or banana cream pie, fresh, frozen, or canned fruit, custards.

Nutmeg Whipped Cream

½ cup heavy cream
1 tablespoon granulated or brown
sugar

⅛ teaspoon Ground Nutmeg or
grated Whole Nutmeg
Dash salt

Whip cream until it forms soft peaks; stir in sugar, Nutmeg, and salt. Continue whipping until smooth and glossy. Serve on pumpkin pie, bread or rice pudding, custards, fruit cobblers or shortcakes. Makes 4 servings.

BEVERAGES

COFFEE AND TEA, lemonade and cider, chocolate, punch, and liqueurs—we've included a sampling of each of them here. However, you'll find that these are not the usual beverages. We have added some new and out-of-the-ordinary ingredients to dress them up in special ways. They are excitingly different and worthy of the most elegant service.

Tea with a refreshing mint flavor is combined with fruit juices in a deliciously cooling punch, or used to give an extra flavor lift to lemonade. Coffee, spiced with Cinnamon, Cloves, and Allspice, becomes a summertime favorite when chilled and topped with a fluff of whipped cream. Cold, blustery days call for Hot Spiced Cider served in sturdy mugs in front of a warming fire. A demitasse of Espresso Cioccalata—hot chocolate in wonderful combination with Instant Espresso Coffee—is a perfect finale to a splendid dinner.

Especially worthy of comment are the two liqueurs and the Vanilla Brandy on page 148. Served alone, they are wonderful after-dinner drinks; but you'll find them mentioned, too, in other sections of this book as important ingredients in sauces and toppings for pastries and desserts. Pour any one of them over plain ice cream or sherbet, and even that simple dessert takes on a special air. Add Vanilla Brandy or Antigua Liqueur to whipped cream to make an especially delicious dessert topping.

Café Brûlot

🌟 One of the traditional after-dinner coffee drinks, Café Brûlot makes a spectacular end for your nicest dinner party.

1 whole Stick Cinnamon	12 lumps sugar
10 Whole Cloves	1 cup cognac or brandy
1 teaspoon Orange Peel	4 tablespoons Antigua Instant Coffee
½ teaspoon Lemon Peel	4 cups boiling water

Break Cinnamon into three or four pieces; combine in top of deep chafing dish with Cloves, Orange and Lemon Peel, and sugar. Add cognac or brandy. Place chafing dish over flame. Meanwhile, add Antigua Coffee to boiling water. When cognac or brandy is warm, set aflame. Let burn for about a minute. Pour hot Coffee over flaming liquor. Stir, then ladle into demitasses. Serve at once. Makes 8 servings.

Frosted Viennese Cooler

🌟 Coffee, in the European tradition, is delightful to serve at a midsummer morning get-together.

6 tablespoons Antigua Instant Coffee	8 Whole Allspice
½ cup sugar	½ cup heavy cream
6 cups boiling water	3 tablespoons powdered sugar
1 whole Stick Cinnamon	1 teaspoon vanilla
8 Whole Cloves	

Combine Antigua Coffee and sugar in large heat-proof bowl or pitcher. Pour boiling water over Coffee and sugar. Stir to dissolve. Break Stick Cinnamon into three or four pieces and add to Coffee along with Cloves and Allspice. Let stand for 1 hour. Strain out spices. Chill. Whip cream until stiff; stir in powdered sugar and vanilla. Pour spiced Coffee into tall glasses over ice cubes. Top with whipped cream. Serve at once. Makes 6 servings.

Hot Spiced Cranberry Punch

2 cans (6 oz. each) frozen concentrated lemonade	¼ teaspoon Ground Cinnamon
	¼ teaspoon salt
2 bottles (1 pint each) cranberry juice cocktail	2½ cups water
½ teaspoon Ground Allspice	

Combine lemonade, cranberry juice cocktail, Allspice, Cinnamon, salt, and water in kettle or saucepan. Heat just to boiling and simmer for 10 to 15 minutes. Serve hot in punch cups or mugs. Makes 2 quarts.

Espresso Cioccalata

Make the hot chocolate with an instant chocolate mix or use your favorite recipe. Or heat a cup of dairy chocolate drink.

4 tablespoons Instant Espresso
  Coffee
1 cup boiling water
1 cup hot chocolate

½ cup heavy cream
2 tablespoons sugar
½ teaspoon Orange Peel
Dash Ground Nutmeg

Combine Espresso Coffee with boiling water. When Coffee is dissolved, add hot chocolate. Pour into chocolate cups or demitasses. Whip cream until stiff. Fold in sugar and Orange Peel. Spoon whipped cream on top and sprinkle with Nutmeg. Serve hot. Makes 4 servings.

Hot Spiced Cider

2 quarts cider
½ cup brown sugar
¼ teaspoon salt

1 whole piece Stick Cinnamon
1 teaspoon Whole Allspice
1 teaspoon Whole Cloves

Combine cider, brown sugar, and salt in saucepan. Add stick of Cinnamon, Allspice, and Cloves. Slowly bring to simmering; cover and simmer for 20 minutes. Remove spices with slotted spoon. Serve hot. Makes 2 quarts.

Tea Lemonade

2 quarts cold water
5 tablespoons Orange Pekoe and
  Pekoe Tea

¾ cup water
¾ cup sugar
¾ cup lemon juice

Bring freshly drawn cold water to a full rolling boil; pour immediately over Tea. Let steep for 4 minutes; stir and strain. Meanwhile, combine water and sugar; bring to a boil and boil for 10 minutes. Add syrup to Tea along with lemon juice. Pour over ice cubes in tall glasses. Serve at once. Makes 8 servings.

Sparkling Strawberry Cooler

2 cups boiling water
1 tablespoon Bouquet of Spice Tea
1 package (1 lb.) frozen whole
  strawberries

½ can (6-oz. size) frozen
  concentrated limeade
2 cups sparkling water

Pour boiling water over Tea. Let steep for 5 minutes; stir Tea and strain. Cool and add strawberries and limeade. Chill. Stir in sparkling water just before serving. Pour over ice cubes in tall glasses. Makes 1½ quarts.

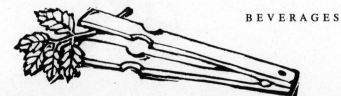

Vanilla Brandy

 Serve as a liqueur, or use to flavor whipped cream, ice cream, hard sauce, cakes, pies, and puddings.

2 whole Vanilla Beans ½ pint brandy

Cut Vanilla Beans into 1-inch pieces. Split pods open. Drop into brandy. Close bottle tightly and let stand about one month. Makes ½ pint.

Antigua Liqueur

 Interesting as an after-dinner liqueur with or without a float of cream. Good, too, poured over vanilla, chocolate, or coffee ice cream, or used as a flavoring for whipped cream.

1 jar (2 oz.) Antigua Instant Coffee
4 cups sugar
2 cups boiling water

1 pint brandy or Bourbon whiskey
1 whole Vanilla Bean

Combine Antigua Coffee, sugar, and boiling water. Stir until coffee and sugar are dissolved. Cool. Add brandy or Bourbon; pour into two bottles, approximately 26-ounce size. Cut Vanilla Bean in two. Split each half and add a half bean to each bottle. Close bottles tightly and let stand about one month. Makes about 6 cups.

Citrus Liqueur

 Serve as a liqueur, or pour an ounce or two over ice cubes in a tall glass and fill with sparkling water for a most refreshing beverage. Good, too, as a topping for ice cream or sherbet. Flavor is best when fresh fruit juice is used.

1¼ cups grapefruit juice
½ cup orange juice
¼ cup lemon juice

2 cups sugar
2 whole Vanilla Beans
1 fifth gin

Sterilize a half gallon jar or jug. Combine fruit juices and sugar; strain into jar or jug. Split Vanilla Beans and cut into 1-inch pieces. Add to fruit juices along with gin. Let liqueur stand for about two weeks; shake jar daily. Makes about 6 cups.

A GUIDE
TO YOUR
SPICE SHELF

THE WORD "SPICES" is an all-inclusive term that encompasses not one substance, but four distinct categories.

Spices are derived from the bark, root, fruit, or berry of perennial plants (for example: Cinnamon from the bark, Ginger from the root, Nutmeg from the fruit, Pepper from the berry).

Herbs are the leaves only of annual and perennial low-growing shrubs (Basil, Marjoram, Tarragon, Thyme, Rosemary, Dill Weed, Chervil, etc.).

Aromatic seeds are the seeds of graceful, lacy annual plants (Anise, Caraway, Coriander, Fennel).

Seasonings generally are blends of spices and/or herbs and/or seeds. They are usually intended for one specific purpose (Poultry Seasoning, Spaghetti Sauce Seasoning, Bouquet Garni for Beef or Lamb or Soup, Chili Con Carne Seasoning, Chili Powder, Salad Herbs, Curry Powder).

To the four categories above might be added yet another that could be called *Vegetable Spices*. This group would include Garlic, Onion, Bell Peppers, Paprika, Chili Peppers, Cayenne, Horseradish, Mushrooms.

In the following special section of this book, we present some of the fascinating stories of the individual spices—their origins, history, appearance, culture. We also give some suggested uses for each of them.

Allspice

ALLSPICE is so called because its aroma and flavor resemble those of several spices, principally Nutmeg, Cinnamon, and Cloves. Native to tropical America, it has the distinction of being the only spice produced exclusively in the Western Hemisphere. Most of the world's better quality Allspice comes from Jamaica. However, it is also produced in Mexico and other Central American countries.

When picked, the berry is approximately ¼ of an inch in diameter and green in color. The characteristic reddish-brown color results from the sun-drying process.

The Allspice tree is an evergreen of the Myrtle family, growing to a height of 25 to 35 feet, depending on soil and climatic conditions. The early Spanish explorers mistook it for pepper, and thus in some quarters Allspice is also known as Pimenta (after the Spanish *Pimienta,* meaning pepper). This similarity to pepper also resulted in the name Jamaica Pepper.

USES

There are a myriad of uses for Allspice. The most common ones are in pickles, relishes, cakes and cookies, stewed and preserved fruits, mincemeat, and tomato-base sauces. It is particularly good in pot roasts. For those who enjoy experimenting, Allspice combines well with most other spices.

Ground Allspice

CAKES, COOKIES: Dark fruitcake; spice, applesauce, prune, plum, or black walnut cake; spiced angel or chiffon cake; german honey cakes; molasses or spice cookies.

FRUITS: Mincemeat, cranberry sauce. Sprinkle lightly on fruit cup, fruit salad, or fruit compote.

MEATS: Pot roasts, stews, braised veal, pork, lamb; meat loaf and hamburgers; stuffiings for veal and lamb.

PUDDINGS, PIES: Steamed or plum pudding; pumpkin, chiffon, apple, cranberry, prune, or raisin pie; spiced custard pies.

SAUCES: Chili sauce, catsup, barbecue sauce, spaghetti sauce, brown sauce, and gravies.

Whole Allspice

BEVERAGES: Spiced drinks such as spiced cider or cranberry juice; fruit or wine punches.

HOME CANNING: Pickles, spiced fruits, relishes, catsup, chili sauce.

MEATS, FISH, GAME: Add to court-bouillon for fish; sauces and gravies for beef, lamb, veal, game, stews, pot roasts; stock for boiled beef, corned beef, tongue, corned or smoked pork.

PICKLING LIQUIDS, SPICED SYRUPS: Use in pickled beets, mushrooms and other vegetables; spiced pineapple, prunes, peaches, apricots; pickled shrimp or fish; syrups for stewed or baked fruits.

SOUPS: Add to taste to split pea, vegetable-beef, tomato soups.

Anise Seed

ANISE SEED is native to Asia Minor and Egypt but is now cultivated in practically all countries in the temperate zone. The bulk of the world's supply is produced in Mexico, Spain, Italy, and Turkey.

Probably the oldest known aromatic seed, it is mentioned in early Egyptian writings as well as by such ancient writers as Pliny and Dioscorides. Charlemagne, we read, required the cultivation of Anise in the Imperial German Gardens. During the year 1305, King Edward I taxed all imports of Anise into London and used the revenue therefrom to keep London Bridge in good repair. Our own American history tells us that in the year 1619 the First Assembly of Virginia decreed that "each man unto whom a division (land) is granted must plant thereon six anise seeds."

The Anise plant is a graceful annual and under ideal conditions will attain a height of 3½ feet. The small, whitish flowers, as well as the seeds, are formed in umbels up to 3 inches in diameter and located at the stalk tips.

Anise Seed is a favorite of those with a "sweet tooth." It is used extensively in confections, sweet pastries, and as a flavoring in liqueurs. Try a touch of ground or crushed Anise in your favorite breakfast roll or coffee cake recipe for a truly delightful flavor.

USES

Use ¼ teaspoon for 4 servings.

BREADS, ROLLS: Sprinkle on as garnish or add to dough for sweet rolls, breads, coffee cakes.

CAKES, COOKIES: Add whole or crushed to refrigerator or butter cookies, spritz or springerle-type cookies, sugar cookies, sponge or spice cake.

MEATS, FISH: Add to court-bouillon for steamed cod, crab, shrimp. Crush and add to sauces for fish, shellfish.

PICKLES: Add whole to sweet pickles.

SALADS: Use whole or crushed in fruit or vegetable salads.

Arrowroot

ARROWROOT is perhaps the least known of Nature's gifts to cooks. Technically, it is a starch and does not readily lend itself to any of the spice categories. Also, being relatively new on the scene, it lacks the glamorous and exotic history of its cousins. Yet, this versatile white powder deserves a place on your spice shelf and certainly deserves prominent mention in this book.

Arrowroot is a starch obtained from the rhizome of a West Indian plant, *Maranta arundinacea*. These rhizomes (roots), after being washed and pulped, produce a milky-white fluid from which is precipitated an insoluble powder. This powder is then dried and milled into the form we know.

Arrowroot is neutral in flavor and does not mask or alter natural flavors.

It produces sauces and pastes of remarkable clarity. This translucent quality makes Arrowroot particularly desirable for use as a thickening agent in fruit sauces, pie fillings (such as lemon cream or fruit pies), puddings, salad dressings and dessert sauces. It is also excellent for vegetable sauces and meat glazes. Arrowroot reaches maximum thickening at lower temperatures than other thickeners, thus it is ideal for use with heat sensitive foods. Sauces made with Arrowroot should not be overcooked.

As a thickening agent, use ⅓ to ½ the amount of Arrowroot in place of flour or cornstarch. Since Arrowroot cooks at a lower temperature than flour and becomes clear, it is not recommended for use in making brown country-style gravy.

The Dispensatory of the United States, 1959 edition, reports that Arrowroot "provides a very mild, easily-digested dietary article well adapted for the sick and convalescent."

Basil

BASIL is native to tropical Asia and Africa. In warmer parts of the world, there can be found 30 to 40 different species, but there is only one that is generally used in the spice industry. Botanically, it is known as *Ocimum Basilicum*.

It is difficult to say when man first began using this herb. Early writings indicate that it had achieved a great popularity long before the time of Christ. In our own country, it was being grown commercially in Virginia as early as 1774, but it has been only in relatively recent years that the culture and production of Basil has reached major proportions in America (principally California).

The Basil plant is a low-growing annual approximately 18 inches in height. When seen growing in the field, it is almost succulent in appearance and gives off a sweet fragrance as one brushes by. The leaves are quite large, up to 2½ inches in length and from ½ to 1 inch in width. The taste of fresh Basil is reminiscent of licorice, and the dried leaves have a lemony, anise-like quality. The better quality Basil available on grocery shelves is produced from leaves that are harvested just before the flower bud opens. It is at this point in the life cycle of the plant that flavoring value is at its maximum.

Basil, as is true of most other herbs, is versatile in its uses, which are limited only by the degree of inventiveness of the cook. However, it does have a special affinity for tomatoes and tomato-base recipes, whether they be salads, vegetables, sauces, or main courses.

USES

Use approximately ½ teaspoon for 4 servings, crushing leaves just before adding.
APPETIZERS: Tomato juice, seafood cocktails.
SOUPS: Tomato, turtle, spinach, minestrone.

SALADS: Tomato, seafood, egg, fruit, mixed green, cream cheese, cottage cheese, cucumber.

SAUCES: Tomato, spaghetti, orange (for game), butter (for fish).

FISH: Broiled or scalloped.

VEGETABLES: Eggplant, squash, tomatoes, peas, onions, new potatoes.

EGGS, CHEESE: Scrambled eggs, Welsh rarebit.

Bay Leaves

SWEET BAY or LAUREL is native to the Mediterranean region where it grows to an evergreen tree up to 40 feet high. It can also be found quite extensively in the milder climates of North America. Much has been written about the role of the Bay tree in Roman and Greek mythology, and Bay still plays a part in religious as well as social festivals in many parts of Europe.

There are several varieties of Bay, each one having a slightly different physical characteristic. The Greek and Turkish leaves, for example, are slightly serrated along the edges, are greenish-brown in color and of medium pungency. The leaf of the California Bay Laurel, on the other hand, is long and tapered, bright green in color, and extremely pungent — from two to three times more pungent than that of the European variety.

USES

The uses of Bay are many and varied. Eggs, meats, game, soups, casseroles, and sauces will benefit from the judicious use of this herb. Use it sparingly, however, for it is dominant by nature.

SOUPS: Vegetable, minestrone, tomato.

SALADS: French dressing for tossed green and vegetable salads.

FISH: Court-bouillon for poaching.

MEATS: Pot roasts, corned beef, tripe, stews, venison, marinades.

VEGETABLES: Boiled potatoes, carrots.

DESSERTS: Custards and creams.

Beau Monde Seasoning Salt

BEAU MONDE SEASONING SALT is a balanced blend of primary, essential seasonings which will enhance the flavor of most foods except sweets and bakery goods.

USES

EGGS: Sprinkle on fried, poached, and boiled eggs. Use ¼ teaspoon for each egg in omelets, scrambled or deviled eggs.

HORS D'OEUVRES: Add to taste in dips and spreads.

MEATS, POULTRY, FISH: Use ½ teaspoon per pound to season steaks, chops, roasts, and variety meats. Rub on chicken, duck, turkey before roasting. Sprinkle on broiled or baked fish.

SAUCES AND GRAVIES: Add 1 teaspoon to two cups cream sauce, tomato sauce, or gravy. Add 1 teaspoon to each cup of sauce with butter or oil base. Add to taste to barbecue sauces and marinades.

SALADS AND SALAD DRESSINGS: Tossed green and vegetable salads. Add to taste to French, sour cream, mayonnaise, or cooked dressings.

Beef Stock Base

BEEF STOCK BASE is a blend of pure beef extract and spices. It is more commonly known for its many uses in sauces and gravies, but did you know that it is an ideal seasoning for vegetables?

USES

POTATOES: Peel 3 medium-size potatoes and cut into cubes. Add 4 teaspoons Beef Stock Base and ½ cup water; cover and cook, turning potatoes occasionally, until potatoes are tender and liquid is absorbed. Sprinkle with Black Pepper. Serves 4.

ONIONS: Peel 1 to 1½ pounds small yellow or white onions. Place in 1-quart casserole. Stir 1 tablespoon Beef Stock Base into ¾ cup water and pour over onions. Cover and bake in a 350° oven for about 1 hour or until tender. Serves 4.

CARROTS: Scrape and slice 4 medium-size carrots. Add 1 tablespoon Beef Stock Base and ½ cup water. Cook over low heat until tender, turning carrots once or twice during cooking. Serves 4.

FROZEN VEGETABLES: (Such as lima beans, green beans, or broccoli.) Stir 2 teaspoons Beef Stock Base into ½ cup water. Place frozen vegetables in saucepan and pour liquid over vegetables. Cover and cook until tender, turning vegetables once or twice during cooking. Serves 4.

CANNED VEGETABLES: (Such as green or yellow beans, carrots, mixed vegetables.) Drain liquid from 1-pound can of vegetables. Add 1 teaspoon Beef Stock Base and 1 teaspoon Instant Minced Onions to liquid. Simmer until liquid is reduced to about ¼ cup. Add vegetables, heat thoroughly. Add 1 tablespoon butter if desired. Serves 4.

Bouquet Garni for Lamb

A BOON TO THE CREATIVE COOK, Bouquet Garni for Lamb enlivens a lamb casserole or stew and is almost magical with lamb roasts or chops. While created to enhance lamb itself, the Garni improves the flavor of such vegetables as onions, potatoes, and carrots cooked in a lamb stew or around a roast lamb. It is good, along with other preferred seasonings, in stuffings for lamb shoulder, crown roast of lamb, or stuffed breast of lamb.

The Garni is excellent in soups made with lamb stock and in sauces and gravies to be served with lamb. Cream sauces, curry sauces, barbecue sauces to be served on or combined with lamb are all good with Bouquet Garni. This herb combination is excellent to use with lamb's liver, heart, and kidneys, and can be used to advantage with some of the game meats such as venison, elk, or rabbit.

As with all herbs and herb blends we suggest using a "light hand." Broiled or roast lamb is best with smaller amounts of Garni. When other seasonings are used, then larger amounts of Garni are desirable. For maximum flavor, crush Garni before adding.

USES

ROAST LAMB: For a 3½ to 4-pound leg or shoulder roast, use ½ teaspoon. Rub into roast with salt, Pepper, Garlic or Curry Powder, Ginger, or other preferred spice before roasting. Baste, if desired, with wine, fruit juice, chicken or lamb stock, or any preferred liquid or sauce. Use drippings for gravy.

LAMB CHOPS: For 4 small loin or rib chops, use ¼ teaspoon. Broil chops in range broiler, portable broiler, heavy frying pan or grill. Season with salt, Pepper, and crushed Bouquet Garni.

LAMB LOAF OR MEAT BALLS: For each pound of ground lamb, use ½ teaspoon. Mix into ground lamb with other ingredients.

LAMB PATTIES OR LAMBURGERS: For each pound of ground lamb, use ½ teaspoon. Broil or pan-fry; sprinkle with Garni just before serving. Or, if preferred, mix Garni with ground lamb, shape into patties or burgers; broil or pan-fry.

LAMB STEW: For each pound of lamb stew meat, use ½ teaspoon.

BRAISED LAMB: For each 4 servings, use ½ teaspoon. For cuts with little or no bone, such as shoulder chops, boned shoulder, or boned breast of lamb, use ½ teaspoon for each pound. For braised neck slices, ribs, shanks, etc., use ½ teaspoon for each 4 servings.

Caraway Seed

CARAWAY SEED is a hardy biennial native to Europe and Asia Minor. It attains a height of approximately 2 feet, and its foliage is similar to that of the carrot to which it is related. Although grown to some extent in the Western Hemisphere, the bulk of the supply comes from the Netherlands.

The use of Caraway was recorded as early as the eighth century. Even then it was considered indispensable in certain breads. Although our modern day cook is familiar with the uses of Caraway in rolls, breads, and biscuits, relatively few have experienced the delightful results of using Caraway in many of our other foods.

USES

CHEESE: Add whole to cottage cheese, rarebits, cheese spreads and dips, cheese straws and wafers.

MEATS, POULTRY: Crush or use whole to season roast pork, pork chops, spareribs, pork sausage, braised or sautéed liver, kidneys. Add to beef, lamb, or oxtail stews. Use in marinades for beef, lamb, veal, and pork.

SALADS: Add whole to coleslaw, sliced cucumbers in vinegar, potato and tomato salads. Crush and use to season salad dressings.

VEGETABLES: Use crushed or whole in red or green cabbage, green beans, carrots, sauerkraut, turnips, onions, potatoes, noodles, rice.

Cardamom

CARDAMOM is a perennial plant of the Ginger family. Native to India, it is extensively cultivated in Malabar, Mangalore, Mysore, and Ceylon. To some extent, it is also produced in tropical America, principally Guatemala.

The Cardamom plant is a graceful one, reaching a height of 8 to 10 feet and is composed of fifteen to twenty shiny, green stems bearing alternate, wide leaves. The leaves resemble those of the flax, popular in western gardens. The flower stalks on which the Cardamom is borne grow from the base of the stem and lie on or close to the ground. The plant begins bearing after the fourth year.

Cardamom, in its whole form, is a plump, three-sided seed pod, and the better quality is creamy white in color and approximately ½ inch in length. The pod contains two clusters of dark brown seeds, with each cluster composed of approximately six seeds.

USES

Whole Cardamom

In its whole form, Cardamom is used to flavor hot fruit punches, pickles, mulled wines, and marinades, and is particularly good in a demitasse.

Ground Cardamom

BREADS: Use 1 teaspoon for 4 servings in Cardamom coffee cake, Cardamom buns, Danish pastries, Swedish coffee breads.

CAKES, COOKIES: Fruitcake, honey cakes and cookies, Norwegian almond cookies, sugar or butter cookies.

DESSERTS: Blend into honey, using ½ teaspoon Cardamom per cup; use to sweeten fruit, whipped cream. Add ¼ teaspoon to other spices for pie fillings, frosting, puddings, coffee-flavored desserts.

MEATS, FISH, POULTRY: Use 1 teaspoon for 4 servings in Swedish meat balls, spareribs, roast pork and ham. Add to barbecue or basting sauces for roast beef, steak, chicken, duck, fish.

Celery Seed

CELERY SEED is the fruit of a plant related to the Parsley family and not to be confused with the plant we recognize and serve as a vegetable, although they are similar in growth habits.

It is native to southern Europe and is now grown extensively in France, Holland, India, and the United States.

For a reason unknown to us, Celery Seed has been relegated to a position of minor importance in the family of Spices. Diligent searching through ancient herbals and cook books has uncovered little to recommend this versatile seed. We can only guess that this neglect is due to its tendency to dominate when used to excess. For best and flavorful results, be light handed in its use.

USES

For both the whole and ground seed (not to be confused with Celery Salt), start with ¼ teaspoon for 4 servings.

Whole Seed

BREADS: Sprinkle on or add to dough for herb breads, rolls, bread sticks.

BUTTERS, SPREADS: Combine with butter or oil and other seasonings; spread on French bread or use to season vegetables, noodles.

HORS D'OEUVRES: Sprinkle on canapés. Mix into dips.

MEATS, FISH, POULTRY: Sprinkle on veal roast. Mix into ground meat for meat loaf, hamburgers. Add to marinades and barbecue sauces for spareribs, roast beef. Add to stock for boiled fresh or corned beef, tongue, chicken. Add to court-bouillons for fish, shrimp, lobster. Use in sauces for fish. Add to stuffings for fish, poultry.

PICKLES, RELISHES: Sweet pickles, vegetable pickles, relishes, mustard pickles, pickled beets, chili sauce.

Ground Seed

EGGS, CHEESE: Cheese sauce, rarebits, dips, scrambled eggs, omelets.

JUICES: Tomato, mixed vegetable, sauerkraut.

SALADS, SALAD DRESSINGS: Tomato aspic, sour cream or cooked salad dressing, mustard dressing for potato salad.

SANDWICH SPREADS: Cream or Cheddar cheese, minced ham, tuna, peanut butter.

SAUCES: Sauces for fish, shellfish, chicken; tomato sauce, cream sauce, cocktail sauce for seafood.

VEGETABLES: Creamed or scalloped potatoes, potato soup, eggplant, casseroles, stuffed tomatoes or peppers, buttered noodles.

Chervil

CHERVIL is a low-growing annual related to the Parsley family. It reaches a maximum height of approximately 8 inches and is an attractive sea-green in color. Its origin is unknown, but it is believed to be native to what is now southern Russia. Chervil has been popular in Europe for many years and is grown extensively in Belgium and several other central European countries.

In America, however, this delicate herb has not attained the popularity it richly deserves. The reason for this is that until recent years, it was not grown domestically in commercial quantities and the small quantities have been of disappointingly poor quality. The finest quality Chervil is now being grown in California and certainly deserves a place on the spice shelf.

USES

Use ¼ teaspoon for each serving.

EGGS: Soufflés, omelets, scrambled eggs.

MEATS: Lamb, veal, pork.

FISH: All fish and shellfish.

SAUCES: Sauce Verte, Vinaigrette, Rémoulade, Béarnaise, Ravigote, Poulette.

Chicken Seasoned Stock Base

CHICKEN SEASONED STOCK BASE is a relative newcomer to the seasoning scene. Its versatility, however, has placed it in a position of prominence.

USES

Aside from its use as a quick, flavorful, and low-caloried broth (12 calories per cup), it is a superb flavor enhancer for:

FRESH AND FROZEN VEGETABLES: Add 2 teaspoons to the vegetables two minutes before they are done.

CANNED VEGETABLES: Drain liquid from 1-lb. can of vegetables. Add 1 teaspoon to the liquid and simmer until reduced to approximately ¼ cup. Add vegetables and heat to boiling.

SAUCES: Use as a seasoning for cream sauces, gravies.

SOUPS: Add to taste.

Chili Con Carne Seasoning

THIS UNIQUE BLEND was developed from the original formula of the Brown Derby restaurant in Hollywood, California. Its characteristic flavor is due to a balanced blend of Cumin, Garlic, Coriander, Oregano, and several varieties of Chili pods, principally the Ancho from Mexico and the Hontaka from Japan.

USES

Use 3 tablespoons to each quart for hot chili con carne, 2 tablespoons to each quart for medium hot chili con carne, 1 tablespoon to each quart for mild chili con carne.

While intended primarily for use in chili con carne, this seasoning blend has a variety of other interesting uses.

CHEESE, EGGS: Add to taste to cheese sauce, cheese dips, rarebits, soufflés, baked or scrambled eggs.

MEATS, POULTRY: Use ½ teaspoon for 4 servings in marinades and basting sauces for pork chops, spareribs, roasts, lamb ribs, beef short ribs, chicken.

SAUCES: Add to taste in cheese sauce for vegetables (such as string beans, potatoes, corn), cocktail sauce for seafood, barbecue sauces, sauces for spaghetti or pizza.

VEGETABLES: Add a dash to corn, rice, kidney, pink or lima beans.

Chili Pequins

CHILI PEQUINS are small, fiery, red peppers of the *Capsicum* family. They range from ¼ to ½ inch in length and their orange-red color well represents their nature — *hot!* They are native to tropical America, and the major source is Mexico.

USES

One half of a Chili Pequin will give heat and flavor to meats, sauces, gravies, vegetables, and stews. Excellent in sauces for enchiladas, tacos, and tostados. One of the more common uses is in pickling liquids for cucumber, vegetable pickles, and relishes.

For an unusual flavor treat, make your own Chili Pequin Sauce:

Combine 1 tablespoon Chili Pequins with 4 ounces brandy or dry sherry. Add 1 teaspoon Garlic Wine Vinegar. Let stand 1 week. Shake each day. Use sparingly on meats, fish, gravies, and sauces.

Cinnamon

CINNAMON was one of the treasured spices during the Middle Ages, and over the centuries its popularity has not diminished. There are many varieties of this fragrant bark (all belong to the Laurel family), but only three are important commercially. They are Ceylon Cinnamon, Saigon Cassia, and Batavia Cassia. Although they belong to the same family of plants, they are botanically dissimilar. This probably accounts for the dissimilarity in names, i.e., cinnamon, cassia.

Through common usage, the name Cinnamon is acceptable in all instances insofar as the layman is concerned. Those engaged in the spice industry, however, continue to identify them by their varietal names.

CEYLON CINNAMON is an evergreen tree reaching a height of approximately 50 feet in its wild state, but the cultivated variety is pruned severely which results in a number of shoots growing from the short main trunk. These shoots are permitted to grow to a height of approximately 8 feet, thus giving the plant the appearance of a shrub rather than a tree.

Harvesting is accomplished by cutting the slender shoots and stripping them of their bark. This is usually done during the rainy season, at which time the greater moisture content facilitates the stripping process. The strips of bark are then scraped inside and out and permitted to become semi-dry, resulting in a quill-like appearance. Next, the small-diameter quills are inserted into progressively larger-diameter quills and dried thoroughly. The finished product is a multi-walled quill approximately ⅝ inch in diameter and 3 feet in length.

This variety of Cinnamon is native to Ceylon, India, and the nearby Malabar Coast. It is somewhat mild in pungency and for this reason is not particularly popular in the United States.

SAIGON CASSIA is native to China and is cultivated in Indo-China. Current trade restrictions restrict the importation of Saigon Cassia into the United States to that produced in South Viet Nam. Harvesting and preparation is similar to that of Ceylon Cinnamon except that the bark is not quilled and the semi-rolled strips seldom exceed 12 inches in length. The major difference is flavor. The warm, bitter-sweet, and aromatic taste of the Saigon is recognized as being the best quality. This is the variety from which the best ground Cinnamon is produced.

BATAVIA CASSIA is native to Indonesia where it is still extensively produced. Flavor-wise it is inferior to that of the Saigon. Harvesting and preparation are similar to that of the other two varieties. It, too, is formed into 3-foot quills, but they are single and double-walled rather than multi-walled as in the Ceylon. The better grades of the Batavia variety are ideal for use as Cinnamon sticks because the quills are straight, firm, and smooth.

USES

Ground Cinnamon

BEVERAGES: Add to taste to hot spiced fruit drinks, hot chocolate, eggnogs, milk shakes, spiced tea or fruit punches, iced coffee.

DESSERTS, PUDDINGS: Add to taste to steamed or plum puddings, custard, fruit, rice or tapioca puddings, or sprinkle on ice cream.

FRUITS: Add to taste to applesauce, baked apples, apple dumplings, cranberry sauce, pickled or spiced fruits, broiled grapefruit, fruit compotes, molded fruit salads.

MEATS, POULTRY: Sprinkle lightly on ham, salt pork, lamb or pork chops. Add a dash to lamb or beef stew, stuffing for goose.

PASTRY: Add 1 teaspoon to pumpkin, apple, peach, cranberry pies, cream or custard pies.

Stick Cinnamon

BEVERAGES: Use to flavor hot tea, coffee, chocolate, Café Brûlot, fruit punches, mulled wine, hot spiced cider or cranberry juice. Use as swizzle stick in hot rum drinks.

FRUITS: Add a whole stick when cooking prunes, apricots, or other dried fruits, spiced or pickled fruits such as peaches, pears, apricots, cranberries, apples.

MEATS: Add a 1-inch piece to stock for boiled beef, smoked pork shoulder, corned beef. Use in court-bouillon for fish, shellfish.

PICKLES, RELISHES: Use in pickled beets, sweet pickles, chutney, watermelon pickles, fruit relishes, catsup.

Cloves

THE CLOVE TREE is a small evergreen from 20 to 40 feet high and native to Indonesia. It begins producing after its sixth year, and throughout the year it bears a succession of beautiful red blossoms.

Although Cloves are now being cultivated in the West Indies, Zanzibar Madagascar, and tropical Africa, at one time they were a closely guarded monopoly of the Dutch. The cultivation was confined to only several small islands in the Spice Islands group.

Cloves, as we know them, are the unopened buds of the Clove tree. They are first white, then green, and finally a bright red. On larger plantations, the harvesting is done by pickers from movable, elevated platforms, while on others it is done by striking the branches of the tree and then gathering the fallen buds. After being harvested, they are spread on grass mats and dried in the sun for 4 or 5 days or until they are dry and brittle. The better quality Cloves can be recognized by their bold size and rich reddish-brown color.

There are three areas where top quality Cloves are produced. In the order of their importance they are, Amboyna, Penang, and Zanzibar. Unfortunately, the Amboyna Clove, which is considered the best, is no longer exported to the United States. Strange as it may seem, the producers of this Clove absorb it in their economy by using it in their smoking tobacco.

USES

Whole Cloves

Remove whole cloves before serving except when using as a garnish.

BEVERAGES: Add to hot or cold fruit punches, mulled wines, spiced cider, cranberry juice.

FRUITS: Add 6 or 8 to syrup while cooking fruit or to syrup of canned fruit. Add while heating water or fruit juice for fruit gelatin; remove before chilling gelatin.

HOME CANNING: Use in making chutney, relishes, spiced marmalades and jellies, watermelon pickles, pickled beets, spiced and pickled fruits.

MEATS, FISH, POULTRY: Add 5 or 6 to marinades and sauces for game, beef, pork, lamb, veal. Add to stock for boiling beef, poultry, corned beef, tongue, ham bone, court-bouillon for fish, shrimp.

Ground Cloves

CAKES, COOKIES: Add to spice, prune, or applesauce cakes, dark fruitcake; spice, oatmeal, honey cookies, raisin or nut bars, gingersnaps, molasses cookies; brown bread, spiced muffins.

HOME CANNING: Add to spiced jam, spiced grape jelly, tomato catsup, mincemeat.

MEATS, FISH, EGGS: Use ¼ teaspoon as seasoning in meat loaf. Add a dash to baked fish, scrambled or creamed eggs. Use in sauce for sautéed sweetbreads.

SAUCES: Use a dash in barbecue, spaghetti, or chili sauces. Add to sauce for lobster, spiced fruit or wine sauce.

VEGETABLES: Use sparingly to season Harvard beets, sweet potatoes, tomatoes.

Coriander Seed

CORIANDER is an annual, native to the Mediterranean region. Due to the extensive cultivation over the centuries, it now grows wild in most parts of Europe. Morocco supplies most of the Coriander imported into the United States.

The appearance of the Coriander plant is similar to that of Anise, both in form and in size. As a matter of fact, they belong to the same family (Parsley). Unlike other aromatics, however, the leaves, stems, and even the unripe seed of the Coriander, have an extremely disagreeable taste and odor. Only after the seed has ripened and dried does it attain an agreeable taste and fragrance.

Coriander could very well be the first spice to be used by mankind. Supposedly it was known as early as 5,000 B.C. We know that it was well known to Moses, as well as to the Jews of 1,500 B.C. The Old Testament described Manna as being "white like Coriander Seed." It is also documented that Coriander Seeds were found in the Egyptian tombs of the Twenty-first Dynasty.

Although extensively used by manufacturers of sausage and variety meats, Coriander Seed has been relegated to a position of minor importance in the American kitchen. This is unfortunate because this fragrant spice can do much to enliven everyday meals.

USES

Use ¼ teaspoon ground Coriander for 4 servings.

BREADS, DESSERTS: Danish pastry, coffee cake, apple pie. Use to flavor tapioca, bread or rice pudding, gingerbread, cookies, custards, frostings.

EGGS: Baked eggs, omelets.

FRUITS: Applesauce, fruit sauces.

MEATS, FISH, POULTRY: Broiled or baked fish, meat balls, meat loaf, beef stew, roast pork, lamb, ham, stuffings for poultry or game.

PICKLES, RELISHES: Sweet pickles, sauerkraut.

SAUCES: Curry sauces, Oriental or Mexican sauces for meats, chicken, fish.

SOUPS: Lentil, pea, bean.

Cumin Seed

CUMIN is a low-growing, ungainly looking annual, native to the Mediterranean area, particularly Egypt. The warm, pleasant, balsamic flavor has been popular since the early Christian era and continues to be a favorite in Chinese, Spanish, and Mexican cookery.

The origin of Cumin pre-dates Biblical times, and with the advent of the Christian era, Cumin assumed religious and medicinal, as well as culinary, importance. It is interesting to note that although it was known and used universally, its culinary uses were somewhat regional. The Dutch and Swiss, for example, used it principally to flavor cheese. The Germans seldom used it in anything but sauerkraut. Hebrews used it principally to flavor their unleavened bread.

Over the years, however, these regional likes and dislikes have established a definite pattern of accepted uses.

USES

Whole Cumin Seed

BREADS: Use in rye bread. Sprinkle on bread sticks or toasted crackers.

COOKIES, PIES: Sprinkle sparingly on sugar cookies. Crush and add 3 or 4 to fruit pies.

MEATS: Add ½ teaspoon, crushed, to marinades and basting sauces for roast pork, pork chops, spareribs, shish kebab. Use in chili con carne, sausage and dishes made with sausage.

PICKLES, RELISHES: Use in making chutney, sweet pickles, vegetable relish.

SAUCES: Crush and add ¼ teaspoon to tomato sauce and sauces for baked or broiled fish.

VEGETABLES: Add a few seeds while cooking to potatoes, dry beans, lentils, beets, carrots.

Ground Cumin Seed

EGGS: Add to taste to Mexican-style baked eggs (Huevos Rancheros), scrambled eggs, omelets, deviled eggs, egg salads.

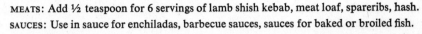

MEATS: Add ½ teaspoon for 6 servings of lamb shish kebab, meat loaf, spareribs, hash.

SAUCES: Use in sauce for enchiladas, barbecue sauces, sauces for baked or broiled fish.

SALAD DRESSING: Add ⅛ teaspoon to 1 cup French dressing or mayonnaise; use for macaroni, chicken, or potato salad.

SOUPS: Add a dash to cream of chicken soup; lobster, shrimp or chestnut bisque; barley, lentil or pea soup.

STEWS, CASSEROLES: Use sparingly in corn pudding, beef stew, veal goulash. Add to taste to chili con carne.

Curry Powder

CURRY POWDER, contrary to the mistaken belief in some quarters, is not one single spice. It actually is a carefully compounded blend of many spices. Curry Powder should not be confused with Curry Leaves which are obtained from a native tree of India. While it is true that these leaves are occasionally used as an ingredient in Curry Powder (in India only) they, in themselves, do not constitute Curry Powder.

There is considerable variation in Curry Powder blends, the compounding of which depends on the preference of the manufacturer. As a general rule, however, a Curry Powder blend will contain six or more of the following items: Cumin, Coriander, Fenugreek, Turmeric, Ginger, Pepper, Dill, Mace, Cardamom, Cloves. As a whole, however, they will all impart the characteristic flavor and aroma of Curry.

Another mistaken belief is that Curry Powder, as a standard blend, is used extensively in India. This is not so. It would be unthinkable there to curry fish, for example, with the same mixture used on lamb. Consequently, the cook prepares her own Curry mixture for each dish.

Although such a practice is commendable, we do not subscribe to it. The preparation of a quality Curry blend not only requires that each ingredient be uniformly ground and sifted, but the final blending operation must be carefully done to insure the uniform color and flavor characteristics of Curry. Generally, these prepared Curry blends will serve their purpose well as is. If desired, additional special flavor overtones can easily be added.

USES

CURRIES: Use 2 teaspoons of Curry Powder for 6 servings for mildly hot Curry, 2 tablespoons for 6 servings for medium hot Curry, and 3 tablespoons for 6 servings for pungently hot Curry.

EGGS, CHEESE: Blend to taste into deviled eggs, egg salad. Slice hard-cooked eggs and add to Curry Sauce.

MEATS, FISH, POULTRY: Add to marinades for lamb, beef, chicken, fish, game. Sprinkle on broiled or baked fish.

SAUCES, BUTTERS: Add ½ teaspoon Curry Powder to 2 cups cream sauce. Blend ½ teaspoon into 4 tablespoons butter; spread on crackers, bread, broiled fish, lamb chops, or use to season cooked vegetables.

Dill Seed

DILL is native to Asia Minor and Europe and can be grown in most of the temperate zones. Most of the Dill Seed used in the United States is imported from India.

It is an annual of the Parsley family and normally attains a height of 3 feet. Under ideal conditions, however, it has been known to attain a height of 6 feet.

Dill Seed is extremely pungent and slightly dominant.

USES

APPETIZERS: Add to cream cheese for dips, spreads. Blend with chopped or deviled ham for canapés, sandwich spreads. Use about ¼ teaspoon per cup of dip or spread.

BUTTERS: Crush 1 teaspoon and blend into 4 tablespoons butter; spread on broiled fish, steak, lamb chops.

MEATS, FISH: Add 1 tablespoon for each quart of stock for boiled beef, lamb, or corned beef, court-bouillon for fish or shellfish. Add ¼ teaspoon to lamb stew.

PICKLES: Combine with Dill Weed and use in recipes calling for dill stalks; use ½ teaspoon Dill Seed and 1 teaspoon Dill Weed to each quart pickling liquid.

VEGETABLES: Add ¼ teaspoon to cooked green beans, cabbage, sauerkraut, summer or winter squash, turnips.

Dill Weed

DILL WEED is the leaf of the Dill plant, which is bright green in color and speckled with yellow blossoms.

Dill Weed is the one herb that reaches its flavoring peak at the bloom stage. To harvest it before or after would result in flavor loss.

The principal difference between Dill Seed and Dill Weed is in the degree of pungency; whereas the seed has a camphorous, slightly bitter taste and fragrance, the Dill Weed has a delightful, delicate bouquet. Its tendency is to enhance rather than to dominate. This characteristic makes it ideal for use in sauces.

USES

Use approximately ½ teaspoon for 4 servings.

SAUCES: Cream, sour cream, butter, fish.

APPETIZERS: Tomato juice, cream cheese spread, pickles and relishes.

FISH: All fish, especially salmon and shrimp.

VEGETABLES: Green beans, squash, beets, turnips, potatoes.

MEATS: Lamb roast, pork roast, boiled beef, spareribs.

SALADS: Vegetable, avocado, cucumber, seafood, coleslaw.

Fennel Seed

FENNEL is a graceful, feathery perennial believed to be indigenous to southern Europe. It may be found growing wild in most areas of the temperate zone;

in fact, its hardy nature has made it somewhat of a pest in vacant lots and along rural roads.

Fennel was well known during the Middle Ages, and the ancient Romans cultivated it extensively for its aromatic seeds as well as its succulent, sweet stalk. One variety, Florence Fennel (Finnochio) continues to be popular with those of Italian extraction. It is eaten much like celery, either cooked or raw. This variety of Fennel is a cultivated annual and seldom grows wild.

Much has been written over the centuries of the curative powers of Fennel. It has been credited, among other things, with preventing witchcraft, giving courage, and improving eyesight.

Culinarily, this fragrant little seed well deserved the high esteem in which it was held. Although somewhat neglected in our modern kitchen, those who use it reap flavor dividends.

USES

MEATS, FISH: Crush ¼ teaspoon and add to meat balls or meat loaf. Mix ½ teaspoon crushed seeds with Lemon Peel and Garlic Powder; rub into pork roast or add to marinades for pork. Crush ⅛ teaspoon and add to sauce or court-bouillon for fish.

PICKLES: Use instead of all or part of Celery Seed in sweet pickles or pickled mushrooms.

SALADS: Add a few whole seeds to macaroni, potato salad. Crush 5 or 6 seeds and add to crab salad.

SAUCES, BUTTERS: Crush 7 or 8 seeds and add to tomato or spaghetti sauces. Crush ¼ teaspoon and blend into 4 tablespoons butter; use to season broiled fish. ,

VEGETABLES: Add ⅛ teaspoon to water when cooking artichokes. Add a few crushed seeds to dry beans or lentils.

Fines Herbes

FINES HERBES is a balanced blend of sweet herbs, each of which has an affinity for the other. It is a traditional blend of French origin.

Although many skilled cooks look with disfavor on the use of pre-blended herbs, such a blend holds a very definite and important position and should not be scorned. Many people, for example, have a prized recipe with which they are particularly successful. Friends and family associate them with this particular dish. It is almost a trademark. Obviously, variations in flavor, texture, appearance, etc., would destroy this illusion. In such a situation, the knowing cook will not risk a possible flavor imbalance by measuring a number of herbs, when, by carefully measuring a pre-determined amount of one blend, she can maintain the continuity of flavor each time the prized recipe is served.

When buying herb or spice blends, look for the uniform particle granulations and blending that is essential to uniform flavor distribution.

USES

Use ½ teaspoon for 4 servings. Crush herbs before adding.

EGGS, CHEESE: Add to omelets, scrambled eggs, cheese sauce, cheese soufflés.

MEATS, FISH, POULTRY: Broiled liver, broiled or braised kidneys, roast pork, pot roast, stews, meat loaf, hamburgers; baked or broiled cod or halibut; broiled chicken; stuffings for fish, poultry, game.

SAUCES, BUTTERS: Add to cream sauce, wine sauce. Use to season gravies and sauces for steaks, chops, roasts.

SOUPS: Use lightly to season asparagus, navy bean, vegetable, and cream soups.

Garlic

GARLIC, a member of the same group of plants as the Onion, is of such antiquity that its area of origin is unknown. With the advent of the dehydrated Garlic on the culinary scene, botanists and agronomists have searched and continue to search every corner of the world in an attempt to find the seed-bearing plant from which Garlic may have originated. The discovery of such a plant would aid immeasurably in the development of improved strains. This is not now possible to any great extent because the Garlic plant does not produce germinating seed and can only be propagated by replanting the clove.

Much was written by the ancients about this robust flavoring. Not all of it was complimentary. Horace detested it mightily and he wrote ". . . is more poisonous than Hemlock," He, as did Shakespeare after him, considered the smell a sign of extreme vulgarity. Both Virgil and Homer, on the other hand, had nothing but praise for this controversial flavor and wrote glowingly of its virtues.

Over the years, Garlic has continued to increase in popularity. The past 15 years, however, have witnessed an unprecedented acceleration in its use. This sudden spurt in usage is undoubtedly attributable to the convenient forms in which Garlic has been made available.

The production of Garlic Powder, Garlic Salt, Garlic Chips, and Garlic Seasoning Powder is an exacting science beginning in the rich, sandy loam of sun-drenched fields and ending with modern, sparkling-clean processing and packaging machinery.

An interesting sidelight to Garlic in a dehydrated form is its flavor enzyme which can only be released by being combined with moisture. This is the reason why your bottle of pure white Garlic Powder doesn't appear to have the pungency you may have expected. Once the dehydrated Garlic is added, the moisture in the food will "trigger" an almost instantaneous flavor release.

Dehydrated Garlic is available to us in many forms. Judging by sales volume the most popular is Garlic Salt. One word of caution, taste before adding additional salt to your recipe.

USES

Garlic Salt

APPETIZERS: Add to taste to canapé mixtures, cheese spreads, dips.

MEATS, FISH, POULTRY: Mix ½ teaspoon into each pound of ground meat for hamburgers, meat balls, meat loaf. Sprinkle to taste on broiled steaks, chops, fish, chicken just before serving.

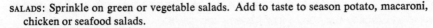

SALADS: Sprinkle on green or vegetable salads. Add to taste to season potato, macaroni, chicken or seafood salads.

SAUCES, GRAVIES: Use to replace all or part of table salt in stews, gravies, barbecue sauces, cream sauce, cheese or tomato sauce.

VEGETABLES: Sprinkle on raw vegetables. Add to butter to season cooked vegetables.

Garlic Powder

Can be used in any recipe calling for garlic. Quantity to be used depends principally on individual taste. For your guidance, ⅛ teaspoon equals 1 average-size garlic clove. When flavoring stews, soups, gravies, sauces and meat dishes, blend the measured quantity of Garlic Powder with a small amount of liquid from the recipe and then add to the recipe. This will give a more instantaneous and uniform distribution of flavor.

When adding Garlic Powder to acid foods, such as relishes, pickles, salad dressings, etc., blend the measured quantities of powder with a small amount of water, then add to recipe. If this is not done, the acid will slow the enzymic activity and the full flavor will not be released.

Garlic Seasoning Powder

A lightly salted seasoning which will not only give a mild garlic flavor but will also enhance natural food flavors. Use it in:

APPETIZERS: Add to taste to dips, canapé mixtures.

MEATS, FISH, POULTRY: Mix into meat loaf, hamburgers, meat balls; use 1 teaspoon for each pound of meat along with other seasonings. Sprinkle on roasts, fried chicken, fish. Sprinkle on meat as it barbecues.

SALAD DRESSINGS: Add 1 teaspoon to 1 cup French dressing or mayonnaise.

SAUCES: Blend 1 teaspoon Garlic Seasoning Powder into 4 tablespoons butter, add ¼ teaspoon Cracked Black Pepper and 1 teaspoon Shredded Parsley; spread on broiled meats, or use to season vegetables. Add Garlic Seasoning Powder to taste to cream sauce, tomato or herb sauce.

Garlic Chips

⅛ teaspoon Garlic Chips equals 1 average-size clove of garlic or ⅛ teaspoon Garlic Powder.

To use in garlic mill: Grind in garlic mill over green salads just before tossing. Grind ¼ teaspoon Garlic Chips and blend into 4 tablespoons butter; spread on French bread or split hard rolls and toast. Grind and use in recipes calling for crushed garlic.

To use Whole Chips: Use Whole Chips to replace chopped or whole cloves of garlic. Use ⅛ teaspoon Garlic Chips in soups, stews, sauces, marinades. Good also in pickling liquids or to insert in lamb or beef roasts before roasting.

Ginger

GINGER is the dried and peeled root of a colorful plant native to tropical Asia. It is now grown extensively in Africa, India, and the West Indies, principally Jamaica. The Jamaica Ginger is recognized as being the finest quality.

The Ginger plant has a perennial, creeping rhizome from which rises solid, somewhat cylindrical stems with alternating lanceolate leaves. Ginger foliage, which in appearance resembles that of a young corn stalk, is annual and dies down every year. Ginger root is harvested immediately after the foliage has

withered. This timing is important because if the root is left in the ground too long, it becomes tough and fibrous.

The best quality ground Ginger can be recognized by its creamy, light buff color, and uniform grind. It must be free of membranous fiber. The fragrance should be rich and extremely pungent. The taste should be clean, hot, and without a resinous aftertaste.

Whole Ginger should be smooth-skinned, light buff in color, and free of discoloration.

USES

Ground Ginger

DESSERTS: Use ½ teaspoon for each cup of flour in making gingerbread, gingersnaps, ginger cookies. Use in steamed puddings. Add a dash to bread or rice pudding.

MEATS, FISH, POULTRY: Add ¼ teaspoon to pot roasts. Rub ½ teaspoon over steak before broiling. Rub on leg of lamb. Add a dash to stuffings for poultry. Sprinkle lightly on fish before broiling or baking.

PICKLES, PRESERVES: Use in relishes, chutney, spiced or pickled fruits, pickled vegetables, jams and jellies, preserves and conserves.

SAUCES: Add to taste to sauces for baked or broiled ham, pork or veal, barbecue or basting sauces for fish. Use in fruit or wine sauce.

VEGETABLES: Add a dash to candied sweet potatoes, glazed carrots or onions, steamed or mashed winter squash.

Whole Ginger

FRUITS, PICKLES: Use ½ piece for each quart of chutney, pickled or spiced fruits, cooked or canned fruit, preserves, conserves.

MEATS, FISH, POULTRY: Split 1-inch piece and add to marinades for chicken or Beef Teriyaki. Soak piece of Whole Ginger in cold water several hours; chop finely and use in recipes calling for fresh Ginger. Grate or shred Whole Ginger; add ½ teaspoon to sauces and marinades. Rub over leg of lamb, in body cavity and on skin of turkey before roasting. Combine ½ teaspoon grated Ginger with salt and Pepper and rub on steak before broiling.

Horseradish

HORSERADISH in its dehydrated, granular form is becoming more and more popular in the American kitchen and has taken its rightful place on the spice shelf. This popularity is understandable. These convenient granules with the locked-in flavor need but a little moisture to turn them into Horseradish equally as good as the fresh product.

The origin of Horseradish is not definitely known. Some authorities place it in what is now Hungary, while others consider it indigenous to the Caspian Sea area. Whatever its origin, we do know that during the Middle Ages it was used universally as a medicine, and about the turn of the fifteenth century it became popular as a condiment.

As to the Horseradish plant itself, it belongs to the Mustard family and is cultivated as a perennial. The plant has a large, parsnip-like, light-colored root noted for its pungency. The foliage is approximately 24 inches high and is characterized by long-stalked, coarse, notched or fringed leaves. The plant occasionally produces seeds which seldom mature. When they do mature, they are generally infertile. Propagation is accomplished through root cuttings or division.

Although Horseradish can be harvested anytime during the year, the better qualities are harvested and processed during the cold months. Horseradish requires frost to "set" the flavor, color, and texture.

In the dehydration of Horseradish all but 6% of the free moisture is removed. To rehydrate Horseradish you need merely to add water. A good rule of thumb is 2 parts of water to 1 part of Horseradish granules. Dehydrated Horseradish, like Garlic and Onion, requires the addition of moisture to trigger the flavor-releasing enzymic activity. It is always good practice to rehydrate the Horseradish before adding to the recipe without regard to the amount of liquid that may be contained in the recipe.

USES

Use rehydrated Horseradish in pickling liquids, sauces for oyster or seafood cocktails, dips and spreads, salad dressings, vegetable and seafood salads, relishes. Add to barbecue sauce for pork, beef, lamb.

HORSERADISH CREAM SAUCE: Moisten 1 tablespoon Horseradish in 2 tablespoons water. Whip ½ cup heavy cream. Stir in Horseradish and ¼ teaspoon salt. Let stand for about 30 minutes for flavor to develop.

Juniper Berries

THE JUNIPER is a small evergreen shrub ranging in height from 5 to 8 feet. It is believed native to southern Europe but now grows extensively in Europe, North Africa, and Asia. Most of the imports into the United States are Hungarian or Italian.

The Juniper Berry requires from 2 to 2½ years to mature, so it is quite common to see dark blue as well as bright green berries on the same plant. Only the ripe, blue berries are picked. These are then spread on drying trays. During the drying process, they acquire the characteristic blackish-blue color. In size and appearance, the Juniper Berry resembles the huckleberry that grows wild in the foothills of Pennsylvania.

Although mentioned in many ancient writings, most references to the Juniper Berry have dealt with its medicinal properties rather than its culinary uses. Apparently, its acceptance in the kitchen is relatively recent.

USES

Use Juniper Berries sparingly. Three to six berries will season 4 servings.

MEATS, POULTRY, GAME: Add to marinades and sauces for wild duck, pheasant, quail, goose, other game birds, venison, elk, bear, other game meat, rabbit. Add to kidney or liver sauté, beef or lamb stew. Crush and rub well into leg of lamb, loin or leg of fresh pork before roasting.

SALADS: Crush 3 or 4 and add to duck, turkey, or chicken salad.

SOUPS: Add 3 or 4 to vegetable, beef, oxtail, or lamb soup.

VEGETABLES: Crush 3 or 4 and add to sauerkraut. Add to casseroles made with dry beans.

Lemon Peel

THE LEMON TREE *(Citrus limonia)* is native to Asia and is known to grow wild in northern India and southeastern Asia.

It is believed to have been introduced into Europe from what is now Iran and Afghanistan. Toward the end of the first century, cultivation of the Lemon was begun in Greece and shortly after that in Italy, Spain, and the north-central seaboard of Africa. The advances in hybridization now make it possible to cultivate the Lemon in practically every part of the world. Commercial cultivation, however, is limited to the warmer climates.

Lemon Peel is the thinly pared outer rind of matured, tree-ripened fruit. A good quality peel is pared very carefully so as not to include an excessive amount of the inner, white, spongy covering which is inodorous and flavorless. After being removed, the peel is then carefully dried and milled.

USES

One teaspoon Lemon Peel equals 1 teaspoon grated fresh peel or ½ teaspoon Lemon Extract.

BREADS: Add to dough for sweet rolls, muffins, tea breads. Combine 1 teaspoon with ¼ cup sugar; sprinkle on sweet rolls, buttered toast, cookies, hot biscuits.

CAKES, COOKIES, DESSERTS: Use 1 teaspoon in cooky recipes, chiffon and angel cakes, sponge cake. Add to taste to custards, bread puddings, sauces and fillings for cake, meringues.

SAUCES, MARINADES: Add ¼ teaspoon to cream sauces and gravies for veal, basting and barbecue sauces for chicken and lamb, glazes for ham, marinades for pot roasts, veal and lamb chops, court-bouillon for fish.

M. S. G.
(Monosodium Glutamate)

THE UNIQUE FLAVOR-ENHANCING properties of M. S. G. were first recognized in Japan at the turn of the century. Subsequently, plants were built in Japan and China. The first commercial M. S. G. was produced in Japan.

M. S. G. is the sodium salt of Glutamic Acid (one of the Amino acids) which is present in virtually all animal and vegetable protein. Although M. S. G. occurs naturally in many of the protein-type foods, its presence is not at sufficient level as to appreciably affect flavor. Sugar beets, corn, and wheat, however, are very high in Glutamic Acid and consequently are the major source material in the manufacture of M. S. G.

Although M. S. G. has only recently achieved popularity (commercial production in the United States began in 1932), conservative estimates place the current consumption at well over twenty-five million pounds per year in the United States alone.

USES

M. S. G. is ideal for use in vegetables, seafood, poultry, and meats. It does not improve or enhance the flavor of dairy foods, fruits, cereals or bakery goods.

POULTRY: ½ teaspoon per pound when stewing for aspics, pies, or fricassées. Rub in same amount before roasting.

MEATS: 1 teaspoon per pound before cooking roast and braised meats, stews, meat loaf, hamburger.

FISH: ½ teaspoon per pound for broiled, fried, sautéed fish.

SAUCES, GRAVIES: ½ teaspoon per cup.

SOUPS, CHOWDERS: ⅛ teaspoon per serving in canned soups.

CREAMED DISHES: 1 teaspoon for each 3 cups.

VEGETABLES: Add ¼ teaspoon to water when cooking fresh, canned, frozen vegetables.

Mace

MACE (see Nutmeg) is the lacy, membranous aril or skin covering the Nutmeg. It is brilliant red in color and turns to a yellowish-orange when dried.

Mace and Nutmeg have the interesting distinction of being separate spices produced from the same fruit of the Nutmeg tree.

In whole form, Mace occurs as flat, branched, irregularly shaped pieces.

USES

Whole Mace

CHEESE: Add a blade while making rarebit; remove before serving.

FRUIT: Add a blade to cooked apples, cherries, applesauce, prunes, apricots, fruit compote, fruit salad.

PICKLES, PRESERVES: Add one blade to each quart of pickles, fruit preserves, spiced fruit, fruit jellies.

SAUCES, MARINADES: Add a blade to marinades and basting sauces for fish, veal, chicken.

Ground Mace

Use ⅛ teaspoon for 6 servings, or add sparingly to taste.

BREADS, CAKES: Add ¼ teaspoon to sweet roll dough, doughnuts. Use in spice cake, fruit cake, popovers. Add a dash to your favorite pancake recipe.

DESSERTS: Add a dash to chocolate pudding, chocolate sauce. Use ⅛ teaspoon in apple, cottage, custard puddings.

FRUITS, VEGETABLES: Add ¼ teaspoon to French dressing for fruit salad. Add a dash to baked apples, applesauce, cooked prunes, apricots. Sprinkle lightly on buttered carrots, cauliflower, squash, Swiss chard, spinach. Add a dash to mashed or creamed potatoes.

MEATS, FISH: Sprinkle sparingly on trout before frying or broiling. Use ¼ teaspoon to season 4 servings veal or lamb chops, sausage, scalloped fish.

Marjoram

MARJORAM, native to Portugal, is a perennial of the Mint family. It is a compact, low-growing shrub from 12 to 18 inches in height. Marjoram grows well in southern France and in other European countries along the Mediterranean, in the Orient, and in California. It is not generally known in the tropical areas of the world.

Although Marjoram has a long and interesting history, culinarily it is a relative newcomer. Only in the past 200 years has it achieved any prominence in the kitchen. Its early history was associated principally with medicine and religious rites.

The cultivation, dehydration, and processing of Marjoram, as is true of the other culinary herbs, is a relatively new facet in American agriculture. The convenient, high quality dried herb on the grocery shelf is due to the skill and imagination of young farmers who chose to discard the traditional and antiquated methods still being practiced in many countries. That they have been successful is attested to by the natural color and full flavor of this aromatic seasoning.

USES

Use lightly for delicious, mellow flavor. Use approximately ½ teaspoon for 4 servings, crushing leaves just before adding.

SOUPS: Spinach, clam bouillon, mock turtle, onion.

SAUCES: Cream, sour cream, brown sauce.

FISH: Broiled, baked, creamed.

EGGS: Omelets, scrambled eggs, soufflés.

VEGETABLES: Mushrooms, carrots, peas, spinach, zucchini.

MEATS: Rub on pork, beef, veal roasts, pot roast before cooking. Add to stuffings.

Meat Tenderizer

AN EFFECTIVE MEAT TENDERIZER contains as its principal constituent Papain, the dried latex (a milky fluid secreted by many plants) of the green Papaya fruit. Papain contains the protein-digesting enzyme which reacts on the fibrous tissue of meat and softens it. It is obtained by scratching the fruit with a sharp instrument. The Papain then exudes and flows into a container, or clots to a pasty mass on the skin of the fruit and is then manually scraped into the container. The latex is always taken while the fruit hangs on the tree. As long as the fruit is green, the plant will continue to replenish the supply of latex. After the latex has been gathered, it is dried, purified, and ground into a fine powder.

Tests have shown that the Papain enzyme works from the surface of the meat inward. For this reason, best results are obtained by distributing the Meat Tenderizer throughout the meat (as by puncturing with a fork).

USES

Use ½ teaspoon to 1 pound of meat. Use no additional salt.

STEAKS, CHOPS, STEWS, LIVER, FISH, FRIED CHICKEN: Sprinkle surface evenly, piercing generously with fork. Leave at room temperature for 30 to 40 minutes for each ½-inch thickness of meat before cooking. (Frozen meat must be thawed first.)

POULTRY, CHICKEN, TURKEY, WILD GAME, ETC.: Rub into cavity; follow above instructions.

ROASTS OF BEEF, LAMB, PORK, VEAL, VENISON: Sprinkle evenly, piercing all sides generously and deeply with cooking fork. Leave at room temperature for 1 hour. Place in cold oven and cook slowly at 300-325°. If treated in advance and refrigerated overnight, start in pre-heated 325° oven.

Mei Yen Seasoning

MEI YEN SEASONING is a blend of seasonings designed to enhance the natural flavor of most foods without introducing flavor overtones of its own.

Mei Yen (free translation from the Chinese is "Delicate Seasoning") has long been a favorite in Oriental cookery. It was first introduced in the Hong Kong market and in recent years has achieved prominence in the American kitchen.

Although originally intended for seasoning vegetables and mild-flavored meats, extensive kitchen use has brought to light the fact that Mei Yen also has an affinity for dishes with acid ingredients, such as tomatoes and wine.

USES

GRAVIES, SAUCES: Use ½ teaspoon for each cup of cream sauce, pan or cream gravy, barbecue sauces and marinades.

MEATS, FISH, POULTRY: Use 1 teaspoon along with other seasonings for 1½ pounds meat. Sprinkle on pot roasts and stew meat while browning. Sprinkle on chicken, fish, steaks, chops before broiling or frying.

SOUPS: Add 2 teaspoons to each quart of chicken or beef bouillon or consommé, chicken or vegetable soup, cream soups, tomato soup.

VEGETABLES: Use 1 teaspoon to each pound of fresh vegetables. Add ½ teaspoon to canned, frozen, or leftover vegetables.

Mint

THERE ARE MANY VARIETIES OF MINT, but only two, Spearmint and Peppermint, are commercially important. Understandably, there is some confusion in the minds of many cooks as to what constitutes the difference between these two varieties.

In comparing the two, one finds that Peppermint is bright green, sharply pungent (almost peppery), and the stems are lightly tinged with purple.

Spearmint is more delicate in fragrance, and its color is a uniform, light grayish green. The Mint found in most gardens is Spearmint.

Mint is a hardy perennial native to the Mediterranean region. It is cultivated extensively in England, France, Germany, Japan, and in our own states of Oregon, Indiana, Washington, and Michigan. Commercial cultivation is principally for its essential oil which is extracted and used as a flavoring in confections, oral medications, and as a scent in toiletries.

Over the centuries, man has held Mint in high esteem. It was important in the cultures of the early Egyptians, Romans, and Greeks as well as to the bandit, nomadic tribes of the northern climates. Aside from the exaggerated curative powers attributed to this fragrant herb by early man, its modern-day uses parallel those of the ancient civilizations. Its use in Mint Sauce is recorded as early as the third century. By the sixth century, it had become important in the crude tooth cleansing preparations of that period. The early Romans not only decorated their dining "boards" with sprigs of Mint, but they also rubbed it into the "boards" prior to setting them. Then, as now, fragrance and aesthetics went hand in hand with relaxed, enjoyable dining.

USES

Peppermint

Use approximately ½ teaspoon for 6 servings, crushing leaves just before adding to dish.

APPETIZERS: Fruit cocktails, fruit juices, cream cheese spreads.

SALADS: Fruit, gelatin.

SAUCES: Mint sauce for lamb or veal.

VEGETABLES: Carrots, potatoes, peas, zucchini.

DESSERTS: Mint ice. Add 1½ teaspoons crushed mint to plain white loaf cake batter.

BEVERAGES: Hot and iced tea, hot chocolate, juleps.

Spearmint

Use approximately ½ teaspoon for 6 servings, crushing leaves just before adding to dish.

SALADS: Fruit, gelatin, coleslaw.

VEGETABLES: Carrots, peas, potatoes, cabbage, zucchini.

MEATS: Sauces for lamb and veal.

FRUIT: Cocktails, pears, applesauce, melons. Mix into syrups for fruits.

DESSERTS: Ices, gelatin, fruits, frostings.

BEVERAGES: Sprinkle in fruit punch, tea, wine, chocolate.

Mushrooms

MUCH HAS BEEN WRITTEN about Mushrooms. Their history, use, culture, and superstitions have been the subject of many volumes. Although extensively covered over the years, one aspect of the subject has been somewhat neglected —that is the use of Powdered Mushrooms as a seasoning. In a broad sense and aside from the technical aspects, the Mushroom is a vegetable and is so treated in most kitchens. As a seasoning (in powdered form) it has the essential capacity for accentuating desirable flavors and suppressing undesirable flavors without overly masking the identity of the food. It must be used judiciously, however, for it tends to be dominant.

USES

Substitute 1 tablespoon Powdered Mushrooms for 3 tablespoons whole dried Mushrooms. Substitute 1 tablespoon Powdered Mushrooms for 4 ounces fresh or 2 ounces canned Mushrooms for flavor in soups, gravies, sauces, stews.

MEATS, FISH, POULTRY: Use 1 tablespoon for 4 servings. Add to stews, goulashes, ragouts, meat loaf, hash, liver or kidney sauté. Use in meat, chicken, or fish croquettes, and in casseroles of meat, fish, poultry.

SAUCES: Use 1 teaspoon for each cup of mushroom sauce, cream sauce, gravies, spaghetti or pizza sauce.

SOUPS: Use 1 tablespoon for each quart of mushroom soup made with stock, or cream of mushroom soup, vegetable soup, oyster stew.

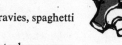

Mustard

THERE ARE NUMEROUS VARIETIES OF MUSTARD SEED of which two are in most common use. Black Mustard (*Brassica nigra*) is native to Europe and southwest Asia. The seed is yellowish-brown in color and has a very pungent and acrid taste. White or yellow Mustard Seed *(Brassica alba)* is native to Europe. It is pale yellow in color and less pungent and acrid than the black variety.

The plant is a hardy annual which grows well in practically every part of the temperate zone. It re-seeds itself very readily and as a result is somewhat of a weed pest. Legend has it that when the Padres were establishing their famous Mission Trail in California, they planted Mustard Seed along the way. On their return trip the trail was marked by the conspicuous Mustard plants.

The recorded use of Mustard as a condiment and a medicine goes back to the year 75 A.D. It is interesting to note that over the years, even to the present time, the use of Mustard for medicinal purposes has kept pace with its growing popularity as a seasoning. In the year 1663, a well-known doctor by the name of Nicholas Culpepper, had this to say about Mustard:

". . . Let such whose stomach are so weak they cannot digest their meat, or appetite it, take of Mustard Seed a dram, Cinnamon as much, and having beaten them to a powder, and with Gum Arabic dissolved in Rosewater, make it up into traches, of which they may take one of about half a dram weight an hour or two before meals." While we cannot vouch for the results of this recipe, it does reflect the high esteem in which Mustard and other spices were held by our ancestors.

Dry Mustards, whether hot or mild, are blended from a number of varieties of Mustard Seeds. Blending, as is true of coffee, is necessary to achieve full flavor and desirable characteristics. The degree of "heat" in Mustard is derived from the particular seed varieties used as well as the portion of the seed used. Generally speaking, the portion of the seed immediately under the skin or hull is "hotter" than the portion at the center.

USES

Whole Mustard Seed

APPETIZERS: Crush and add to dips for chilled shrimp, lobster tails.

MEATS, FISH: Add a tablespoon to liquid for pickled or spiced meats, shrimp. Add to stock for boiled beef, corned beef.

PICKLES: Use according to recipe in cucumber pickles, vegetable relishes, chutney, green tomato pickles, mustard pickles, pickled onions.

SALADS, SALAD DRESSINGS: Add 1 teaspoon to coleslaw. Sprinkle over salad greens and toss lightly. Add to mixed vegetable salad or potato salad. Add ½ teaspoon to French dressing.

VEGETABLES: Add 1 teaspoon to cooked cabbage or sauerkraut. Sprinkle lightly over buttered beets. Sprinkle on creamed vegetables.

Hot Mustard

CASSEROLES: Add ½ teaspoon to macaroni and cheese. Use ¼ teaspoon in casseroles of ham, turkey, eggs, seafood. Add to soufflés, baked beans, crusts for meat pies, croquettes.

MEATS, FISH, POULTRY: Add 1 teaspoon to glaze or sauce for baked ham or fresh pork. Combine with equal amount of olive oil; spread over steak before broiling. Add to taste to stews, pot roasts, deviled crab, coating mixture for fried chicken.

SALADS, SALAD DRESSINGS: Add ¼ teaspoon to French dressing. Add to taste to potato, tuna, macaroni, seafood salads.

SAUCES: Use to make mustard sauce for ham, corned beef, cold cuts. Add ¼ teaspoon to gravies, cream sauce, Newburg sauce, cheese sauce.

VEGETABLES: Add ¼ teaspoon to buttered or creamed asparagus, broccoli, Brussels sprouts, cabbage, celery, green beans, pickled beets.

Mild Mustard

MEATS, FISH, POULTRY: Sprinkle lightly on fish before broiling or frying. Add ½ teaspoon to fine crumbs for breading meats, fish. Add ½ teaspoon to coating mixture for fried chicken, Swiss steak, beef stew.

SALADS, SALAD DRESSINGS: Add ½ teaspoon when making French dressing, cooked salad dressing, mayonnaise. Add to taste to vinegar and sugar dressing for coleslaw. Add ¼ teaspoon to prepared mayonnaise dressing for meat, seafood, potato, macaroni, chicken salads.

SAUCES, BUTTERS: Add ⅛ teaspoon to raisin sauce for ham, cream sauce for creamed meat, fish, vegetables.

VEGETABLES: Add ¼ teaspoon to scalloped potatoes or potatoes au gratin. Mix with butter and lemon juice to taste; use on steamed cabbage, Brussels sprouts, asparagus, broccoli.

Nutmeg

THE NUTMEG TREE is an attractive evergreen native to the Spice Islands. It attains a height of approximately 30 feet and its foliage is, in many respects, similar to the Rhododendron. Aside from its native habitat, it is cultivated in the West Indies, principally Grenada.

The Nutmeg tree is a prolific producer. After it reaches maturity (approximately 8 years) it bears almost continuously for 50 years or more. In its native region, the tree produces 3 crops per year. The ripe fruit, which is intermingled with the flowers, resembles an apricot in size and color. Harvesting is accomplished by means of long, hooked poles which are used to break the fruit loose from the branches. After the fruit is gathered, the outer husk is stripped and discarded. The stripping is carefully done so as not to destroy the Mace which clothes the Nutmeg nut. After the Mace has been carefully removed for drying, the Nutmeg nut is also dried. The drying is done by spreading in the sun or over charcoal fires. After drying is completed, the nut is cracked, thus exposing the kernel which we know and recognize as Whole Nutmeg.

USES

Whole Nutmeg

One whole Nutmeg makes approximately 3 teaspoons grated Nutmeg. Use in Nutmeg grater or grate on kitchen grater.

BEVERAGES: Just before serving, grate over eggnog, milk shakes, milk punch, hot rum drinks.

CAKES: Add ½ teaspoon to spice cake or fruit cake. Grate generously over fruit for upside-down cake or fillings for coffee cake.

FRUITS: Grate over applesauce, baked apples, fruit compotes. Grate 1 to 2 whole Nutmegs and add to home-made mincemeat.

PASTRIES, PUDDINGS: Grate generously over fillings for apple, peach, pear or plum pies, rice pudding, baked custard. Add ½ teaspoon to soft custards, cream fillings, date or nut fillings for pie, meringue, pumpkin or sweet potato pie.

Ground Nutmeg

BEVERAGES: Sprinkle on milk shakes, eggnog, hot lemonade, hot spiced drinks, hot chocolate.

BREADS: Add ½ teaspoon to doughnut or fritter batter. Add to mixture for French toast.

CAKES, PIES, DESSERTS: Use ½ teaspoon in spice cakes, cookies, steamed puddings, custards. Add ¼ teaspoon to whipped cream. Sprinkle lightly over ice cream, rice pudding.

MEATS, FISH, POULTRY: Mix ¼ teaspoon into Swedish meat balls, meat loaf, cream sauce for chicken, seafood, or veal. Add a dash to toppings for meat or chicken pie, stuffing for baked fish, fish croquettes. Sprinkle lightly on broiled chicken, baked or broiled fish.

Old Hickory Smoked Salt

THE MANUFACTURE OF OLD HICKORY SMOKED SALT is a patented process by which Hickory wood smoke is fused to pure table salt.

The process involves the charring of Hickory wood in the form of small chips. The resultant smoke is passed through a series of cleansing baths which remove objectionable tars. The smoke is then passed through a long (30-foot), narrow, revolving cylinder mounted on an inclined plane and equipped with a high-voltage apparatus. As the smoke-borne microscopic particles travel through the electrical field they are given a positive (+) charge. Thus charged they are attracted to the negative (−) pole or metal sides of the cylinder.

Simultaneous to the entry of the smoke into the cylinder, pure salt is also fed into the cylinder in a calibrated flow. As the salt enters the cylinder, it acquires a negative (−) charge and fuses with the smoke solids.

This fusion of pure salt and true Hickory smoke imparts a sweet, fragrant, smoky flavor without the objectionable, acrid after-taste of synthetic preparations.

USES

EGG DISHES: Add 1 teaspoon to 4 eggs for omelets or scrambled eggs. Sprinkle lightly on fried, poached, or soft-cooked eggs. Use to season deviled eggs.

SANDWICHES: Add to taste to egg, tuna, or chicken salad spreads. Sprinkle on sliced turkey, chicken, or roast meat fillings.

SOUPS: Add to taste to split pea, bean, lentil, vegetable soups, or fish chowder.

MEATS, FISH: Mix 1 teaspoon with 1 pound ground beef for hamburgers. Add to taste to breaded pork or veal chops, sweetbreads, fried oysters, fish filets. Sprinkle on spareribs, roasts, steaks.

SAUCES: Add to taste to cream sauce, barbecue sauce, or marinade.

Onions

THE ORIGIN OF THE ONION is not definitely known, but it is believed to be native to central Asia. It has been, and continues to be, cultivated extensively in practically every part of the world.

Over the centuries, the Onion has retained its seed identity. This has been most fortunate for it has permitted geneticists to develop and improve specific strains for specific purposes.

These special seed strains, particularly adapted to the West, have made possible the convenient, high quality, dehydrated Onion products such as Onion Powder, Onion Salt, Instant Minced Onions, and Instant Toasted Onions.

In producing dehydrated Onion products, quality control actually starts in the field. Before the Onions are permitted to be sacked, preparatory to being hauled to the processing plant, they must pass stringent inspection on portable tables. When the Onions reach the processing plant, they are carefully graded according to size. This operation insures that only sound, fully matured Onions go into manufacturing.

From the graders, the Onions are passed through a flame peeling device which removes the membranous skin without injuring the Onion itself. After being peeled, they are rooted, topped, and thoroughly washed. Prior to drying, the Onions are sliced mechanically with rotary razor-sharp knives.

After they have been dried, the Onions are again inspected on conveyor belts. The inspected and approved material is then conveyed to the milling and screening equipment.

The great advantage in using dehydrated Onion products is the constant, uniform flavor. This, plus the convenience in using and storing, undoubtedly accounts for the popularity of these products.

USES

Onion Powder

One tablespoon equals 1 medium-size onion. Blend Onion Powder with small amount of liquid from recipe, then add to soups, stews, gravies, sauces, meat dishes. Blend Onion Powder in small amount of water before adding to such acid foods as relishes, pickles, salad dressings.

Onion Salt

Use in place of all or part of table salt where onion flavor is desired.

MEATS, FISH, POULTRY: Use 1 teaspoon for each pound of ground meat for hamburgers, meat loaf. Add 1 teaspoon to coating for fried chicken. Add to taste to season oven roasts, steaks, chops. Use ½ teaspoon per pound of meat or chicken in pot roasts, stews, meat or chicken pies.

SALADS, SALAD DRESSINGS: Add 1 teaspoon per cup of French dressing. Use to season molded seafood or chicken salads. Add to potato, chicken, or turkey salads.

SAUCES: Add to taste to cream sauce or gravy.

VEGETABLES: Add to taste to cooked vegetables.

Instant Minced Onions

One tablespoon of Instant Minced Onions soaked in 1 tablespoon of water for 5 minutes will equal 1 medium-size onion, chopped. Use to flavor soups, salads, meat dishes, sauces, gravies, stuffings, cocktail canapés, relishes, omelets. Use wherever minced onions are called for in recipes.

Instant Toasted Onions

Instant Toasted Onions have the mild flavor of sautéed onions but with a crisp crunchy texture. Use them without rehydrating.

DIPS: Stir into sour cream, cream creese, cottage cheese, avocado dips.

EGGS: Add to scrambled eggs, omelets, sauces for baked eggs or creamed hard-cooked eggs.

SALADS: Add to tossed green salads, coleslaw, potato, cooked vegetable, seafood salads.

SAUCES: Add 2 tablespoons to 1½-2 cups cream sauce, or canned mushroom, celery, or chicken soup thinned with milk. Combine sauce with cooked vegetables, leftover meat or fish. Use as sauce for croquettes, cutlets, broiled or fried fish, poultry, meat.

CASSEROLES: Add to casseroles, or use as topping.

Orange Peel

THE ORIGIN AND HISTORY OF THE ORANGE, as well as the processing of the Peel, parallels, in many respects, that of the Lemon (see Lemon Peel).

Early Arabic writings lend credence to the opinion of most researchers that man's first Orange was small, bitter, and to our taste, unpalatable. Over the centuries, hybridization by both man and nature has resulted in the delectable Sweet Orange in all its varieties. From one these varieties comes the dried, versatile Orange Peel.

The so-called Bitter Orange, however, is still very much in evidence. From its rind is extracted an excellent Oil of Orange, and for this reason it continues to be cultivated in most Orange-producing areas, particularly southern Italy, Sicily, and southern France.

USES

One tablespoon Orange Peel equals 1 tablespoon fresh grated peel. Two teaspoons Orange Peel equal 1 teaspoon Orange Extract.

BREADS: Add 1 teaspoon to muffin batter, dough or fillings for coffee cake, sweet rolls or bread, date or nut bread, shortcake.

CAKES, DESSERTS: Add to fruit, spice, cheese cakes. Add to puddings.

MEATS, POULTRY: Add ¼ teaspoon to glazes, marinades for pork, ham, lamb chops, chicken, or duck. Add to stuffings for poultry, pork.

VEGETABLES: Use 1 teaspoon in candied sweet potatoes, glazed carrots, baked squash, rice pilaff.

Oregano

OREGANO is a perennial of the Mint family and believed to be native to the Mediterranean region. It is closely related to Marjoram—indeed it is often called "Wild Marjoram." Botanically it is known as *Origanum vulgare*. According to ancient herbals, the name Origanum is derived from two Greek words: "Oros" (mountain) and "Ganos" (joy). Supposedly this is in allusion to the jolly appearance of the plant, an attractive shrub, growing on the hillsides.

There are two strains of Oregano available. One is common to the Mediterranean region, the other is common to Mexico. The Mediterranean strain is rather delicate in fragrance and taste, while the Mexican strain is quite pungent.

Although Oregano has been known and used since the early days of ancient Rome, until twenty-five years ago the American kitchen chose to ignore it. Once it received recognition, however, it leap-frogged into popularity.

USES

Use ⅛ teaspoon for 6 servings, crushing leaves before adding.

SALADS: Aux Fines Herbes Salad Dressing, tomato salad.

SAUCES: Spaghetti, meat, barbecue.

VEGETABLES: Zucchini, eggplant, tomatoes.

MEATS: Hamburgers, meat loaves, stews, stuffings.

Paprika

PAPRIKA is the ground, dried pod of a variety of *Capsicum*. Its growth habits are similar to those of the Bell Pepper to which it is closely related. Paprika is native to Central America where it was found by the early Spanish and Portuguese explorers. It is now grown extensively in central and southern Europe as well as in the rich valleys of Southern California.

The bulk of the Paprika consumed in the United States (well over 8,000,-000 pounds per year) is imported from Spain. However, within the past 20 years, a domestic variety produced in California has met with ever-increasing acceptance.

Of all the spices, Paprika is perhaps the most misunderstood. Many of us think of Paprika as a garnish rather than a seasoning. However, aside from its aesthetic value, its "go with almost anything" flavor makes it an ideal food enhancer.

USES

Use as a garnish or seasoning. Dust generously on creamed meat, fish, and vegetables. Just before serving sprinkle on crumb-topped casseroles, baked potatoes, canapés and hors d'oeuvres, soups.

APPETIZERS: Mix into cheese mixtures and pâtés.

MEATS, FISH, POULTRY: Add ¼ teaspoon per pound ground meat for meat loaf or meat balls. Use generously in dipping mixture for fried chicken, fish, pork chops, veal cutlets.

SALAD DRESSINGS: Add ¼ teaspoon per cup to French dressing, cooked salad dressing, sour cream dressing.

SAUCES, BUTTERS: Add to cream sauce or gravies to serve with meats or vegetables.

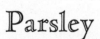

Parsley

PARSLEY is a low-growing biennial belonging to the celery family. The nativity of this popular herb is rather obscure, but it was definitely known as early as the third century, B.C. It is interesting to note that in early times Parsley was cultivated when celery was still in a wild state. So in contrast to celery, Parsley has a deep and definite ancient history as a food. Both the ancient

Greeks and Romans used Parsley generously as a flavoring and a garnish. A little reading into this subject has brought to light the fact that both the curled and plain types of this herb have been in common use since the first century but did not find a general acceptance in Europe until the thirteenth century. It is generally agreed that Parsley was introduced in England in 1548. The first plants came from the Island of Sardinia; later, in the seventeenth century, the colonists brought it to America.

There has been considerable controversy regarding the difference, if any, between the wild and cultivated Parsley. There are those who believe the wild would grow like the cultivated if it were sown in rows, fertilized, and given the technical supervision that is now given to the cultivated plant. Quite to the contrary is the fact, for regardless of how carefully the wild plants are cared for, they will still be wild plants. It is true, they may grow somewhat larger and give greater yields than they would without the added attention, but if the seeds are replanted each year, only wild plants will result. The cultivated variety is a result of many generations of planned selections by growers. The original appearance, good values, and uses of Parsley many years ago were definitely different from their counterparts of today. Present leaves are larger and the stems are smaller. The leaves are also richer in natural vitamin potency and mineral values.

There are many problems involved in the production of dehydrated Parsley, not the least of which is the fact that 50% of the weight of Parsley as it comes from the field is made up of stems which are discarded before the Parsley is dried. After drying, there is an additional stem loss of 20%. It requires 12 pounds of de-stemmed fresh Parsley to make one pound of the dried product.

Healthwise Parsley is a very valuable herb. It is very high in Vitamins A and C. It also contains iron, iodine, manganese, and copper.

USES

MEATS, FISH, POULTRY: Add to basting or barbecue sauces for broiled or fried fish, roast or broiled poultry, roasts, steaks, chops. Use in stuffings for fish, poultry, meats.

SALADS, SALAD DRESSINGS: Add to tossed green salad, molded vegetable salads, coleslaw, potato salads. Use in Green Goddess, French, or Thousand Island dressings.

SAUCES, BUTTERS: Use in herb sauces and butters, Italian-style tomato and meat sauces, sour cream, tartar, green sauces.

SOUPS: Add ½ teaspoon to minestrone, vegetable, beef or chicken broth.

Pepper

PEPPER is the berry of a perennial vine which attains a height of from 8 to 12 feet and is native to the East Indies. Both Black Pepper and White Pepper are produced on the same vine. Black Pepper is picked when slightly underripe and then dried in the sun or over charcoal fires. During the drying process, it attains the characteristic black, wrinkled appearance. White Pepper, on the other hand, is picked when fully ripened. It, too, is dried and becomes black and wrinkled (when fully ripened it actually is dark red in color). Then the outer hull is removed by attrition, thus exposing the creamy-white core which we know and recognize as White Pepper. White Pepper is less pungent than the black and is more popular in Europe than in the United States.

Pepper is now cultivated extensively in tropical and sub-tropical countries, particularly India, British Malaya, Java, Sumatra, Borneo, and in recent years equatorial Brazil.

It is believed that Pepper was first found and recognized growing wild on the Malabar Coast of India. Undoubtedly, it was there that it was first cultivated. Its cultivation spread from the Malabar Coast to Java, where Marco Polo saw it in the thirteenth century, and to Sumatra in the fourteenth century, probably brought by either Hindus or Moslems. Its introduction into the Malayan region was accomplished by the Portuguese during the sixteenth century.

Pepper, perhaps more than any other spice, had the strongest influence in the Age of Discovery. Columbus, Magellan, Vasco de Gama, and the other explorers of their period sought Pepper as avidly as any other treasure. Indeed, Pepper was literally worth its weight in gold.

Columbus first thought he had reached his goal when he found small dark berries similar to Peppercorns growing in the West Indies. They turned out to be Allspice and to this day this spice is known as "pimento" (meaning Pepper).

Included in the amazing diary of Pepper — a history that covers over 5,000 years — is a fascinating chapter in American history. Early in the Spring of 1797, a small American schooner with the imposing name of "Rajah" sailed into the Port of New York. As her cargo, she carried 75 tons of Black Pepper. Although her captain would not divulge where he had been, word soon leaked out that the voyage had been extremely successful and the cargo most profitable — the profit on the Pepper cargo was estimated at 700%.

In the 50 years following the successful voyage of the "Rajah," America's Pepper trade with the Far East did much to establish a strong Merchant Marine for our fledgling nation. Hundreds of fast schooners were built just

for the Pepper trade alone, and they brought back millions of pounds of this coveted spice. More than $5,000,000 in Pepper duties was added to the United States Treasury.

There is no doubt that Pepper has been, and continues to be, the spice shelf favorite.

USES

Whole Black Peppercorns

For use in Pepper grinder. Grind and sprinkle over food to season and garnish wherever freshly ground Pepper is desired.

MEATS, FISH, POULTRY: Add 3 or 4 whole Peppercorns to court-bouillon for fish, boiled beef, tongue, corned beef, stewed chicken, stews, pot roasts, spiced shrimp, pickled pigs' feet, spiced or pickled meats. Crush and add to marinades, basting and barbecue sauces for beef, lamb, and poultry.

PICKLES: Add 4 or 5 whole Peppercorns to each quart of dill or sour, sweet or mixed pickles.

SOUPS: Add 4 or 5 whole Peppercorns to chicken or beef stock, oxtail, vegetable, bean or split pea soups.

Cracked Black Pepper

Cracked Black Pepper is crushed and screened for full flavor. Sprinkle to taste just before serving on eggs, meat, fish, poultry, salads, cheese dishes, hors d'oeuvres, vegetables, all creamed foods.

Use ⅛ teaspoon or season to taste: French dressing, marinades, basting and barbecue sauces for roasts and steaks, soups, salads, sauces for meats, eggs, fish, poultry, vegetables.

Medium Grind Black Pepper

Use in Pepper shaker for table or kitchen use. Sprinkle to taste just before serving on eggs, meat, fish, poultry, salads, cheese dishes, hors d'oeuvres, vegetables, creamed foods.

Sprinkle before or during cooking on roasts, steaks, chops, broiled or fried chicken, fish, hamburgers, stews.

Use ⅛ teaspoon or season to taste: Salad dressings, marinades, basting and barbecue sauces for roasts, steaks, fish and poultry. Add to meat, fish and poultry dishes, sauces, stuffings for poultry and meats, egg and cheese dishes, vegetables.

Fine Grind Black Pepper

Use in Pepper shaker for table or kitchen use. Just before serving sprinkle to taste on eggs, meat, fish, poultry, salads, cheese dishes, vegetables, creamed foods.

Sprinkle before or during cooking on roasts, steaks, chops, hamburgers, poultry, fish, stews.

Whole White Peppercorns

For use in Pepper grinder. Use on light-colored foods such as cream sauces, clear or cream soups, mashed potatoes, sliced cold turkey and chicken, roast meats, fish.

PICKLING, SPICING: Add to pickled fruits, light-colored vegetables such as onions, cauliflower, mushrooms, celery. Add to pickled meats and seafood, such as veal, pigs' feet, oysters, or shrimp.

SOUPS, COURT-BOUILLONS: Add 5 or 6 whole Peppercorns to chicken, fish and cream soups, bisques, court-bouillon for fish.

Ground White Pepper

Use in Pepper shaker for table or kitchen use. Use as a seasoning interchangeably with Ground Black Pepper. Especially good in light-colored foods where Black Pepper might detract from the appearance of the food, such as white or light cream sauces, clear or light cream soups, mashed potatoes, creamed white vegetables, chicken, fish or veal stock, court-bouillon for fish, poached or steamed white fish, cream cheese dips, spreads.

Cayenne Pepper

CAYENNE is not related in any way to the true Pepper vine. It is, in fact, of the *Capsicum* family and as such is closely related to Paprika, Chili Pequins, and Bell Peppers.

It is native to Central America and was first introduced into Europe by Columbus. From Europe, its cultivation spread to the Near East, Africa, and the Orient. It is now being cultivated extensively in Africa, Japan, Louisiana, California, and Mexico.

The Cayenne pod ranges in size from 1 to 3 inches in length and from ½ to 1 inch across at its base. Its orange to bright-red color well represents its fiery character. Cayenne should be used with care and restraint.

USES

Use sparingly (1/16 teaspoon or less) in:

APPETIZERS: Dips, spreads, sauces for seafood appetizers, chilled tomato or vegetable juices.

EGGS, CHEESE: Deviled eggs, omelets, cheese soufflés, scrambled eggs.

MEATS, FISH, POULTRY: Pot roasts, stews; broiled, baked, or roast meats; broiled, baked, or fried fish and chicken.

PICKLING, SPICING: Use according to specific recipe in pickled or spiced meats, fish, vegetables, catsup, chili sauce, chutney.

VEGETABLES: Corn pudding; baked, stuffed or fried potatoes; fried eggplant, creamed onions, cooked tomatoes.

SAUCES: Combine with Paprika and herbs and butter for a pungent sauce. Add to barbecue and basting sauces, tomato sauce, sauces for game, fish, cream sauces, Hollandaise sauce.

Poppy Seed

THE POPPY FAMILY is believed native to southwestern Asia. Its many subspecies have adapted themselves in one form or another to practically every part of the world.

Two varieties of this colorful plant have achieved prominence in the fields of food and medicine. Of culinary importance is *Papaver Rhoeas* from which we obtain the tasty, nut-like flavored Poppy Seed. The other is *Papaver somniferum,* the principal source of opium.

Poppy Seed, which incidentally does not have any narcotic properties, has a long history of cultivation dating back several thousand years B.C. As early as the year 1500 B.C., the Egyptians were cultivating it as a source of cooking oil. Ancient monastery writings record the cultivation and use of Poppy Seed as a food and flavoring adjunct.

Commercial production of Poppy Seed is now centered in Holland, Poland, and Iran, with lesser quantities being produced in Turkey and Argentina. The best quality comes from Holland and can be recognized by its uniform slate-blue color.

USES

BREADS: Sprinkle lightly over yeast breads or rolls before baking. Combine ¼ cup with candied or dried fruits for filling for coffee cakes.

CAKES, COOKIES: Sprinkle lightly over cake batter or cooky dough before baking.

CHEESE, EGGS: Toast and add 1 tablespoon to scrambled eggs, cheese sauce and rarebits, cream cheese spreads.

SALADS: Sprinkle lightly over fruit salad. Toast 1 tablespoon and add to vegetable or tossed green salads.

VEGETABLES: Brown 2 tablespoons in butter and stir into cooked noodles or rice. Use to season carrots, celery root, turnips, peas, spinach, cauliflower, potatoes.

Rosemary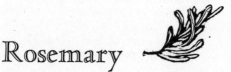

THE ROSEMARY PLANT is an attractive perennial of the Mint family and native to the Mediterranean area. Commercially it is produced in Spain, Portugal, France, and California.

Commercial cultivation of Rosemary in California is relatively new, having been begun by Spice Islands in 1943. This domestically produced product can be recognized by its green, bold leaf as well as by its strong pungency, free of any resinous overtones.

As is true of so many herbs and spices, the history of Rosemary dates so far back into antiquity that it is very difficult to determine just when it first received recognition. We do know that by the year 500, it had already achieved a position of importance in the herbals, cook books, and kitchens of that period.

Interestingly enough, one of the popular uses of Rosemary during that period was in the form of a simple wine sauce. It was prepared by boiling together 1 part of crushed Rosemary leaves and 3 parts of wine. Although it is not clear as to how it was used, we suspect that the primary purpose of the sauce was to mask the flavor of "over-ripe" meats. No doubt the idea of the sauce originated from the practice of using Rosemary as a wine preservative. In an early herbal, we read: "Take the leaves (Rosemary) and put them into wine and it shall keep the wine from all sourness and evil savours and if thou wilt sell thy wine thou shalt have goode speede."

While we do not recommend either of the above practices, the wine and Rosemary combination is still very much in "style," particularly in marinades.

USES

Use ¼ teaspoon for 4 servings. Crush leaves before adding to dish.

SOUPS: Split pea, minestrone.

FISH: Salmon, stuffing for all fish.

BREADS: Cornbread, biscuits, dumplings.

VEGETABLES: Add to liquid when cooking potatoes, green beans, peas, spinach, chard, zucchini, pickles, cucumbers.

POULTRY: Partridge, capon, duck, rabbit, chicken; stuffings for poultry.

MEATS: Lamb, beef, and veal roasts; beef stew, ham loaf.

FRUITS: Compotes, punches, jellies.

Saffron

SAFFRON is obtained from the dried stigmas of a fall-flowering Crocus believed native to Spain, where most, and the best, of the world's Saffron supply continues to be produced. The Saffron plant, related to the Iris, is somewhat bulbous in appearance and seldom exceeds 6 inches in height. Its delicate, light purple blossom bears the scarlet-yellow stigmas which must be picked by hand. The stigmas resemble pieces of colored string, about ¾ inches long. Approximately 225,000, stigmas are required to make 1 pound of Saffron. Is it any wonder, then, that it always has been, and continues to be, the world's most expensive spice? Fortunately, only minute quantities are required for the average recipe.

Because of its beautiful golden color, Saffron supposedly was associated with royalty, great wealth, and the higher stratas of early society. We suspect that the association was not so much social tradition as it was simple economics — only the wealthy could afford it.

Saffron is not to be confused with Safflower (an annual that grows to 2 to 3 feet and is thistle-like in appearance). The two plants are not related and they have but one thing in common — both were used as dyes prior to the advent of the fast dyes now available.

When used in proper amounts and with foods for which it has an affinity, Saffron will impart a pleasant, distinctive "old world" flavor.

It should be measured carefully and recommended amounts should not be exceeded. If too much is used, it will impart a most unpleasant, medicinal flavor.

USES

Use 1/32 teaspoon or less for 6 to 8 servings. To measure this amount, fill a ¼ teaspoon measuring spoon. With a sharp knife, push half the Saffron from spoon. Cut the remaining half in two and push half of the Saffron back into the envelope. Again bisect the remaining 1/16 teaspoon. The amount left in spoon is 1/32 teaspoon. (Not too difficult to do, for Saffron packs down firmly into spoon.) Use to season or flavor:

BREADS: Saffron buns, sweet breads with fruit and nuts, dumplings.

FISH: Bouillabaise, fish stews and soups, butter and wine sauces for fish.

RICE: Saffron rice, Risotto Milanese, casserole dishes with rice.

CHICKEN: Arroz con Pollo, Chicken and Rice Valenciana, chicken recipes from Mediterranean and South American cuisine.

MEATS: Veal fricassee, veal sauté.

SAUCES: Sauces for meats, fish, fowl, and vegetables typical of Mediterranean and Latin countries.

 # Sage

OF ALL THE HERBS, SAGE is undoubtedly the most commonly known. The popularity that it has maintained over the centuries is well deserved. There are few foods, indeed, that cannot be enhanced by the judicious use of this ancient and traditional herb.

Sage is native to south-central Europe where most of the world's supply is still produced. In the United States, it is cultivated commercially in California, Oregon, and Washington from seed and plants introduced from Dalmatia, Yugoslavia. Although there are over 400 varieties of Sage, only one, *Salvia officinalis,* is recognized as being of the best quality for use as a food adjunct. The common Sagebrush growing so profusely in the western and southwestern United States bears no culinary relationship to *Salvia officinalis*.

The uses of Sage are so many, varied, and traditional as to make a selection extremely difficult. In spite of the many developments in foods and their preparation, many of the uses for Sage parallel those of the ancients. For example, Sage's affinity for pork was recognized hundreds of years ago, as illustrated by the following recipe taken from "Ancient Cookery," published in 1790:

"Take pork and seeth (boil) it well and grinde it smale (small) and medle (mingle) it with ayren (eggs) and ygrated (grated) brede (bread). Do thereto salt sprinkle and Saffron. Take a close litull (little) ball of it in foiles (leaves) of Sawge (Sage). Wet it with a bator (batter) of ayren (eggs), fry and serve forth."

You will note that ancient recipes were anything but clear as to directions and quantities. Apparently much was left to the imagination and originality of the cook.

USES

Use approximately ¼ teaspoon for 4 servings.

SOUPS: Cream soup and chowder.

FISH: Add a dash to melted butter for basting broiled fish.

STUFFINGS: Meat roasts, pork chops, baked fish, poultry.

DUMPLINGS: A dash of Sage will add interest.

VEGETABLES: Add to liquid when cooking lima beans, eggplant, onions, tomatoes.

MEATS: Rub lightly on pork, veal, lamb before roasting. Use in sausage, meat loaves, meat stews.

Salad Herbs

OVER THE CENTURIES salads and herbs have gone hand in hand. Indeed, early man often used the herbs themselves as his salad greens. Lovage, Borage, Chervil, Basil, Marjoram, Burnet, and even Violet leaves found their way into the salad bowls of ancient gourmets. An account written in the year 1500 records that the royal salad bowl of England included 35 roots and herbs, including the humble carrot and parsnip.

Many of the salad herbs known to our forefathers have since vanished from the culinary scene. In their place we have new varieties of crisp, green vegetables and fruits. These, too, need to be "dressed" with the mouth-watering fragrance and sprightly flavor that only herbs can impart.

Of the herbs that have an affinity for salads, three seem to stand out. They are Tarragon, Basil, and Thyme. In combining these three into a balanced, all-purpose blend, Spice Islands has added an unusual and distinctive touch by replacing the Common Thyme with a commercially exclusive herb — Lemon Thyme. This herb, in addition to its Thyme characteristics, also imparts a delightful, lemony fragrance. Spice Islands maintains the only major commercial planting of Lemon Thyme in the world and uses it exclusively as an ingredient in Salad Herbs.

USES

Use approximately ½ teaspoon for 4 servings, crushing leaves just before adding to dish.

APPETIZERS: Fruit cup, vegetable, tomato juices, seafood cocktail sauce, garnish for chicken broth.

SALADS: All.

BROILED FISH: Garnish before serving.

MEATS: Meat loaves, pot roasts, meat stews.

Savory

THERE ARE TWO DISTINCT VARIETIES OF SAVORY — Summer Savory and Winter Savory. Their names, however, have no relationship to the time of year they are produced.

Summer Savory is a bushy annual that attains a height of up to 2 feet. Its flavor and aroma are somewhat more delicate and much less resinous than those of Winter Savory. For that reason, it is more generally preferred. Winter

Savory, on the other hand, is a perennial and because of its sharp, resinous character has not attained popularity.

Savory is native to southern Europe, and its use and cultivation were recorded before the first century. Over the centuries, it has received frequent and favorable mention by contemporary writers. The accounts of early American colonists record the culinary and medicinal uses of Savory. Of particular interest is the fact that the ancient Romans used Savory as a flavoring for vinegar used in the salad courses of their religious and political feasts.

Principal cultivation is now in California, France, and Spain.

USES

Use approximately ¼ teaspoon for 4 servings, crushing leaves just before adding to dish.
SOUPS: Fish, consommé, lentil, bean.
SALADS: Mixed green, vegetable, potato.
FISH: Use as garnish, or add to court-bouillon.
SAUCES: Horseradish, fish sauces.
STUFFINGS: Pork, chicken, turkey.
VEGETABLES: Green beans, peas, sauerkraut, rice, lentils, zucchini, cauliflower.
POULTRY: Chicken, turkey.
MEATS: Meat loaves, hamburgers, pork or veal roasts.

Sesame Seed

SESAME, also known as Benne, is the seed of a sturdy annual which attains a height of approximately 2 feet. It is native to south-central Asia and is now cultivated extensively in China, Africa, India, South and Central America, and in the southwestern United States.

Sesame Seed does not lend itself readily to any of the categories in the family of spices. It lacks the aromatic qualities of its cousins and its claim to distinction is in its sweet, "nutty" flavor. What it lacks in glamour, however, is more than compensated for by its versatility. Aside from its common uses in appetizers, breads, meats, and vegetables, this easily cultivated seed yields a fine cooking oil which has been, and continues to be, an important diet item in many parts of the world.

USES

Use untoasted, or toast briefly in heavy frying pan.
APPETIZERS: Sprinkle toasted seed over canapés. Add to cheese dips and spreads.
BREADS: Sprinkle generously on bread, rolls, biscuits, and scones before baking.
MEATS, FISH, POULTRY: Sprinkle on fish before broiling or baking, or on chicken before roasting. Add 2 tablespoons to coating for fried chicken or fish. Add to stuffing for roast chicken or turkey. Mix 2 teaspoons into 1 pound ground beef for hamburgers or meat balls.
VEGETABLES: Toast in oil or butter and add to cooked cabbage, spinach, green beans, carrots, noodles, rice, boiled potatoes.

Shredded Green Onions

SHREDDED GREEN ONIONS are produced from the young, tender tops of a special strain of spring Onions. Although new to the spice shelf, this product is becoming increasingly more popular. This popularity is undoubtedly due to its similarity to Chives in both flavor and color. As a matter of fact, Shredded Green Onions and Chives are very closely related.

USES

Use approximately ½ teaspoon for 4 servings.

APPETIZERS: Cream cheese and sour cream dips, garnish for canapés.

SALADS: Mixed green, tomato, vegetable.

SAUCES: Cream, meat, gravies, butter, tomato.

STUFFINGS: Vegetable, meat, fish.

FISH: Sprinkle on lightly before serving.

VEGETABLES: Green beans, peas, potatoes, carrots, tomatoes.

MEATS: Beef, lamb, kidneys, steaks, chops, roasts, scallopini.

Spice Parisienne

SPICE PARISIENNE is a unique blend of spices and herbs patterned after a continental formula which has long been a favorite of European and Scandinavian chefs.

Its distinctive flavoring properties, serve as an unusual change from Pepper alone, with which it is both interchangeable and complementary.

USES

Use sparingly to taste or ¼ teaspoon for 4 servings.

APPETIZERS: Add ⅛ teaspoon to dips and dunks or canapé mixtures, cheese spreads, seafood mixtures.

MEATS, FISH, POULTRY: Add to sauce for broiled or sautéed chicken, fish, or chops. Use as a seasoning for goulash, Stroganoff, sauerbraten, meat balls, meat soups, grilled meats, variety meats.

VEGETABLES: Add to mushroom sauce, cream or cheese sauce for peas, spinach, whole onions, broccoli. Use to season macaroni or noodles, spaghetti sauce.

Tarragon

LITTLE IS KNOWN about the nativity and origin of Tarragon. It is believed that it is native to Siberia and from there was introduced into central and eastern Europe. The move from the cold northern climate to the relatively warmer climate of Europe apparently resulted in a more pungent strain. That being produced in Europe (principally France) is of a superior quality to that produced in Russia. Although Tarragon can be grown in most parts of the United States, commercial production is centered in California. Spice Islands currently maintains the largest acreage of Tarragon in the United States.

The Tarragon plant, an attractive bright-green perennial, attains a height of approximately 18 inches. It does not produce fertile seed and consequently must be propagated by root division.

USES

Use ¼ teaspoon for 4 servings.

SALADS: Chicken, seafood, mixed green, fruit.

FISH: Salmon, lobster thermidor, crab, tuna.

SAUCES: Tartar, Béarnaise, egg, mushroom, fish.

EGGS: Omelets, deviled or scrambled eggs.

MEATS: Veal, lamb, sweetbreads, chicken.

Tea

THE TEA PLANT is a perennial evergreen shrub related to the Camellia, which it resembles in appearance and growth habits. Under cultivation, it is kept pruned to a height of 3 to 4 feet.

The original home of all Tea is said to be a small range of mountains known as the "Bohea Hills" located in southern China. However, some Tea experts believe that certain species of the plant are indigenous to India and Japan. In any event, the bulk of the world's supply of Tea is now produced in India, Ceylon, Indonesia, Japan, and Formosa. In recent years, Africa has become increasingly more active in the production of Tea.

Although there are many varieties of Tea, there are but four basic types: Black, Green, Semi-fermented (Oolong), and Scented. However, regardless of the type or variety, *all* Tea can be produced from the leaf of the same plant. It is true, of course, that because of soil and climatic conditions, as well as "know-how," some areas produce better grades and quality of one type than of another type.

The characteristic difference in the four basic varieties is the degree of fermentation to which each is subjected:

BLACK TEA is produced by inducing full fermentation of the fresh leaf. This accounts for the color and flavor. The better quality is consistently produced in Ceylon and India.

GREEN TEA is the dried leaf without any fermentation. It thus retains its natural green color and delicate flavor. The better quality comes from Japan.

OOLONG TEA is produced by subjecting the fresh leaf to partial fermentation. Prime quality is produced in Formosa.

SCENTED TEA is a semi-fermented leaf to which is added the blossom of a fragrant flower. The most popular scents are Jasmine, Orange, and Rose. Better quality comes from Formosa.

Thyme

THYME is the leaf of a bushy, low-growing (approximately 1 foot in height) perennial native to southern Europe. It belongs to the Mint family. The principal producing areas are California and France.

There are many varieties of Thyme, but only two are commercially important. They are the narrow leaf or French Thyme and the variegated or Lemon Thyme. The French Thyme is a tiny leaf about ⅛ inch in width. It is gray-green in color and pungently balsamic in fragrance. A good quality Thyme should be relatively free of brown leaf and woody stem. The Lemon Thyme is characterized by its fragrant, lemony aroma and is an essential ingredient in Salad Herbs. Spice Islands maintains the only major planting of Lemon Thyme in the world.

Although Thyme was well known to early civilization, apparently it was not culinarily important and was used principally to flavor certain cheeses, a practice which is still being followed in some areas of Scandinavia. The Thyme blossom has always been a favorite of the honey bee, and the Thyme Honey of ancient Greece was noted for its sweetness and flavor. An early English writer once wrote: "Thyme, for the time it lasteth, yieldeth most and best honie and therefore in old time was accounted chief."

USES

Use approximately ⅛ teaspoon for 6 servings, crushing leaves just before adding to dish.

APPETIZERS: Tomato juice, clam juice, seafood cocktails.

SOUPS: Gumbo, borscht, clam chowder, pea, vegetable.

SALADS: Tomato, aspics.

FISH: Sprinkle lightly on broiled, baked, fried fish.

SAUCES: Creole, Espagnole; herb bouquets for sauces.

VEGETABLES: Onions, carrots, beets.

POULTRY: Stuffings, fricassee, roast chicken and turkey.

Turmeric

TURMERIC is the rhizome or root of a plant belonging to the Ginger family. Unlike Ginger, with its aromatic fragrance, Turmeric is somewhat medicinal in aroma and should be used with restraint.

The plant is native to China and Indonesia and is also being produced in India, Haiti, and Jamaica. It is generally agreed that the best Turmeric is produced in Allepy, India.

During Biblical times, Turmeric was used not only as a flavoring but as a perfume and dye as well. Although the use of Turmeric dates back to Biblical times, it has not attained an important role in the average kitchen. It is used principally in commercial preparation of Mustard, Curry Powder, and certain pickles.

USES

EGGS: Add to cream sauce for eggs. Sprinkle on scrambled eggs.

MEATS, FISH, POULTRY: Add ¼ teaspoon to basting sauces and marinades for broiled chicken, salmon, lobster, shrimp. Add ⅛ teaspoon to curried lamb or beef.

PICKLES, RELISHES: Use according to specific recipe in bread and butter pickles, mustard pickles, chow chow, chutney, corn relish.

SALAD DRESSINGS: Use ½ teaspoon per cup in dressings for seafood salads. Use ¼ teaspoon for color in mustard sauces and dressings.

SOUPS: Add a dash to color cream soups and chowders.

Vanilla Beans

IN THE FRAGRANT FAMILY OF SPICES, none is more fragrant or exotic than Vanilla—the exquisite fruit of a delicate orchid.

The Vanilla Bean, which, when extracted or "percolated" with alcohol and water produces Vanilla extract, is native to tropical America, particularly Mexico. Although it is now being produced in Madagascar, Islands of Reunion and Comores, Tahiti and Java, the finest quality continues to be produced in Mexico.

The Vanilla vine is an epiphyte, a plant that draws a substantial portion of its sustenance from the air. It is generally planted immediately adjacent to a young sapling which ultimately serves as a living support for the vine. To facilitate harvesting, the vine is kept carefully pruned so that it does not grow beyond the reach of the workers.

The Vanilla blossom is a delicate, pale yellow orchid which is formed in clusters of 12 or more blossoms. Although it may take 5 or 6 weeks for the buds to open, once they do, the blossom is relatively short-lived, often lasting but a single day. The fruit or Vanilla Bean is, in many respects, similar to the familiar string bean, both in appearance and growth habit.

The amazing diary of Vanilla dates back to long before the Aztec reign; Vanilla was already being cultivated during Montezuma's rule. To the rest of the world, however, the diary is opened to the year 1560. It was then that the Spanish adventurer, Hernando Cortez, discovered this exotic flavoring in the palace of Montezuma.

While being received at court, Cortez was served a delectable beverage which Montezuma called "Xoco-Latl." The beverage was made from the powdered bean of the cocoa tree flavored with what the Aztecs called "Thil-xochitl," meaning black pod. The Spaniards later named this black pod *Vainilla,* meaning "little scabbard."

The acceptance of Vanilla by the Europeans was instantaneous and clamorous because this exciting new flavor did much to enliven the monotonous fare of that period. So, for over three centuries, Mexico enjoyed a lucrative monopoly in the Vanilla trade. This monopoly did not go unnoticed by the European powers. England, France, Spain, and Portugal attempted time after time to establish the cultivation of Vanilla in their own tropical and subtropical colonies. They studied the methods of the Aztecs, duplicated climatic and soil conditions, but to no avail. The Vanilla vine would not produce anywhere except in its own native land.

It was not until the year 1835 or 1836 that a French botanist, after years of research, discovered that the reason was biological—the vanilla blossom was not being pollinated, thus could not reproduce. He further learned that in its native land Vanilla was pollinated by a tiny little bee named *Melipona.* This tiny member of the bee family was the only one that could traverse the complex structure of the Vanilla blossom and accomplish the important function of pollination. Lacking this functional insect, the curious botanist did the next best thing—artificial pollination. His efforts met with success and he, Charles Morren, became the first man to produce the coveted Vanilla pod outside of Mexico. As a result of Morren's discovery and research, France to this day produces over 75% of the world's supply of Vanilla Beans.

But the story does not end there. When fully matured, and harvested, the Vanilla Bean is green in color, completely odorless and flavorless. How, then, is the fragrant chocolate-colored bean that we know and recognize produced?

The process is man-induced fermentation. During this process, the beans are alternately sun-heated and covered with woolen blankets to induce fermentation or "sweating." This cycle of heating and covering is repeated over and over (every day for several weeks) until the beans are of a dark chocolate, almost black, color. Simultaneously to the change in color, the chemistry changes induced by fermentation result in the characteristic fragrance and flavor.

The entire process of curing and drying requires almost 6 months of careful and skillful labor.

USES

For flavoring ice cream, fruit sauces, cakes, custards, puddings. For 1 quart custard or pudding, split a 2-inch piece of Vanilla pod, scrape out seeds, and scald seeds and pod with milk. Put a 2-inch split piece in your sugar bowl for delicious flavor.

TABLE OF EQUIVALENTS

For the cook who is temporarily out of a particular seasoning ingredient, and for the cook who wishes to substitute Spice Islands products for other products called for in recipes, here is a convenient guide to equivalents.

ARROWROOT

1 teaspoon	1 tablespoon flour
1 tablespoon	3 tablespoons flour
2 teaspoons	1 tablespoon cornstarch
1 tablespoon	1 tablespoon flour plus 1 teaspoon cornstarch

BAY LEAF

¼ teaspoon CRACKED	1 WHOLE BAY LEAF

BEEF STOCK BASE

4 teaspoons dissolved in 1¼ cups water	1 can (10½ oz.) condensed, undiluted beef bouillon or consommé
4 teaspoons dissolved in 2½ cups water	1 can (10½ oz.) condensed beef bouillon or consommé diluted with 1 can water
2 teaspoons	1 beef bouillon cube
1 teaspoon	1 teaspoon beef extract

BELL PEPPERS (GREEN)

1 tablespoon, rehydrated	3 tablespoons chopped fresh green pepper

BELL PEPPERS (RED)

1 tablespoon, rehydrated	3 tablespoons chopped fresh red pepper
1 tablespoon, rehydrated	2 tablespoons chopped pimiento

BEAU MONDE SEASONING

1 teaspoon	1 teaspoon seasoning or seasoned salt
1 teaspoon	½ teaspoon table salt
1 teaspoon	1 teaspoon MEI YEN SEASONING

Bouillon (see BEEF STOCK BASE or CHICKEN SEASONED STOCK BASE)

CHICKEN SEASONED STOCK BASE

1½ teaspoons	1 chicken bouillon cube
1 tablespoon dissolved in 1 cup water	1 cup canned or homemade chicken broth or stock

Chives (see ONIONS, SHREDDED GREEN)
Consommé (see BEEF STOCK BASE or CHICKEN SEASONED STOCK BASE)
Cornstarch (see ARROWROOT)
Flour (see ARROWROOT)

GARLIC CHIPS

⅛ teaspoon	1 medium-size clove garlic
⅛ teaspoon, ground or crushed	⅛ teaspoon GARLIC POWDER

GARLIC POWDER

⅛ teaspoon	1 medium-size clove garlic
⅛ teaspoon	⅛ teaspoon ground or crushed GARLIC CHIPS

GINGER

1 teaspoon WHOLE (soak in cold water for several hours, then chop finely or grate)	2 teaspoons chopped fresh ginger
2 teaspoons CRYSTALLIZED, chopped or slivered (wash sugar from ginger or leave on if flavor is compatible)	1 teaspoon chopped fresh ginger
¼ teaspoon GROUND	1 teaspoon chopped fresh ginger
¼ teaspoon GROUND	2 teaspoons chopped CRYSTALLIZED GINGER

HORSERADISH

1 tablespoon, rehydrated in 1 tablespoon water and mixed with 1 tablespoon vinegar and sugar and salt to taste — 2 tablespoons bottled prepared horseradish

LEMON PEEL

1 teaspoon — 1 teaspoon grated fresh lemon peel
1 teaspoon — Grated peel of 1 medium-size lemon
1 teaspoon — ½ teaspoon lemon extract

MEI YEN SEASONING

1 teaspoon — 1 teaspoon BEAU MONDE SEASONING
1 teaspoon — ½ teaspoon table salt

Mint (see PEPPERMINT or SPEARMINT)

MUSHROOMS (POWDERED)

1 tablespoon — 3 tablespoons whole dried mushrooms
1 tablespoon — 4 oz. fresh or 2 oz. canned mushrooms for flavor in soups, gravies, sauces, stews

MUSTARD

1 teaspoon MILD — 1 tablespoon mild prepared mustard in sauces, salad dressings, marinades
1 teaspoon HOT — 1 tablespoon hot prepared mustard in sauces, salad dressings, marinades

ONION POWDER

1 tablespoon, rehydrated — 1 medium-size onion, chopped
1 tablespoon, rehydrated — 4 tablespoons chopped onions

ONIONS (INSTANT MINCED)

1 tablespoon, rehydrated — 1 small onion, chopped
1 tablespoon, rehydrated — 2 tablespoons chopped onions
1 tablespoon, without rehydrating — 1 tablespoon INSTANT TOASTED ONIONS

ONIONS (INSTANT TOASTED)

1 tablespoon — 1 tablespoon INSTANT MINCED ONIONS
As casserole topping or in salads — Use instead of French-fried onions

ONIONS (SHREDDED GREEN)

½ teaspoon — 2 teaspoons finely chopped chives
½ teaspoon — 2 teaspoons finely chopped green onion tops

ORANGE PEEL

1 tablespoon — 1 tablespoon grated fresh orange peel
1 tablespoon — Grated peel of 1 medium-size orange
2 teaspoons — 1 teaspoon orange extract

PARSLEY

1 teaspoon — 3 teaspoons chopped fresh parsley

PEPPER

CAYENNE — NEPAL PEPPER (equal amount)

PEPPERMINT

1 tablespoon — ¼ cup chopped fresh mint

Pimiento (see RED BELL PEPPERS)

SPAGHETTI SAUCE SEASONING

1 tablespoon — 2 tablespoons packaged spaghetti sauce mix
2 tablespoons — 1 package (1½ oz.) spaghetti sauce mix

SPEARMINT

1 tablespoon — ¼ cup chopped fresh mint

VANILLA BEANS

1-inch piece, split and simmered in part of the milk or water called for in recipe — 1 teaspoon vanilla extract or flavoring
1-inch piece — 1 teaspoon pure vanilla extract

HERB CHART

	BASIL	BAY LEAVES	CHERVIL	DILL WEED	MARJORAM	OREGANO
Appetizers	Cheese Spreads Seafood 　Cocktails Tomato Juice	Court Bouillon 　for Shrimps 　and Prawns Pickles	Avocado Dip Butters Canapés Cheese Dips 　and Spreads	Cheese Dips 　and Spreads Pickles Seafood 　Cocktails Seafood Spreads Stuffed Eggs	Butters Cheese Dips 　and Spreads Liver Patés Mushrooms	Avocado Dip Cheese Spread Mushrooms Pizza Canapés Tomato Juice
Soups and Chowders	Chowders Minestrone Pea Spinach Tomato Vegetable	Bean Beef Stock Bouillabaisse Bouillon Corn Oxtail	Chicken or 　Beef Stock Vegetable Garnish for all 　Soups	Bean Borsch Chicken Chowders Pea Tomato	Chicken Noodle Clam Broth Onion Oyster Stew Spinach Tomato	Bean Minestrone Mushroom Onion Tomato Vegetable
Salads	Chicken Cucumber Fruit Mixed Green Seafood Tomato	Aspics Marinade for 　Beef and 　Onion	Beet Cole Slaw Cucumber Fruit Mixed Green Tomato	Beet Cole Slaw Cucumber Potato Seafood Vegetable	Asparagus Chicken Fruit Mixed Green Seafood	Avocado Bean Mixed Green Potato Seafood Tomato
Fish and Shellfish	Crab Halibut Mackerel Salmon Shrimps Tuna	Court Bouillon 　for Lobster, 　Shrimps Poached 　Halibut 　Salmon	Court Bouillon Garnish or 　Seasoning for 　all Seafoods	Halibut Salmon Shrimps Sole	Clams Creamed 　Crab 　Tuna Halibut Salmon	Clams Creamed 　Crab Lobster Shrimps
Poultry and Game	Chicken Duck Rabbit Turkey Venison	Fricasseed 　Chicken Rabbit	Garnish or 　Seasoning for 　all Poultry 　and Game Stuffings	Chicken Pie Creamed 　Chicken	Chicken Duck Goose Rabbit Turkey Venison	Chicken Guinea Hen Pheasant Stuffings
Meats	Beef Lamb Liver Pork Sausage Veal	Pot Roast Shish Kebab Stews Tongue Tripe	Stews Ground Meats Garnish for 　Steaks, Chops	Beef Corned Beef Lamb Pork Sweetbreads Veal	Beef Pork Pot Roast Sausage Stews Veal	Ground Beef Lamb Liver Sausage Stews Veal
Sauces	Butter Orange for 　Game Spaghetti Spanish Tomato	Barbecue Curry Spaghetti Spanish Sour Cream Tomato	Barbecue Butter Cream Spaghetti Sour Cream Tartar	Cream for Fish Tartar	Brown Cream Spanish Sour Cream Tomato	Barbecue Brown Mushroom Spaghetti Spanish Tomato
Eggs and Cheese	Cheese Soufflé Cream Cheeses Omelets Rarebits Scrambled Eggs		Cream Cheeses Deviled Eggs Omelets Rarebits Soufflés	Cottage Cheese Omelets Scrambled Eggs	Omelets Rarebits Scrambled Eggs Soufflés	Boiled Eggs Cheese Soufflé Omelets Rarebits Scrambled Egg
Vegetables	Beans Eggplant Onions Peas Squash Tomatoes	Beets Carrots Potatoes Stewed 　Tomatoes	Beets Eggplant Peas Potatoes Spinach Tomatoes	Beans Beets Cabbage Celery Parsnips Potatoes	Brussels Sprouts Carrots Onions Peas Spinach Zucchini	Broccoli Cabbage Lentils Mushrooms Onions Tomatoes
Desserts and Beverages	Fruit Compotes	Cooked 　Cream Sauces Custards			Fruit Juices Fruit Punches	

PARSLEY	PEPPERMINT	ROSEMARY	SAFFRON	SAGE	SUMMER SAVORY	TARRAGON	THYME
Avocado Dip Butters Canapés Cheese Dips and Spreads	Cranberry Juice Garnish for Fruit Cups, Melon Balls, etc.	Fruit Cup Pickles	Saffron Butter	Sharp Cheese Spreads	Cheese Spreads Liver Patés Stuffed Eggs Tomato Juice Vegetable Juice	Cheese Spreads Liver Patés Seafood Cocktails Seafood Spreads Stuffed Eggs Tomato Juice	Liver Patés Sauerkraut Juice Seafood Cocktails Seafood Spreads
Chicken or Beef Stock Vegetable Garnish for all Soups	Bean Pea	Chicken Chowders Pea Potato Spinach Turtle	Bouillabaisse Chicken Turkey	Chicken Minestrone Pea Potato Tomato Vegetable	Bean Chicken Chowders Lentil Pea Vegetable	Bean Chicken Mushroom Pea Tomato	Borsch Clam Chowder Consommé Gumbo Pea Vegetable
Fruit Mixed Green Potato Seafood Vegetable	Fruit Aspics Celery Cole Slaw Fruit Mixed Greens Waldorf	Fruit	Chicken Seafood		Bean Mixed Green Potato Tomato Vegetable	Chicken Cole Slaw Egg Fruit Mixed Green Seafood	Aspics Beet Chicken Cole Slaw Tomato
Court Bouillon Garnish for Seasoning for all Seafoods	Garnish for Broiled Shrimps and Prawns	Poached Halibut Salmon Broiled Salmon	Baked Halibut Sole	Baked Halibut Sole Poached Salmon	Broiled Halibut Shrimp Sole Crab Salmon	Baked Salmon Crab Halibut Lobster Shrimps Sole	Cod Crab Creamed Tuna Halibut Scallops Sole
Garnish or Seasoning for all Poultry and Game Stuffings	Garnish for Poultry	Capon Duck Fricasseed Chicken Quail Rabbit	Creamed Chicken Turkey Rabbit	Chicken Duck Goose Rabbit Turkey Stuffings	Chicken Duck Squab Turkey Venison Stuffings	Chicken Duck Goose Squab Turkey	Chicken Duck Pheasant Quail Turkey Stuffings
Stews Ground Meats Garnish for Steaks, Chops	Hamburger Lamb Stew Roast Lamb Veal	Beef Ham Loaf Lamb Pork Stews Veal	Lamb Curry Veal	Beef Lamb Pork Sausage Stews	Kidneys Lamb Shanks Meat Loaf Pot Roast Spareribs Veal Cutlets	Lamb Pork Chops Pot Roast Stews Sweetbreads Veal	Beef Lamb Pork Veal Variety Meats
Barbecue Butter Cream Spaghetti Sour Cream Tartar	Cranberry Currant-Mint Mint	Barbecue Brown Butter Cream Spanish Tomato	Cream for Fish Curry	Brown Butter Cheese for Eggs	Butter for Fish, Steak Horseradish	Béarnaise Mustard Sour Cream Tartar Vinaigrette	Creole Curry Mustard Spaghetti Spanish Tomato
Cream Cheeses Deviled Eggs Omelets Rarebits Soufflés	Cream Cheese	Deviled Eggs Scrambled Eggs Soufflés	Cream Cheese Scrambled Eggs	Cottage Cheese Creamed Eggs Soufflés	Deviled Eggs Omelets Scrambled Eggs Soufflés	Cottage Cheese Deviled Eggs Omelets Scrambled Eggs	Cottage Cheese Deviled Eggs Omelets Shirred Eggs Soufflés
Carrots Potatoes Tomatoes Garnish for all Vegetables	Carrots Peas Potatoes Spinach Zucchini	Cauliflower Cucumber Mushrooms Peas Potatoes Spinach	Rice Squash Zucchini	Carrots Eggplant Lima Beans Onions Peas Tomatoes	Artichokes Asparagus Beans Lentils Rice Sauerkraut	Cauliflower Celery Root Mushrooms Potatoes Spinach Tomatoes	Asparagus Beans Beets Carrots Onions Zucchini
	Frostings Frozen Desserts Fruit Compotes Fruit Juices Tea Wine Punch	Fruit Compotes Fruit Punch Wine Coolers	Cake Frostings Fruit Compotes Fruit Juices Sweet Buns	Hot Milk Tea	Stewed Pears		Custards Fruit Compotes

AROMATIC SEED CHART

	ANISE	CARAWAY	CARDAMON	CELERY	CORIANDER
Appetizers	Crackers*	Liptauer* Corn Crisps*	Fruit Cup**	Corn Crisps* Canapes* Crackers*	
Soups	Cabbage Cream	Clam Chowder Cabbage*	Pea**	Celery* Any*	Pea** Almond**
Bread and Rolls	Coffee Cake* Tea Sandwiches Bread*	Rye Bread* Roll Topping*	Danish Pastry** Buns** Coffee Cake**	Seed Rolls* Celery Toast*	Buns* Bread** Biscuit**
Fish, Eggs and Cheese	Cottage Cheese*	Cheddar* Gorgonzola* Cream Deviled Eggs		Fish Stews* Stuffings* Scrambled Eggs*	Cream Cheese** Cheddar**
Meat and Poultry	Stews*	Pork Liver Kidneys Goulash*		Meat Loaf* Stuffings* Stews*	Pork Roast Sausage Stuffing Frankfurters
Vegetables	Carrots*	Turnips** Sauerkraut Rice* Potato Pancakes		Stewed Tomatoes*	Rice Fried Potatoes Spiced Beets*
Salads		Cole Slaw* Beet*	Orange**	Aspics* Fish Salads* Potato*	Mixed Green
Cakes and Cookies	Cookies* Pain d'Epice** Springerle** Anise Cake*	Seed Cake*	Danish Pastry** Cookies**		Gingerbread* Cakes** Cookies** Applesauce Cake**

Desserts and Beverages	Stewed Fruits*
	with Raw
	   Apple*
	Fruit Pies*
	Tea*
		Baked Pears
		Baked Apples
			Baked Apples**
			Coffee
			   Gelatine**
			Demi-Tasse**
					Apple Pie**
					Stewed Pears
					Baked Apples
					Rice Pudding*

Miscellaneous	Candy*	Candy*	Jellies** Honey** Pickles**	Boiled Salad Dressing* Pickles*	Game Sauce Pickles* Candies**

*Indicates whole seed.   **Indicates ground seed.

VINEGAR CHART

TARRAGON RED WINE VINEGAR
GARLIC RED WINE VINEGAR
ESCHALOT RED WINE VINEGAR
BASIL WHITE WINE VINEGAR

CUMIN	DILL	FENNEL	MUSTARD	POPPY	SESAME
Cheese Spread*	Fish Cocktail* Avocado Spread*	Seed Crackers*	Many	Corn Crisps* Cheese Spreads*	Corn Crisps* Sesame Butter* Canapés*
Chicken Pea Bean	Bean* Borscht* Tomato*	Cream* Garnish*	Potato**	Garnish*	Garnish*
Bread*		Roll Topping*	Sandwiches**	Rolls* Bread*	Rolls* Bread or Toast* Tea Sandwiches*
With Cheddar* With Edam* Deviled Eggs	Halibut* Salmon* Boiled Fish* Cottage Cheese*	Halibut* Codfish* Bel Paese* Omelets*	Garnish (For Fish)* Scalloped Fish** Scalloped Eggs** Any Cheese		Cheese Spread*
Mexican Dishes Meat Loaf Chili Con Carne Chicken	Lamb Stew* Creamed Chicken* Chops*	Liver* Pork*	Steaks** Chops** Ham** Cold Cuts**		Casserole Topping*
Mexican Beans Sauerkraut* Cabbage* Rice*	Sauerkraut* String Beans* Beets*	Sauerkraut* Lentils* Pickled Beets*	Baked Beans** Green Beans** Macaroni**	Noodles* Mashed Potatoes*	Hash Browned Potatoes* Noodles*
	Cole Slaw* Potato* Cucumber* Avocado*	Fish* Mixed Green*	Cole Slaw* Mixed Green* Salad Dressing	Pear*	Potato* Garnish*
Sugar Cookies*		Seed Cake* Cookies*		Cake* Cookies*	Cookies* Cakes*
Fruit Pies	Apple Pie*	Baked Fruit* Apple Pie* Pudding*		Tarts*	Nut Substitute*
Cheese Toppings*	Fish Sauce* Olives* Pickles Sour Cream*	Fish Sauce* Pickles* Candy*	Bearnaise Sauce Mayonnaise Pickles* Cheese Sauce		Candy* On Icings*

Salads	*Vegetables*	*Meats*	*Fish*	*Sauces*	*Gravies*
Fruit Green Potato Fish	Baked Beans Beets Chard Spinach Water Cress	Stews Roasts. Broiled Chicken Butter Sauce	Baked Broiled With Butter Sauce	Fish Game Ravigote Vinaigrette Spanish	A few drops in Meat Gravies to taste
Fish Green Potato Vegetable	Baked Beans Artichokes Sprouts Water Cress	Pot Roast Roast Lamb Stews	Baked Broiled With Butter Sauce	Tartar Fish	
Sliced Onion or Cucumber Lobster, Crab or Shrimp Green Potato	Artichokes Cucumbers Onions	Ragouts	Au Gratin	Fish Mushroom	
Fruit Green Tomato Lobster Crab	Tomatoes Beets String Beans Carrots Julienne	A few drops on Roast Lamb and Stews to taste	Frog Legs Deviled Crab Lobster	Tomato Fish	A few drops in Lamb Gravy to taste

INDEX TO SEASONINGS

INDEX TO RECIPES